BAPTISM

BAPTISM

God's Gift of Holiness

Jim Petty *&* Miles Cotham

WIPF *&* STOCK · Eugene, Oregon

BAPTISM
God's Gift of Holiness

Copyright © 2022 Jim Petty. All rights reserved. Except for brief quotations in critical publications or reviews, no part of this book may be reproduced in any manner without prior written permission from the publisher. Write: Permissions, Wipf and Stock Publishers, 199 W. 8th Ave., Suite 3, Eugene, OR 97401.

Wipf & Stock
An Imprint of Wipf and Stock Publishers
199 W. 8th Ave., Suite 3
Eugene, OR 97401

www.wipfandstock.com

PAPERBACK ISBN: 978-1-6667-4090-5
HARDCOVER ISBN: 978-1-6667-4091-2
EBOOK ISBN: 978-1-6667-4092-9

November 3, 2022 11:47 AM

All Scripture quotations are from The New American Standard Bible Update® unless otherwise indicated.

The Bible text designated (NASU®) is from THE NEW AMERICAN STANDARD BIBLE UPDATE® Copyright © 1995 by The Lockman Foundation. Used by permission. All rights reserved.

Scripture quotations designated NIV® are taken from The Holy Bible, New International Version® NIV® Copyright © 1973, 1978, 1984, 2011 by Biblica, Inc. TM Used by permission. All rights reserved worldwide.

Scripture quotations designated ESV® are from The ESV® Bible (The Holy Bible, English Standard Version®), copyright © 2001 by Crossway, a publishing ministry of Good News Publishers. Used by permission. All rights reserved.

The following translations are in the public domain:

American Standard Version (ASV), *Darby Translation* (Darby), *Douay-Rheims* 1899 American Edition (DRA), *King James Version* (KJV), *Revised Version* (RV), *Updated King James Version* (UKJV), and *Young's Literal Translation* (YLT).

In Memory of Miles Cotham

who loved God and his word with sincerity and courage.

On October 24, 2021, pneumonia claimed the life of Miles Stanley Cotham, a brave warrior and faithful servant of God. As we were in the final stages of the production of this book the virus attacked and killed Miles.

His participation in this project, with our many hours conversing together on the phone over its many facets, gave this book a much higher quality and accuracy. Struggling together over the concepts we dealt with and refining words into sentences together was a rare treasure of an experience. Miles had a way to make difficult concepts clearer and easier for readers to follow. His input is evident on every page.

Miles was blessed by God with a beautiful mind that quickly absorbed the most complicated matters, collated a vast amount of information, and recalled with amazing speed his storehouse of knowledge. His greatest enjoyment was to bring enlightenment to everyone he encountered.

Along with his beautiful mind, Miles had a heart molded by God that blessed a multitude of people throughout his five plus decades of ministry. He had a true shepherd's heart. In his many years of preaching and teaching he enlightened many minds, healed many hearts, and brought God's grace to many souls.

Miles was dedicated to spreading the Gospel, both as a local preacher in Nashville and abroad. Not only did he work in various mission fields, but he also helped numerous missionaries to raise the funds they needed to carry on their ministries.

I will miss you, my friend, my brother.

Jim Petty, October 27, 2021

Contents

Preface		ix
1	That Grand Old Book	1
2	Pagan Baptismal Rituals	7
3	The God of the Hebrews	13
4	Holiness	18
Excursus 1: Ephesians 5:25–26		39
5	The Baptism of John the Baptist	42
Excursus 2: On the Meaning of *Eis* in the New Testament		66
6	Baptism in the Ministry of Jesus	79
7	Baptism in the Preaching of the Early Church	100
8	Baptism in the Letters to the Churches	127
9	Baptismal Postscripts	172
Appendix: Baptismal Quotes in Church History		195
Bibliography		253
Subject Index		261
Scripture Index		275

Preface

IF THE GOSPEL WERE the King in the Royal Court, and all the doctrines of the Bible were attendants present before the King, then the doctrine of baptism would stand among the more noble. It would stand in the court along with other such nobles as atonement, redemption, sanctification, justification, grace, faith, hope, love, church, creation, judgment, eternal life, etc.

We, your authors, Jim and Miles, are thankful and proud to be Christians. Our pride is not grounded in ourselves, but in our King, who, in his gracious love, has made us citizens of his kingdom. We both came from families whose names—Petty and Cotham—we bear with pride. God has blessed us both with a strong Christian heritage. As much as we have the highest respect for our family names, we give our ultimate allegiance to an even higher name. To bear the name of Christ, the name above all names, is a humbling blessing given to us that we do not deserve. However, it is the name that God has granted, so we cherish it.

> "And there is salvation in no one else; for there is no other name under heaven that has been given among men by which we must be saved."[1]

As God bore us into our parents' families, so he has born us, in our baptism, into his spiritual family, the church. That moment in the waters of baptism was the juncture that determined who we are and our commitment to the life God has chosen for us. We look back to the significance of that event in our lives and pray that this book will lead others to surrender their life to him in baptism, or if already inducted into his family through baptism, may it help them to better appreciate the blessings he has given.

---

1. Acts 4:12.

Our salvation is of ultimate importance. We want to know with confidence that heaven is our eternal destiny, and we have a great desire to teach others that they, too, can enjoy such confidence. There may be some areas of doctrine in which there is some room for misunderstanding, but in our relationship with God we want to know just what, where, when, and how God has made this marvelous salvation available. To err in this has eternal consequences.

In this life when men go in search of riches, they spend much time and resources in their quest. Our treasure in heaven is infinitely more valuable than earth's greatest wealth. Therefore, we ask you, our readers, to consider very carefully the things we cover in this project. If you find herein things that are contrary to where you have been led in your understanding, please look closely before you decide whether we are right or wrong. If you find that the facts of the Gospel are different than what you have always thought, we pray to God that you will have the courage to accept truth at any cost. If you find that we have erred in our presentation, we would love, if possible, to hear from you.

> Our major concern, therefore, must be the concern for reality. We want to know, if possible, not what would be nice but what is! . . . for a doctrine is of little permanent interest if there is no evidence that it is true . . . If any religion or any part of religion is not true, we ought to give it up . . . If a religion is not true it is evil![2]

An important thing to realize as we delve into this exploration of baptism is that baptism is something that cannot be really understood as an individual doctrine, separate unto itself. It is wrapped up and intertwined with many other grand concepts found in the Bible. Particularly, it is important to realize its connectedness to the meaning of holiness (to be explored in chapter 4), hence the subtitle of the book: "God's Gift of Holiness." Baptism is also related to other great themes of the Bible, such as righteousness, faith, confession, repentance, grace, hope, love, etc. As we shall see, to divorce baptism from these great themes is not only to divest baptism of its beauty and greatness, but to sap glory from those other themes as well. They are all hues of color that give the Bible its masterful glory; they are like a complex tapestry with themes that weave in and out of each other.

---

2. Trueblood, *Philosophy of Religion*, 20, 33.

Miles and Jim have known each other for many years. Over the years we have endeavored to be known by what we are *for* rather than what we are *against*. To *proclaim* truth is a higher calling than *refuting* error. However, we recognize that error often rears up as a deterrent to the search for truth. Therefore, when errors stand to obscure the truth, they must be addressed, not as the prime substance of our proclamation, but to "clear the air" so that the truth shines forth. In the early years of Jim's ministry, an elderly brother informed him that he perceived his gift to the church was the ability to detect and expose false doctrine! Witch-hunting diminishes faith; preaching the Word enhances faith. It's always easier to find fault than it is to search out and declare truth.

Our important guiding method of interpretation is that we seek to begin with the text of Scripture. It is critical to ascertain, to the best of our ability, exactly what the text says by defining terms, looking at the grammar, considering the context in which the text under examination is found, etc. Then we can move to consider its original setting and try to ascertain all we can about the occasion(s) of the people to whom it is addressed and what impact the message had on them. Only then will we be in a good position to decipher what application(s) of that teaching fits our modern situation.

> So we have the prophetic word made more sure, to which you do well to pay attention as to a lamp shining in a dark place, until the day dawns and the morning star arises in your hearts. But know this first of all, that no prophecy of Scripture is a matter of one's own interpretation, for no prophecy was ever made by an act of human will, but men moved by the Holy Spirit spoke from God.[3]

This is a joint effort by the authors of this undertaking. Jim, in Salem, Oregon, drafted the original chapters, then, as a chapter began to take shape, it was sent to Miles in Nashville, Tennessee, who worked through it. We conferred extensively over what to add or delete and the accuracy of content, grammar, structure, word usage, etc. Our relationship of many years has proven to be a valuable asset, and it has been a wonderful experience to work with each other on this project.

We would like for our readers to know that we, the authors, have no allegiance to any church creed, tradition, or dogma. We are both faithful Christians whose loyalty is to God, in whom we have placed all ultimate

---

3. 2 Pet 1:19–21.

confidence. We are also both loyal members of the congregations of the Churches of Christ, in which we serve God in fellowship with other like-minded Christians. This has given us the freedom to seek truth without the necessity of making our investigations dependent on any ecclesiastical authority, or church tradition. Both of us hold advanced degrees in biblical studies (Miles, DMin and Jim, MAR). Both of us have ministered from pulpits for several decades. Both of us have been Bible teachers on many different levels. Miles has been very involved in mission efforts, both of his own and through giving assistance to others entering the mission field. During those years, we have both encountered several differing and conflicting understandings about the purpose of baptism. There are many very fine works on this topic on the market . . . and, there are some not so fine. To those who have gone before us in this endeavor, we offer our thanks for the insights they have given us.

You will notice as you go through the following pages that we have worked to give our confidence and loyalty to the text of God's Word as the final and only authority. That is why we have included chapter 1, "That Grand Old Book," in which we have explained our apologetic for such loyalty. The non-biblical sources referred to throughout the book, while helpful aids to our inquiries, are recognized as valuable but not authoritative. These sources have helped open our eyes to see things that we might otherwise have missed. We have tried to be faithful to give credit to each of these sources. The fact that we have utilized their work does not mean that we endorse everything they have to say. If any of them have been misrepresented or misunderstood in any way, we offer our apology, and the blame can be attributed to our human fallibility.

There may be some who will read this endeavor with a strong critical mind. This we welcome and encourage. Our understanding and maturity are always growing and changing (Ephesians 4:11–16). *We are open to consider any feedback so long as it is done in a spirit of love and desire to find truth.* There may be others who will find the more detailed examination of certain passages too tedious or beyond their level of expertise. To you, we implore your patience and ask you to wade through the more technical sections and glean understanding from those not so technical.

We would like to extend our gratitude to the various people who have read this manuscript with their astute and discerning suggestions, encouraged its compilation, but most of all, have petitioned God for his hand to guide its writing and bring it to completion. A special thanks is due to Makyra Williamson for her insightful and detailed critique. She caught minute errors that would have escaped our eyes, corrected poor wording and sentence structure, and offered excellent suggestions to make it clearer and easier to read.

The first three short chapters provide some background for this thesis. Chapter 4 is a close look at the oft misunderstood doctrine of holiness and sanctification, which becomes a major theme throughout the rest of the book. Chapters 4–8 form the main body of the book with a close examination of the text of the New Testament. Chapter 9, "Baptismal Postscripts," provides some short wrap-ups of major points covered in the previous chapters and some brief subjects that are related to the theme of the book. The appendix provides a list of quotes found throughout church history that relate to baptism. This list of quotes is obviously not exhaustive, but it should give the reader a feel for the way the church has dealt with the topic of baptism down through the centuries. The aim of this work is to ascertain the purpose for baptism as it is taught in the New Testament. Other aspects of the doctrine of baptism—such as methods of baptizing, subjects for baptism, who may perform baptisms, etc.—will be touched on briefly only as they pertain to the purpose of baptism.

May God bless you and guide you as you grow daily in His grace.

1

That Grand Old Book

> Every word of God is refined [*tsahraph*[1]];
> He is a shield to those who take refuge in him.
> Do not add to his words
> Or he will reprove you,
> And you will be proved a liar.
>
> —PROVERBS 30:5–6

> The words of the Lord are pure [*tahor*[2]] words;
> As silver tried in a furnace on the earth, refined seven times.
> You, O Lord,[3] will keep them;
> You will preserve him from this generation forever.
>
> —PSALM 12:6–7

> All Scripture is inspired by God and profitable for teaching, for reproof, for correction, for training in righteousness; so that the man of God may be adequate, equipped for every good work.
>
> —2 TIMOTHY 3:16–17

---

1. *tsahraph*: pure, refined. Used of goldsmiths and silversmiths in the process of refining metals before they were worked into fine vessels. See also: Ps 18:30.

2. *tahor*: pure, clean, without alloy.

3. In some translations the word "Lord" is rendered in all capital letters, with the first letter larger than the other three (LORD).

IN ONE OF THE CONGREGATIONS where I (Jim) ministered, we used to have an elderly gentleman who, every time he led a prayer in our assemblies, prayed, "Thank you, Lord, for that grand old book, the Bible." I had great respect for those prayers, and though Norm passed away several years ago, that expression of thanksgiving to God has become more and more precious to me. Yes, indeed, thank you, Lord, for that grand old Book!

> Reading the Scriptures with a clean heart is a basic rule. It prevents what is intended to be medicinal from becoming noxious. You must maintain at all times a high regard for the revealed word. It is genuine because *it has its origin in the very mind of God*. If you approach the Scriptures in all humility and with regulated caution, you will perceive that you have breathed upon the Holy Will. It will bring about a transformation that is impossible to describe.[4] (italics added)

In that Book, we have Words of Life from the Creator and Lord of life himself. As referenced above in Prov 30:5, the Word of God is said to be refined (*tsahraph*). The word *tsahraph* is used of smiths who use the blazing furnace for the purpose of refining metals, such as gold and silver, before making them into fine vessels. In this is their value, that the impurities are incinerated out and only the precious metal remains. The Word of God is genuine; it is no cheap imitation and is completely reliable. This is the wonder expressed in Ps 12:6 above: "the words of the Lord are pure [*tahor*] words." The Bible has stood in its superiority and purity throughout the tests of time.

It tells about both the fullness of life we can enjoy in our present existence in this world and the eternal glory of life beyond this life. When God created man, he did not hand down a textbook and say to us, "Here, study this and you will have eternal life." Rather, he came to us and walked among us, saying, "Here, let me show you how to live the fullness and joy of life as I made it to be lived."

From Genesis to Revelation, the greatest story ever told unfolds as God walked among his people. The Bible is His-story, God with us, Immanuel! With Paul Tillich, we can readily assert,

---

4. Erasmus, *The Handbook*, 36–37.

> His Word is an event created by the divine Spirit in the human spirit. It is both driving power and infinite meaning. The Word of God is God's creative self-manifestation . . .[5]

The following passages illustrate this blessing of God with us:

> Enoch lived sixty-five years, and became the father of Methuselah. Then Enoch *walked with God* three hundred years after he became the father of Methuselah, and he had other sons and daughters. So all the days of Enoch were three hundred and sixty-five years. Enoch *walked with God*; and he was not, for God took him.[6]

> Moreover, I will make my dwelling among you, and my soul will not reject you. I will also *walk among you* and be your God, and you shall be my people.[7]

> And the Word became flesh, and *dwelt among us*, and we saw his glory, glory as of the only begotten from the Father, full of grace and truth.[8]

Because the Bible is from the Creator, and because words of Life fill its pages, our diligence in searching out the vast storehouse of treasures contained therein ought to be approached with much diligence and excitement.

> Be diligent to present yourself approved to God as a workman who does not need to be ashamed, accurately handling the word of truth.[9]

All through history, the Bible has been the spark that has ignited innumerable reforms and restorations to bring people back to God. For example, in the seventh century BC, the twenty-year-old king of Judah, Josiah, instigated a spiritual reform that restored the nation from the degradation that was brought on by his grandfather, Manasseh, and his father, Amon.[10] The spark that ignited the restoration was his command for the Levites to clean up and restore the temple from its neglected

---

5. Tillich, *Biblical Religion*, 78.
6. Gen 5:21–24.
7. Lev 26:11–12.
8. John 1:14.
9. 2 Tim 2:15.
10. For the story of the Restoration of the Law by King Josiah, see 2 Kgs 22:1—23:30 and 2 Chr 34:1—35:19.

condition. While at this work, the priests found the *Book of the Law*! All those years it lay stashed on some obscure shelf in the temple gathering dust. It was immediately taken and read to King Josiah who, upon hearing it read, had the temple purged of its idolatrous past and restored true worship to God throughout Judea.

Today, we live in a time when many churches in every city claim the Bible as their authority. Yet, vast differences of doctrine exist among them. Is this because the Bible is too complicated, or confusing, or insufficient? Can we lay the blame for all the confusion on God and his word? If we could take the Bible simply for what it says without the cloud of presuppositions and traditions that cast shadows over its glory and majesty, how far would it go to restoring the unity of the churches and thus bring glory to the God who gave us this great Book? The Bible can be found in the pews, in homes, and in many public places. Many people wear out the cover, carrying it wherever they go. Much lip service is given to the Bible. Few open it to discover its heights of glory or probe its depths of meaning, or when they do read it, they read through glasses colored by a host of presuppositions. If the massive ignorance of the Bible among our church members could be resolved, what glorious restoration of the Gospel might we expect to occur?

There are numerous attitudes and methods by which people approach the Bible. Some simply ignore it. Some scholars read it with a critical literary eye but have no thought for its message or impact on daily life. Perhaps the most subtle danger lies with those who devise mutations of the biblical text to make it fit their preconceived traditions. This, for example, is especially true when baptism is reduced to a mere symbol of a previously completed conversion. When people encounter a text that contradicts their beloved tradition and say, "That's what it says, but that's not what it means," we are on extremely shaky ground. We enter this shaky ground if we use our traditions and theologies to determine the meaning of the text rather than rely on the text to shape our traditions and theologies. Some would prefer the theologian tell us what the text means before the exegete has completed his work. Would it not be wiser that the theologian must himself first be an exegete?

In the following pages, we delve into numerous passages of Scripture. There are risks involved when we take on the responsibility to handle accurately the word of truth.[11] Yet, we are instructed to do so.

---

11. 2 Tim 2:15.

While many portions of the Bible are easier to understand than others, it is a cop-out to neglect the more difficult portions; it is easy to offer up a plethora of excuses to sidestep these passages.

> Its study demands our full attention and the mental discipline of concentrated effort to grasp the import of the words before us if we are to penetrate to their true meaning. It is a counsel of despair to turn away from serious Bible study because it is difficult, in preference for the easy way of impressionism.[12]

In a project of this nature, there is a danger when excerpting passages out of the Bible in an effort to validate the conclusions we have already formed. Any serious student of the Bible will recognize that there are passages, whether short or long, that provide evidence for the various doctrines in our Christian faith. We want to avoid, however, approaching the text

> . . . as an arsenal of proof-texts to be arranged, without much regard given to their literary form, historical context, theological purpose, or even their best translation into modern English, to form a network of probative evidence.[13]

The Bible is a special and unique Book. As our word from God, it can survive the most intimate scrutiny and still stand as the reliable foundation on which to build our doctrines and our lives. It was God who chose what should be in its pages and how *the words he chose* should be presented. The Bible contains many words that carry life-and-death in their meaning. It is our responsibility to critically examine them (exegesis) and study how they should be applied to our daily lives (hermeneutics); our eternal destiny depends on it. We cannot afford to take our own modern perceptions of the biblical words—as an individual or as a church—and force that definition back into the biblical text. Nor can the biblical student afford to equate the passage before him with whatever emotional impressions possess him at the moment. The Bible is meant to produce strong emotions in its readers. Emotions are the result of study, not a source to define the meaning of the text. Such impressionism destroys objectivity when trying to discover the truths of the Bible as God's Book and promotes oneself to the Author's chair to determine what are to be considered eternal truths.

---

12. Martin, "New Testament Exegesis," 221.
13. Martin, "New Testament Exegesis," 220.

For one reason or another, many biblical words, such as "baptism," have been redefined down through church history, resulting in much confusion and debate. Often, such words are given definitions that conform more to church dogma than the way they are actually used in the Bible. Harsh lines are then drawn with much wrangling and debate that bring disgrace to the church and lack of respect from those outside the church. The purpose of this study is to open and examine the text of the Bible anew, with a fresh mind every day. When we read the Bible solely for the purpose of discovery, we will experience a freedom and thrill of discovery that will open our eyes to see many lofty and mighty things of God. In this project, we desire to rediscover the richness of its teaching about baptism and what it means for us today. Our challenge is to come to the text with openness and honesty by being faithful to its revealed inerrancy and authority. Our ambition is to approach this project with an open mind and a compassionate heart. Not the kind of open mind that accepts just anything that comes along, but a mind that is willing to apply the diligence and courage necessary to discover and accept what we find in its pages. This process requires much prayer accompanied with hard examination of the text of the Bible.

Once we have done the work of exegesis, our goal is to present to you, our respected readers, the results of our efforts in such a way that it will be easier to understand. We wish to clarify confusing passages, to promote harmony, and to find a common ground that conforms with the Bible rather than to the plethora of our many, often contradictory, traditions.

> Purge our minds, O Lord.
> Clear our minds of all preconceptions.
> Help us to open your grand old Book with a longing for discovery.
> In our praise of your great name, help us to declare your glory.
> O God, may we ever be recipients of your mercy.
> If we have revised, watered-down, or neglected your word, forgive.
> When we read it, may we not read it through eyes blinded by traditions of men.
> Examine us, O Lord.
> Try us; test the intentions of our hearts.
> Try us; know our thoughts.
> See if there is found therein any idol after our own fashioning,
> And lead us always in the everlasting way.

2

Pagan Baptismal Rituals

> Alcmaeon said to Achelous: 'Absolve my sin',
> And he did absolve that son of Amphiarus.
> Ah! Too facile [shallow], to think the dark guilt of murder
> Could be washed away by river water![1]
>
> —OVID, *FASTI*

SERIOUS STUDENTS OF THE BIBLE are eventually confronted with questions about where the New Testament teachings about baptism came from. Was the practice of baptism in the New Testament inherited from earlier traditions? Did the practice of baptism just suddenly appear with the preaching of John the Baptist?

In this chapter we will look at ablutions[2] in cultures that are outside the Hebrew tradition. While our focus in this book is on the Christian doctrine of baptism, it is helpful to look back to see what influence, if any, these pre-Christian ablutions had on the practice of baptism as it is presented in the New Testament.

There are some similarities between Christian and pre-Christian baptismal rites associated with water, and there are also several significant differences. The similarities should not surprise us since many of God's ways and wonders have been recognized by other cultures outside the Hebrew-Christian tradition, even though those cultures did not have the Hebrew and Christian Scriptures. Nor should it surprise us that there

---

1. Ovid, *Fasti* 2.45–46.
2. Ablution is the act of washing oneself; the washing of one's body or part of it as in a religious rite. The word "ablution" comes from the Latin verb *abluere* (to wash away, to purify). It is formed from the prefix *ab* (away, off) and *lavere* (to wash).

are numerous and significant differences, and it is these differences that lift the biblical teaching concerning baptism to its own unique place.

Most ancient religions recognized various forms of cleansing, renewal, initiation, and petition accomplished through rituals of washing and immersion in water. The association of water with these ablutions was accepted from earliest antiquity.

> The use of water as a means of purification is widespread in religions of the world. It was common in the religious activities of Greeks and Romans in the period surrounding the rise of Christianity... An early reference to a dipping for purification occurs in Herodotus. In explaining that Egyptians considered pigs an unclean animal, he says that "If an Egyptian touched a pig, he went to [*ex*] the river and dipped [*ebapse*] himself in his clothes" (Histories 2.47)... The washings were so common that they were taken for granted and seldom commented on, and where they were mentioned, often little or no detail was given as to how one performed the ablutions.[3]

It was often believed that the water itself held supernatural powers and properties. The power, and even in some cases the very essence of the deity himself or herself, resided in the local springs, streams, lakes, and rivers. In fact, it became custom to believe that not only did the god(s) actually inhabit the water, but in many communities, the water was identified as being the god.

The people came to the water seeking solutions to the issues in their lives. Because life is complicated, they found in these water ablutions a wide variety of purposes. The people came to the sacred waters believing that the power of the water's deity could be acquired by contact with its water, especially flowing (living) streams and rivers. At times, the waters were approached for the healing of physical illnesses and ailments. Sometimes, people came seeking favors, such as success in hunting or victory in war. Other times, it was for release from various destructive natural phenomena such as droughts. Sometimes, in their contact with the water, a person would demonstrate honor and homage to the deity by simply bathing in their stream. Contamination from reproductive activities, contact with dead bodies, criminal behavior, immoral activities, body fluids and discharges, and any number of other sources of uncleanness found their cleansing in the water's powers.

---

3. Ferguson, *Baptism*, 25.

When practicing a religious rite, they came to the waters to be baptized for cleansing, not just from physical uncleanness, but from spiritual uncleanness as well. Because water was often associated with cleansing, especially running water, they recognized the need for some power of cleansing that reached beyond the mere washing of their body or physical possessions. The gods were perceived as the access to all power, so it was natural to assume that the gods used these waters to dispense the cleansing of their souls as well as their bodies. However, warnings, as can be seen in this quote from Philo, were issued against coming to the rituals with impure passions.

> And besides this, they wash their bodies with baths and purifications, but they neither desire nor endeavor to wash off the passions of their souls, by which their whole life is polluted; and they are eager to flock to the temples in white garments, clothed in robes without spot or stain, but they feel no shame at bringing a polluted mind up to the very inmost shrine.[4]

It is quite understandable how these waters came to acquire such magical and mythical associations in their daily lives. The flowing, bubbling streams seemed to have a life in themselves, and the larger rivers also exhibited a moving power. From the earliest times, there were traditions of fascination with various running waters, which were thought of as "living water" in contrast to still or stagnant water. The Greek philosopher Heraclitus of Ephesus[5] (approximately 570–536 BC), about the same era as Ezra's ministry, was quoted by Socrates as saying, "No man steps into the same river twice."[6] When one stands on a river's bank, the river that flowed by a moment ago is replaced by new water, and thus the river becomes a new river every moment. Heraclitus went on to apply

---

4. Philo, *On the Cherubim*, 28.95.

5. Heraclitus of Ephesus was an ancient Greek philosopher and a native of the city of Ephesus. Little is known of Heraclitus' life; most of what has been handed down consists of stories, apparently invented to give him a historical credibility. It is generally believed that Heraclitus was of a distinguished (and likely royalty) family, but he turned from his privileged life for the more lonely life as a philosopher. Heraclitus is said to have produced a single work on papyrus, which has not survived; however, over 100 fragments of his writing survive in quotations by other authors.

6. Plato, *Cratylus*, section 402.a.:
   Hermogenes: "What do you mean by that?"
   Socrates: "Heracleitus says, you know, that all things move and nothing remains still, and he likens the universe to the current of a river, saying that you cannot step twice into the same stream."

this ever-changing process to his core evolutionary understanding of how the universe, especially human life with its many aspects of social interaction, unfolded. Ever-changing and flowing, the continuously renewed river with its swirling and sometimes boiling currents invited all kinds of enchanting imaginations.

Besides the minor local streams and rivers that were looked to for their magical powers, many of the larger more famous rivers of the world, such as Egypt's Nile River, also played a significant role in religious mythology. The Nile was the god who nourished Egypt and was itself regarded as a deity.[7] It was also associated with the worship of other gods, especially Isis, the god of motherhood, marriage, protection, and the fertility of the people and their land. Even in our modern times, there are many who still look to rivers as holding spiritual powers. For about 3,000 years the Hindu people of India have considered their river, the Ganges, to be the "Mother of All Rivers," and thus divine. Large crowds come daily to plunge into it, seeking in their baptism the divine river's favor and forgiveness of their sins. Missionaries to India find it much easier to explain the Christian practice of baptism since it is already so much a part of Indian culture.

Many other of the world's famous rivers, such as Mesopotamia's Euphrates River, Judea's Jordan River, and the Sindhu River, which is fed by snow from the Himalayan Mountains, have been, and continue to be, venerated to the status of deity. It would be intriguing to consider the role of other great and small bodies of water, such as India's Bhramaputra River and the Indus River, and likewise, the Turag River of India's neighbor, Bangladesh.[8] The gods associated with Earth's rivers are as numerous as the rivers and the people associated with them. The Greeks had numerous river gods known as the *Potamoi*, and the *Potamoi* had numerous offspring known as *Naiades*.

---

7. Plutarch, *On Isis and Osiris*, 5.
   ... nothing is so venerated by Egyptians as the Nile, but because drinking the water of the Nile is supposed above all other to fatten, and produce corpulence ...
8. Reeve, "Sacred Rivers."
   I was visiting Gish Abay [in Egypt at the source of the Nile], revered by millions as the source of the world's longest river, while filming *Sacred Rivers*, a new TV series for which I travelled the length of the Nile, the Yangtze and the Ganges ... There was [at Gish Abay] both wailing and joy. One young woman told me, with the certainty of piety, that her kidney infection had just been cured by contact with the water.

There are several characteristics that stand out in the practice of these water ablutions by the ancient people, some of which are still practiced even in modern times:

1. The powers sought in the waters were only temporary, requiring repeated ablutions that were necessary for life's many and complicated issues. Sometimes multiple baptisms a day were required.
2. The divine power was believed to be inherent in the water itself. Whether the god of the water impregnated the water with power, was present in the water, or was considered synonymous with the water, the cleansings and blessings were received as gifts upon contact with the power in the water.
3. They often came to the water for spiritual insight, healing, and cleansing.
4. The stimulating power of the living waters was thought to bring them heightened mental and spiritual awareness, especially chilling waters.
5. The practice of baptism ranged from dipping only part, or parts, of the body in the water to the submergence of one's entire body.
6. They often looked to their baptisms to appease the anger of their gods or in some way to gain their favor. Fear was often a factor that drove the devotee to the water; at other times, it might be fear of the god himself/herself that kept them away from the water. After all, the gods were big and powerful. In contrast, human life was fragile and susceptible to the selfish whims and lusts of these flighty divinities.
7. Almost all of the ancient religions revolved around a large plurality of gods (*polytheism*), whereas the uniqueness of the Hebrew religion was its devotion to one God (*monotheism*) who permeates his creation yet is not contained exclusively in the creation.[9]

---

9. Polytheism is the combination of two Greek words: *polus* (many) and *theos* (god); hence, the worship of many gods. In contrast, *monos* (one, only) identifies monotheism as the worship of one god. For a brief time in Egypt's history, Atenism, sometimes called by the Egyptian polytheists the Amarna heresy, professed belief in a monotheistic god. In the 14th century BC, Atenism was Egypt's state religion for around 20 years. Subsequent rulers returned to the traditional plurality of gods, and the Pharaohs associated with Atenism were erased from Egyptian records.

Ancient pagan worship of the gods involved many other objects besides the waters, including such inanimate objects as the sun, moon, stars, mountains and hills, rocks, buildings, etc. Many of their objects of worship were man-made idols, images created by man to represent their various religious beliefs. It is hard for us, in our modern western mindset, to understand why people should follow such pagan pseudo-religious superstitions until we realize that if we did not have the knowledge and insights of the Bible that bless our minds, we might, like them, turn to whatever explanation of life our minds could conjure up. We do, in fact, see in our culture of today the worship of many gods—e.g., wealth, fame, power, and raw lust. Such noble things as family, church, and even the Bible itself have become idols when they become an end in themselves, usurping the God who created them.

Did any of these animistic practices have any influence on Christian baptism? We have no evidence that they did, but neither do we have evidence that they didn't. However, we do know, as we will come to see in later chapters, that there are several critical differences between these pagan rites and the practice and meaning of baptism found in the New Testament.

> As the Bible sees it, there is no possibility of comparing the forgiveness of the sins of believers, which stands at the very heart of biblical religion, with the external washings of paganism or Judaism. Any sacral, magical, ritualistic, or legalistic emphasis on the external cleansing by water would be a relapse into pagan ablutions.[10]

---

10. Oekpe, "*louo, apolouo, loutron*," 4:303.

3

The God of the Hebrews

> For great is the Lord, and greatly to be praised;
> He also is to be feared above all gods.
> For all the gods of the peoples are idols,
> But the Lord made the heavens.
>
> —1 CHRONICLES 16:25–26

> I am the Lord, and there is no other;
> Besides me there is no God.
> I will gird you, though you have not known me;
> That men may know from the rising to the setting of the sun
> That there is no one besides me.
> I am the Lord, and there is no other,
> The One forming light and creating darkness,
> Causing well-being and creating calamity;
> I am the Lord who does all these.
>
> —ISAIAH 45:5–7

THERE IS SUCH A DRAMATIC difference and distance between the pagan deities and Yahweh, the God of the Hebrews, that to make even a cursory comparison of the two would be an exercise in futility. It would be like comparing—well, like what? Maybe sports? What does football have to do with Monopoly? They are such completely different sports that to draw similarities between them would be laughable. True, there are some similarities of the most basic nature between them. Both are games. Both involve competition. Both involve some type of strategy. But beyond such generic characteristics, they involve two totally different concepts.

The vast void between the pagan religions and the Hebrew religion defies any attempt at compatibility. To bridge that void would be more difficult than the attempt to travel from one "side" of the universe to the other. The monotheistic Yahweh of the Old Testament turns all pagan polytheistic "gods" inside out, exposing them for the frauds they really are. The worship of Yahweh and the worship of the pagan gods may have some general things in common, such as the recognition of guilt and various moral issues, but they can no more be of the same mold than football and monopoly. Therefore, with King David, we declare, "I hate those who regard vain idols, but I trust in the Lord."[1]

In contrast to pagans who worshipped the Baal of the Palestinian area, the Greek Zeus, Roman Jupiter, and the Egyptian Ra, the Hebrews recognized that people were created by God, not the other way around.

> Know that the Lord himself is God;
> It is he who has made us, and not we ourselves;
> We are his people and the sheep of his pasture.[2]

These would be strange words to pagans who were governed solely by the five senses and whose concept of deity was contained within the natural realm. For them, the gods were understood in terms of the nature of mankind. Pagan gods were identified with human emotions and restricted to physical—especially national—boundaries.

All of Israel's neighbors were henotheistic[3] in that while they worshipped many gods, they elevated one as supreme who was identified with the nation and/or the nation's ruler. In their eyes, Yahweh was simply the god of the Hebrews. They failed to recognize the vastness of Yahweh as the one and only God of the whole universe.[4] When the Israelites lost in war, their opponents concluded that it was because their god, e.g., Baal,

---

1. Ps 31:6.
2. Ps 100:3.
3. Henotheism is the practice of believing in many gods but exalting one god within a particular territory to be elevated as supreme over all the other gods. For example, we see Zeus and Jupiter respectively with the Greeks and Romans being the supreme god, yet a whole plethora of other gods were still worshipped.
4. Num 35:34: "You shall not defile the land in which you live, in the midst of which I dwell; for I the Lord am dwelling in the midst of the sons of Israel." While it is true that "the land"—the nation of Israel—was considered as special to Yahweh, unlike the gods of other nations, he was not restricted to a territory.

was more powerful than Israel's Yahweh. However, the Bible explains that Israel's losses in battle were due not to the competition between Yahweh and the pagan gods, but rather because of Israel's failure to adhere in their loyalty to Yahweh. While the pagan gods were located and limited in space and time, the Hebrew Scriptures revealed God as One so big that the whole of the universe could not contain him. To place boundaries on him who has no bounds would be to reduce him to just another god among the many other gods. When the Israelites finished building the temple and the priests placed the Ark of the Covenant in its Most Holy sanctuary, King Solomon, in his prayer of dedication for the temple, said,

> O Lord, the God of Israel, there is no God like you in heaven above or on earth beneath, keeping covenant and showing lovingkindness to your servants who walk before you with all their heart... But will God indeed dwell on the earth? Behold, heaven and the highest heaven cannot contain you, how much less this house which I have built![5]

He who created the universe is too majestic and too vast to be contained within the universe that he created. Can a painting justly contain the artist who paints it?

How can we describe him who is indescribable? How can our human language describe spiritual realities that transcend our verbal skills as light transcends darkness? If we were to set out on a mission to discover God, where would we look? The mystery is too great. Where would we even begin our search? We would not even know we needed to find him if he had not first come to us. All the other gods could easily be located. They were in the rocks, the rivers, the idols, and some were far away in the heavenly bodies.

All the while that Job and his three "friends" pontificated back and forth with each other, Elihu waited to speak. These sages, Job, Eliphaz, Bildad, and Zophar, were his seniors by many years. But when they finally ran out of words, he then had to have his say. In his concluding comments, Elihu declared, "The Almighty—we cannot find him; he is exalted in power..."[6] Is this then the end of the matter? Is he so far off we cannot find him? Elihu was right. We cannot find him. But, *he has found us*. Who is this unknowable God who has made himself known? Who is this God who dominates the pages of the Bible, who permeates all of life

---

5. 1 Kgs 8:23, 27.
6. Job 37:23.

from the beginning of time to the present times and all the way to the end of all time? It is the Christian's joy to spend the days of their life exploring and discovering his magnificent glory. He has transcended the great gulf between him and us and has made himself known.

The amazing thing is that this great unknowable One has not only made himself known, but he desires intimate connection with his people. This is the key to understanding the meaning of baptism. It is in baptism that he reaches out, lays claim to his own, and takes us in wedlock to himself.

The Israelites in their lust and pride had difficulty remaining loyal to the monotheistic Yahweh. To be "like all the nations" (1 Sam 8:4–9) drove them to substitute the pure and genuine ways of God for the cheap and crude ways of the pagan artificial gods. We, as Christians, need to realize how spiritually confusing and difficult it was for the Israelites. They, like the nations surrounding them, came to think in terms of a national religion focused on their national god(s). Was Yahweh merely the God of the Jews? The Israelite's move to a nationalistic focus in which their religion became limited to a local territory left them with a mentality that Yahweh belonged to their nation, rather than vice versa. Given such an ingrained tradition that permeated most of the nations, it should not surprise us how hard it was for those nations to see the universal reign of Yahweh. Even though they knew of the powerful signs and wonders performed by Yahweh (such as the crossing of the Red Sea), they found it difficult to accept Yahweh as anything other than merely Israel's God.

They allowed their ingrained traditions to blind them from seeing beyond the borders of their own self-imposed mental prisons. The Hebrews themselves were often subject to such nearsightedness. An example of such ingrained loyalty can be seen in the Sanhedrin's attitude toward Jesus. Nicodemus, who came one night to see Jesus,[7] gives us some insight into this attitude when he said, "Rabbi, *we know* that you have come from God as a teacher; for no one can do these signs that you do unless God is with him."[8] He did not say, "I know," but "we know." Being a "ruler of the Jews," Nicodemus admitted that he and his fellow Sanhedrin rulers knew that Jesus came from God. These men knew what Jesus taught and what he did. It was their business to know such things, and at least some of them had witnessed Jesus' marvels first-hand. Their

---

7. John 3:1–12.
8. John 3:2.

position of influence and membership among the elite was threatened by Jesus, and they did not have the courage to be converted. To accept Jesus as the Messiah would require of them a whole new outlook on life.

So it is in our time. Traditions can form a formidable barrier to conversion. It is the same with the doctrine of baptism. The doctrine of baptism as a post-conversion event has become so ingrained in many evangelical churches that to consider any other possibility would bring a price that few are willing to pay. Family and social loyalties are so tied to church dogma that to make such a change becomes a threat to them.

All down through church history and into our time, differing traditions concerning the purpose of baptism and its chronological relationship to conversion have divided the church. This might cause a person to wonder whether the battles fought over baptism can be justified. The answer to that rests on understanding the biblical purpose of baptism. In this project, we hope to make clear why a close examination of the purpose of baptism is necessary. It is our goal to discover what the biblical view is and to do so as simply as possible.

4

Holiness

> Moreover, they shall teach my people the difference between the holy and the profane, and cause them to discern between the unclean and the clean.
>
> —EZEKIEL 44:23

> I thank Thee, O Lord,
> for Thou hast redeemed my soul from the Pit,
> and from the Hell of Abaddon
> Thou hast raised me up to everlasting height . . .
> Thou hast cleansed a perverse spirit of great sin
> that it may stand with the host of the Holy Ones,
> and that it may enter into community
> with the congregation of the Sons of Heaven.[1]

FROM GENESIS 1:1 TO Revelation 22:21, a common thread runs throughout the biblical text. The beauty of holiness illuminates the vast rainbow of doctrinal themes in the Bible, giving them their glow and wonder. Purity is the essence of God's nature; holiness is what gives his grace its radiance and glory. What would God's grace be without holiness? Holiness is the essence of salvation and brings hope to the Christian's life. *Holiness illuminates the practice of baptism, giving it its significance and purpose.* In this chapter, we will explore the meaning of holiness and sanctification as used in the Bible; then, in subsequent chapters, we will

---

1. Vermes, "Hymns," 158.

examine the relationship between holiness and baptism in various New Testament passages.

It is generally assumed by most Bible commentaries and dictionaries that holiness and sanctification mean "set apart" (i.e., distinctness). Although the idea of distinctness is a biblical concept and is closely associated with holiness, they are not the same; they are bound together as cause and result. That which is pure must be set apart as distinct from that which is unclean.

We shall see in this chapter, concerning holiness and sanctification, for one thing, that in both the Old Testament and the New Testament, holiness and sanctification are identical in meaning since they both come from one Hebrew word in the Old Testament and one Greek word in the New Testament. Second, holiness and sanctification both mean to make pure, clean, and flawless. It will be our purpose in this chapter to restore the wonder of the essential meaning of holiness and sanctification as used in the Bible. Purity and cleanness are what give these two words their majestic beauty.

God is Holy

Life is full of flaws. All things living and animate, be it the "perfect" rose or the "perfect" diamond, fall short of the glory of perfection. Even the most carefully cultivated rose will have its blemishes. Diamonds develop small inclusions (imperfections) as they are formed from carbon deep within the earth under extreme heat and pressure. In reality, there is no such thing as a flawless diamond, but when they are examined under a standard magnification of 10x and have no *perceivable* flaws, they are recognized as "perfect." Diamonds that have scarcely perceivable inclusions under 10x magnification are called "VVS" (very, very slight) and sell as flawless. The purity of gold is measured in karats. The highest grade of gold is 24 karats. That means it is 99.9 percent free of any impurities, which accounts for its distinctive bright yellow color. Like the "flawless" diamond that has no *visible* inclusions, gold of this quality is *called* "pure."

The fact that we are aware of such imperfection means that we realize that the True Perfect exists; 100 percent purity does exist. In heaven, 99.9999 percent pure is still impure, and the Lord of heaven will not permit anything in heaven, that Most Holy of Holies,[2] that is not 100

2. Heb 9:24.

percent pure. If 0.000001 percent impurity were acceptable there, purity would be compromised, and holiness would be destroyed. That is something God will not allow.

How can we grasp the reality and majesty of God's holiness? The idea of absolute purity boggles our mind; its overwhelming magnitude does not fit in our finite brains. To speak of God without recognizing the reality and loftiness of his holiness would diminish him to an empty, impotent, and useless pagan god. The Hebrew's God, Yahweh, was unique; he stood above all the other gods. Because of his holiness, Yahweh stood in stark contrast to and apart from all the impurities that characterized the foreign deities. The following passages testify to the majestic holiness of Yahweh,

> Holy, holy, holy is the Lord of hosts!
> The whole earth is full of his glory.[3]
> Exalt the Lord our God
> And worship at his holy hill,
> For holy is the Lord our God.[4]
> Who is like you among the gods, O Lord?
> Who is like you, majestic in holiness,
> Awesome in praises, working wonders?[5]

> Then Moses said to Aaron, "It is what the Lord spoke, saying, 'By those who come near me I will be treated as holy, and before all the people I will be honored.'"[6]

> There is no one holy like the Lord,
> Indeed, there is no one besides you,
> Nor is there any rock like our God.[7]

The degree of flawlessness is what gives a diamond its sparkle. The degree of purity is what gives gold its radiance. But what gives God his glory and majesty is the *absoluteness* of his flawless purity in holiness.

On the glorious splendor of your majesty

---

3. Isa 6:3 and Rev. 4:8.

4. Ps 99:9.

5. Exod 15:11. Sung by Moses and the people upon their deliverance from the Egyptians at the Red Sea.

6. Lev 10:3. After the death of Aaron's sons, Nadab and Abihu, who died because they disregarded God's commands and thus made light of His glory.

7. 1 Sam 2:2. Hannah's prayer of praise for the birth of her son, Samuel.

And on your wonderful works, I will meditate.[8]

As he is holy, so is his name; it is high and majestic. No other name carries such respect, awe, and fear. At the mention of his name, the demons tremble; the Devil himself cringes and flees its sound! Numerous warnings against defaming, disregarding, or blaspheming the holy name are accompanied by the promise of severe consequences.

> You shall not take the name of the Lord your God in vain [*shav*[9]], for the Lord will not leave him unpunished who takes his name in vain [*shav*].[10]

> You shall not swear falsely by my name, so as to profane [*chahlal*[11]] the name of your God; I am the Lord.[12]

> You shall not profane [*chahlal*] my holy [*qadosh*[13]] name, but I will be sanctified [*qadash*] among the sons of Israel; I am the Lord who sanctifies [*qadash*] you.[14]

> my holy [*qadosh*] name I will make known in the midst of my people Israel; and I will not let my holy [*qadosh*] name be profaned [*chahlal*] anymore. And the nations will know that I am the Lord, the Holy [*qadosh*] One in Israel.[15]

> Sing to him, sing praises to him;
> Speak of all his wonders.
> Glory in his holy [*qadosh*] name;
> Let the heart of those who seek the Lord be glad.[16]

Notice that the word "holy" in these passages is set in contrast to the words "profane" and "vain." One of the ways to help determine the meaning of a word is to see how it is used in contrast with its opposite. The opposite of profane and vain would be holy and significant. In their commentary

---

8. Ps 145:5.
9. Vain. From *shav*: desolate, useless, ruin.
10. Exod 20:7.
11. Profane. From *chahlal*: defile, pollute, wound, break, stain.
12. Lev 19:12.
13. Holy. From *qadosh* (adjective): clean, pure, sanctified, undefiled.
14. Lev 22:32.
15. Ezek 39:7.
16. 1 Chr 16:9–10.

on Ex 20:7, Keil makes a good point, showing what it means to "take the name of the Lord your God in vain."[17]

> The word [in vain] prohibits all employment of the name of God for vain and unworthy objects, and includes not only false swearing, which is condemned in Lev 19:12 as a profanation of the name of Jehovah [Yahweh], but trivial swearing in the ordinary intercourse of life, and every use of the name of God in the service of untruth and lying, for imprecation, witchcraft, or conjuring; whereas the true employment of the name of God is confined to "invocation, prayer, praise, and thanksgiving," which proceeds from a pure, believing heart.[18]

This lofty respect for the name of God was addressed by Jesus when he gave instructions to his disciples about how they should pray.

> Pray, then, in this way: "Our Father who is in heaven, Hallowed [*hagios*[19]] be your name."[20]

The only way there can be any meaningful relationship with the holy God is not by bringing him down to our level, but for us to somehow be exalted to the state of holiness that he will not reject. This is something that only God can do. In baptism, God's washing of regeneration accomplishes the cleansing that leaves us pure and therefore acceptable to him.

"You Shall Be Holy"

Most people recognize that purity and cleanness are universally viewed with respect and honor—except perhaps for little boys who love to play in the mud and hate baths. Most people naturally go to great lengths to remove uncleanness from their lives. When a bride walks the aisle in her white wedding dress, she radiates the beauty of purity. As she comes down the aisle, all eyes are focused on her. We are attracted by the symbolism of her white dress which exemplifies the value we put on purity. From her birth, great effort is put into preparing the bride for this special moment so that she can march with dignity into the ceremony and

---

17. Ex 20:7; Deut 5:11.
18. Keil, *The Pentateuch*, 398.
19. The Greek word *hagios* in the New Testament is the equivalent of Hebrew word *qadosh* in the Old Testament.
20. Matt 6:9.

be presented to the people, to the groom, and especially to God as the beauty of holiness.[21] In like manner, God demands that his bride, the church, be presented before him as holy. God both cleanses his Bride and takes Her to himself as his holy Wife.

> "Let us rejoice and be glad and give the glory to him, for the marriage of the Lamb has come and his bride has made herself ready." It was given to her to clothe herself in fine linen, bright and clean; for the fine linen is the righteous acts of the saints. Then he said to me, "Write, 'Blessed are those who are invited to the marriage supper of the Lamb.'" And he said to me, "These are true words of God."[22]

Only when the bride has been properly cleansed of all impurity can there be a union that is fit for heaven. This is why God insists that only those whose sins have been forgiven and cleansed by the blood of the Cross can be allowed entrance into that most special and intimate embrace of the Lord.

> For I am the Lord who brought you up from the land of Egypt to be your God; thus you shall be holy, for I am holy.[23]
>
> Speak to all the congregation of the sons of Israel and say to them, "You shall be holy, for I the Lord your God am holy."[24]
>
> You shall consecrate yourselves therefore and be holy, for I am the Lord your God.[25]
>
> Thus you are to be holy [qadosh] to me, for I the Lord am holy [qadosh]; and I have set you apart [bahdahl] from the peoples to be mine.[26]

Peter referred to these verses when applying the same concept to the church:

---

21. Perhaps it ought to be that such purity should be expected and demonstrated by the groom also.
22. Rev 19:7–9.
23. Lev 11:45.
24. Lev 19:2.
25. Lev 11:44; 20:7.
26. Lev 20:26. Notice here that the act of holiness (holy, pure) results in the act of being set apart (divide, sever, separate, distinguish). If holiness means "set apart," this would be a redundancy.

> but like the Holy One who called you, be holy yourselves also in all your behavior; because it is written, "YOU SHALL BE HOLY, FOR I AM HOLY."[27]

"You shall be holy" is an imperative, an absolute command! Compulsory, not elective! Absolute purity in God's people is the only option acceptable to God. If we are not holy, we stand as condemned in our impurity and alienated from the One with whom we most need to be intimate. But who can say, "I am holy; I am righteous"? What a dilemma we face. In this command to be holy, we face a compulsory demand that transcends our ability to obey.

So alas, like Eliphaz, we are confronted with the soul-searching question, "Can mankind be just before God? Can (*even*) a valiant man be pure before his Maker?"[28] Which of us can say we are free from guilt, free from impure thoughts, words, or deeds? Our great lamentation is that "all have sinned and fall short of the glory of God."[29] "If we say we have no sin," the apostle John wrote, "we are deceiving ourselves and the truth is not in us."[30] In like manner Paul declared,

> as it is written, "there is none righteous, not even one; there is none who understands, there is none who seeks for god; all have turned aside, together they have become useless; there is none who does good, there is not even one."[31]

---

27. 1 Pet 1:15–16.
28. Job 4:12–17.
    Now a word was brought to me stealthily,
    And my ear received a whisper of it.
    Amid disquieting thoughts from the visions of the night,
    When deep sleep falls on men,
    Dread came upon me, and trembling,
    And made all my bones shake.
    Then a spirit passed by my face;
    The hair of my flesh bristled up
    "It stood still, but I could not discern its appearance;
    A form was before my eyes;
    There was silence, then I heard a voice:
    "Can mankind be just before God?
    Can a man be pure before his Maker?"
29. Rom 3:23. See also Ps 14:1–3; 53:1–3.
30. 1 John 1:8.
31. Rom 3:10–12. See also Ps 14:1–3; 53:1–3.

Is there any way we can rid ourselves of this hopeless dilemma? Is there any way we can scrub from our lives the filth that has penetrated to the core of our being? Where do we turn to find a cleanser with the power to wash away the stains that condemn us to eternal alienation from God? Because of this dilemma, Jesus told us, "Blessed are those who mourn, for they shall be comforted." We need someone to wash us clean to remove the stain of our sins; we need someone who, while undefiled and pure himself, can go to whatever extreme measure is necessary to scrub our lives clean of *every* spot and wrinkle. This task has fallen on God's Son, Jesus, our Redeemer, whose blood alone wields such cleansing power. In baptism, the sinner bows prostrate before God, imploring him for the cleansing of our sins.[32] His answer:

> Come to me, all who are weary and heavy-laden, and I will give you rest.[33]

The Meaning of the Words "Holiness" and "Sanctification" in the Old Testament

When we speak of the lofty principles handed down to us by God in his Bible, it behooves us to observe two critical criteria: 1). The Bible, having been written in the Hebrew and Greek languages (with a few passages in the Aramaic language), must necessarily be translated into a language that is familiar to the readers. Translators are challenged to exercise a high degree of integrity and intelligence to ensure that modern readers have the most accurate reading possible, as it first came from the pens of the original authors. 2). There are words in the Bible that have high and majestic concepts associated with them. *These words were chosen by God, not men.* Regardless of what the words may have come to mean with the passage of time (tradition), we must discover, to the best of our ability, what God meant to convey by the words when he incorporated them into his book. It is a grave and serious error to misrepresent God's message. When it comes to defining and understanding words that represent such great and noble concepts as holiness/sanctification, "we choose to speak of Bible things by Bible words . . ."[34]

---

32. See 1 Pet 3:21.

33. Matt 11:28.

34. Campbell, *Christian System*, 103. The first edition was entitled *Christianity Restored*, (Bethany, VA: M'Vey and Ewing), 1835. The full quote from Alexander

Each of these inspired words has its own special meaning. Without a common understanding of what these words mean, communication falters and all our relationships, including our relationship with God, spiral into chaos. With Voltaire we declare, "If you wish to converse with me, define your terms." [35] Our prayer is that God will direct, and, when necessary, correct us as we go forward into his word.

Holiness is a major theme throughout the Bible. It is the word that God has chosen to express the high and lofty principle of forgiveness that lies at the heart of his saving grace. Since the word "holiness" was chosen by God, we must take a serious look into its meaning. As we noted above, both holiness and sanctification mean the same thing. They are both translated from the Old Testament Hebrew word *qadosh* and its associated parts of speech. And likewise, in the New Testament, they are both translated from the same Greek word, *hagios,* and its associated parts of speech. Therefore, holiness and sanctification are identical in meaning and will be used interchangeably throughout this study.

As noted above, most biblical commentaries and dictionaries assume that sanctification means "to be set apart" (distinctness). However, upon investigation into how holiness and sanctification are used in the Bible, the primary meanings are "cleanness" and "purity." Therefore, *holiness and sanctification do not inherently convey the idea of distinctness; rather, distinctness is the result of holiness and sanctification.* Every cause produces an effect; every effect is the product of a cause. In this manner

---

Campbell:
> *We choose to speak of Bible things by Bible words,* because we are always suspicious that if the word is not in the Bible, the idea which it represents is not there; and always confident that the things taught by God are better taught in the words, and under the names which the Holy Spirit has chosen and appropriated, than in the words which man's wisdom teaches. (italics in original).

The full text of *The Christian System* can be found at: http://www.gravelhill-churchofchrist.com/ebooks/Campbell,%20Alexander%20-%20The%20Christian%20System.pdf, Gravel Hill Church of Christ, Moreland, Arkansas, 2012, 167.

35. The origin of this quote is lost in obscurity. It is thought that it may have originated with François-Marie Voltaire (1694–1778) who may have adopted this concept from John Locke (1632–1704) who wrote in 1689:
> Words are often employed without any, or without clear ideas. First, in this kind the first and most palpable abuse is, the using of words without clear and distinct ideas; or, which is worse, signs without anything signified . . . without much troubling their heads to examine what are the precise ideas they stand for.

John Locke, *An Essay Concerning Human Understanding,* 3.10.2. pp. 214–215

sanctification and distinctness, while not the same thing, are interdependent. That which is unclean must first be washed (cause), and then, because of that cleansing, the clean must be set apart (effect/result) from the unclean. Sanctification is the cleansing that washes away the guilt of our sins by the powerful blood of Christ; *consequently*, we stand before him as distinct and set apart from those who have not been cleansed. This is the essence of the church.

As an illustration of the meaning of holiness, consider a daily practice we are familiar with in our homes. After a meal it is common practice to take the dirty dishes to the kitchen to be washed. What use do we have for those dishes again unless they are washed? Who wants to eat from dirty dishes? Once the dishes are washed, they are set apart in a clean place, thus fit to be used again. It would be foolish to place the clean dishes back with the dirty dishes or to place them in any other unclean place. The act of cleaning is the primary focus in this process. The act of setting apart that which is washed, though important and even necessary, is a secondary action. Being set apart has no value without the washing. So what if the dirty dishes are set apart? They are still dirty. The cause is always greater than the result, just as an artist is always greater than their work of art.

There are several Old Testament Hebrew words that are translated as "set apart." These words clearly portray a meaning different than *qadosh*. Below are some examples:

> But know that the Lord has set apart [*pahlah*] the godly man for himself; The Lord hears when I call to him.[36]
> *pahlah*: to separate, set apart, sever, distinguish.

> I am the Lord your God, who has separated [*bahdal*] you from the peoples.[37]
> *bahdal*: to divide, separate, distinguish, sever.

> At that time the Lord set apart [*bahdal*] the tribe of Levi to carry the ark of the covenant of the Lord, to stand before the Lord to serve him and to bless in his name until this day.[38]

---

36. Ps 4:3.
37. Lev 20:24.
38. Deut 10:8.

> Thus you shall keep the sons of Israel separated from [*nahzar*] their uncleanness, so that they will not die in their uncleanness by their defiling my tabernacle that is among them.[39]
>
> *nahzar*: to separate, devote, hold aloof.
>
> And Aaron was separated [*bahdal*], that he should sanctify [*qadash*] the most holy [*qadosh*] things, he and his sons forever, to burn incense before the Lord, to minister unto him, and to bless in his name forever.[40]

The words *pahlah, nahzar,* and *bahdal* refer to marking a distinction; none of these words by themselves identify that which causes the distinction. That action is reserved for *qadosh*.

When we look into the origin of the word "holiness," we find that it comes from a very respected family of languages in human history. This historic family includes languages such as Arabic, Aramaic, Hebrew, Ethiopic, and Akkadian (ancient Babylonian and Assyrian). Some biblical linguists have assumed that the Old Testament word *qadosh* is derived from an original Akkadian root, *qd*, which means "to separate by cutting," thus emphasizing "apartness," "distinctness." However, *qadosh* is actually closer to the root *qds*, which signifies "cleanness," "purity," and "holiness."[41] In the ancient Semitic languages and their modern descendants, *qds* is always used in the sense of religious cleanness and purity. The ancient Semitic root *qds* can still be seen in the modern Arabic language with words such as *qadusa* and *yaqdusu*, which are universally translated "clean," "immaculate," "pure."[42] It is important, therefore, for

---

39. Lev 15:31.
40. 1 Chr 23:13.
41. McComiskey, "*qadash*," 786–87.

    The suggestion that the root *qdsh* is derived from an original biliteral *qd* ("cut") is attractive but tenuous in view of the uncertainties surrounding the transmission of biliteral roots to the biliteral form. The meaning "to separate" is favored by many scholars, but the fact that *qdš* rarely, if ever, occurs in a secular sense makes any positive conclusion in this regard difficult because of the limited evidence on which to base philological comparison. The word occurs in several dialects of Akkadian with the basic meanings "to be clean, pure, consecrated." In the Canaanite texts from Ugarit, the basic meaning of the word group is "holy," and it is always used in a cultic sense.

42. Translation results for قدس (*qadusa*): "holiness," "sanctuary," "shrine," "to be holy," to be "pure," "to hallow," "sanctify," "enshrine." See: http://arabic.britannicaenglish.com/en/%D9%82%D9%8E%D8%AF%D9%91%D9%8E%D8%B3%D9%8E.

us to recognize and honor this long and splendid heritage as we try to understand the concept of holiness and sanctification.

With the passage of time, it became necessary for the Hebrew text of the Old Testament to be translated into the Greek language so that it could be read and understood by the Gentiles who had no knowledge of the Hebrew language. This was also necessary for the many Jews who were raised in cultures where the Hebrew language was no longer their native tongue. This Greek translation, which later came to be known as the Septuagint (abbreviated LXX), consistently translated the Hebrew word *qadosh* with the Greek word *hagios*. Consequently, whatever meaning should be given to *qadosh* in the Hebrew text of the Old Testament should also be applied to *hagios* in the Septuagint's Greek text of the Old Testament. This becomes important in the New Testament where the authors used this same word, *hagios*, which has come down to our English as "holy" or "sanctified." Thus, *qadosh* in the Old Testament means the same thing that *hagios* means in the New Testament.

It would be tempting at this point to veer off to look at other words in the Old Testament that are akin to *qadosh*, such as *tahor*, which also means to be clean, pure. The word *tahor* has its roots in the same concept of purity as *qadosh*. However, in this chapter, it will suffice our purpose to deal only with *qadosh* and its relationship to baptism.

The Use of Holiness and Sanctification in the Old Testament

Having examined the etymology of the word "holiness" (*qadosh*) in the above section, we now ask whether that definition fits in the context of the writings of the Old Testament, for the meaning of a word must fit the context in which it is used. *Qadosh* and its other parts of speech[43] occur over 830 times in the Old Testament.[44] Of those, it occurs 91 times in the 27 chapters of Leviticus, an average of about three and one-third times per chapter. The way *qadosh* is used in Leviticus as the book's primary theme provides us with more insight into the true meaning of holiness for the rest of the Bible. The purity of God and his cleansing work upon his people permeated both the cultic rituals and the personal daily lives of the people.

---

43. Adjective: *qadosh*; noun: *qadesh*; verb: *qadash*.
44. Smith and Harrelson, "Holiness," 387.

> For I am the Lord your God. Consecrate [*qadash*][45] yourselves therefore, and be holy [*qadosh*], for I am holy [*qadosh*]. And you shall not make yourselves unclean [*tahmei*: defiled] with any of the swarming things that swarm on the earth. For I am the Lord who brought you up from the land of Egypt to be your God; thus you shall be holy [*qadosh*], for I am holy [*qadosh*].[46]

The significance of this passage lies in the declaration that God is pure and that he requires purity in all of his people. In verse 44 there is a strong contrast between holy (*qadosh*) and unclean (*tahmei*); they are set in antithesis to each other. This same contrast is also illustrated in the following passage concerning the priests:

> Do not drink wine or strong drink, neither you [Aaron] nor your sons with you, when you come into the tent of meeting, so that you will not die—it is a perpetual statute throughout your generations—and so as to make a distinction [*bahdal*] between the holy [*qadosh*] and the profane [*chol*[47]], and between the unclean [*tahmei*] and the clean [*tahor*[48]] . . .[49]

In this passage "holiness" is parallel to "clean," and "profane" is parallel to "unclean." "Holiness" and "clean" are distinct from and contrasted with "profane" and "unclean." Further, in regard to the priests, God instructed:

> You shall consecrate [*qadash*] him [the priest] therefore, for he offers the food of your God; he shall be holy [*qadosh*] to you; for I the Lord, who sanctifies [*qadash*] you, am holy [*qadosh*].[50]

Throughout Leviticus 21, the purity of the priests who serve before God is thoroughly and emphatically described. There were many things that could defile the priest so that he could not serve in the cultic activities. He could return to his religious duties only with a ceremonial washing (consecration, or *qadesh*). *Qadosh* is significant in this passage because it ensures the priest's cleanness.

Another book of the Old Testament that has much to say about holiness is Ezekiel. In the following passage, like the Leviticus passages above,

---

45. *Qadash* in this passage is translated as "consecrate" in NASU, NIV, ESV, NKJV, and RSV; and as "sanctify" in KJV, ASV, and Young's Literal Translation.

46. Lev 11:44–45. See also Lev 19:2; 20:26; and 1 Pet 1:16.

47. *Chol*: exposed, profane, polluted, unclean, common, unholy.

48. *Tahor*: pure, clean, fair, pure.

49. Lev 10:9–10.

50. Lev 21:8.

we can see that the words "holiness" and "cleanness" are set in contrast to the words "profane" and "impure."

> Therefore say to the house of Israel, "Thus says the Lord God, 'It is not for your sake, O house of Israel, that I am about to act, but for my holy [*qadosh*] name, which you have profaned [*chahlal*: defiled, stained, wounded] among the nations where you went.²³ I will vindicate the holiness of [*qadash*] my great name which has been profaned [*chahlal*] among the nations, which you have profaned [*chahlal*] in their midst. Then the nations will know that I am the Lord,' declares the Lord God, 'when I prove myself holy [*qadash*] among you in their sight. For I will take you from the nations, gather you from all the lands and bring you into your own land. Then I will sprinkle clean [*tahor*] water on you, and you will be clean [*taher*]; I will cleanse [*taher*] you from all your filthiness [*tum'ah*: religious impurity] and from all your idols.'"⁵¹

God desires to purify his people so that he can draw them into oneness with him and they can recognize him as the One who purifies and gathers rather than the One who is set apart and stands aloof from them.⁵² Only when there is unbelief does he push them away and scatter them among the nations. Then, when they turn again to him, he stands ready to restore them to himself. "I will gather you . . . I will bring you" is a concept completely foreign with gods of stone and wood. This ingathering of his people to himself was not dependent on their location as it was with the other gods. Regardless of where they were, if they called on his name, he was present and willing to bring them back to himself. In all of Jacob's traveling God promised,

> Behold, I am with you and will keep you wherever you go.⁵³

Even though they were in the farthest corners of the earth, he promised he would bring them home to himself.

> If your outcasts are at the ends of the earth, from there the Lord your God will gather you, and from there he will bring you back.⁵⁴

---

51. Ezek 36:22–25.
52. Ps 100.
53. Gen 28:15.
54. Deut 30:4.

> "You will seek me and find me when you search for me with all your heart.
> I will be found by you," declares the Lord . . . [55]

> For what great nation is there that has a god so near to it as is the Lord our God whenever we call on him?[56]

> I sought the Lord, and he answered me,
> And delivered me from all my fears.[57]

Does this sound like a God who wants to be known for his distinctness, as a deity who is set apart from and alien to his people? Yet, because he is holy, he is also distinct; he is distinct from all the cheap idols, the imitations of deity among the nations. But for his cleansed people, he is near and intimate. He desires to cleanse his people so that he may bring them to himself rather than push them from himself as One who is aloof and distant. He wants to experience his faithful ones and for them to experience him. God wants the nations to look upon Israel and see Yahweh, not as One who is distinct/set apart, but as the God who draws his bride into His intimate embrace. He desires to be known as Immanuel.[58] God has made a highway to himself; he really does want to be near us. In this, we can begin to see the significance of the New Testament meaning of baptism as his work to wash us so that he can draw us unto himself.

Though God desires and goes to great lengths to be intimate, he is different from humans. He is Creator. He is deity. His eternal presence, his absolute knowledge, and his all-encompassing power make him distinct from his creation. The marvel and mystery are how can he be so removed, yet at the same time so near? "Oh, the mighty gulf that God did span . . ."[59] In the Cross, he transformed distinctness into intimacy.

---

55. Jer 29:13–14.
56. Deut 4:7.
57. Ps 34:4.
58. Isa 7:14; Matt 1:23.
59. Newell, "Years I Spent," 381.

The Meaning of the Words Holiness and Sanctification in the New Testament

Having examined the etymology and usage of the Old Testament Hebrew word *qadosh*, we now turn to ask whether this same meaning of holiness and sanctification fits the Greek word *hagios* in the writings of the New Testament. Just as *qadosh* has a long history in the Semitic languages as being associated with holiness, *hagios* has a long and ancient heritage in the languages of the Greek culture as being associated with sanctification. Going back to ancient Greek Hellenistic writings, "the adjective *hageis* . . . approximates to the sense of *katharos*, 'clean.'"[60] It is also used to refer to things that pertain to sanctuaries and temples (*hagion*).[61]

The verb, noun, and adjective forms of *hagios* occur 273 times in the New Testament. Of these it occurs 93 times as the adjective in "Holy Spirit" and 63 times as the adjective in "holy ones" (*hagioi*, the plural form for "saints"). In most English translations, the adjective *hagios* is translated as "holy," and the verb *hagiadzo* is translated as "sanctify."

Although not occurring as frequently as *hagios*, the synonym *hagnos* occurs as an adjective eight times, and in all of the primary English translations, it is rendered as "pure," "innocent," "clear," "guiltless," "blameless," "right," "undefiled," "chaste," and "free from sin."[62] In the same manner, the verb *hagnidzo* (synonym of the verb *hagiadzo*) occurs seven times and in most of the English translations is rendered as "purify" or "cleanse." By far, the most common English translation of *hagnos* pertains to purity.

That *hagios* and *hagnos* are synonyms is supported by their common association with the verbal adjective of *adzomai* (pure, clean) and the English word "innocent."[63] Since both words are closely related by both their common origin and the common root, *hag*, it would seem proper to assume that they both have similar, if not the same, definitions. While many doubt that purity is the central meaning of *hagios*, the same claim cannot be made for *hagnos*.

Of the ninety-three occurrences of the adjective *hagios* describing the Holy Spirit in the New Testament, sixty-eight of them are found in the four Gospels. It would seem quite awkward to translate *hagios*

---

60. Procksch, "*hagios*," 1:88.
61. Procksch, "*hagios*," 1:88.
62. KJV, NKJV, NASU, NIV, RSV, ESV, ASV, NRSV, and Young's Literal Translation. The adjective is used five times by Paul and once each by James, Peter, and John.
63. Hauck, "*hagnos*," 1:122.

pneuma (more frequently occurring as *pneuma hagios*) as the "set apart Spirit," emphasizing that the Spirit is distant from rather than near to us. Throughout the New Testament, the Holy Spirit is said to be near and active in the lives of God's people rather than being set apart from the people. It would make much more sense for *hagios* to refer to the purity and innocence of the Spirit.

Sometimes, *hagios* is used alongside *dikaios* (righteous, just). Righteousness[64] is used to identify a relationship that is right or just. The only way people can have a just relationship with the pure God is if they have been sanctified (*hagiadzo*) by the blood of Christ. It is by the cleansing (*hagiadzo*) power of the blood of Jesus that a person is made right (*dikaioo*) with God. It is a serious offense to God's word to divorce God's work of sanctification from his work of justification. Any attempt to separate those who have been sanctified (cleansed) from those who have been justified (made right) does grave injustice to God's grace, and they can expect the severest of God's wrath.

Paul helps us recognize the meaning of sanctification as it is associated with washing and justification in his first letter to the Corinthians:

> Or do you not know that the unrighteous [*adikaios*] will not inherit the kingdom of God? Do not be deceived; neither fornicators, nor idolaters, nor adulterers, nor effeminate, nor homosexuals, nor thieves, nor the covetous, nor drunkards, nor revilers, nor swindlers, will inherit the kingdom of God. Such were some of you; but you were washed [*apolouo*], but you were sanctified [*hagiadzo*], but you were justified [*dikaioo*] in the name of the Lord Jesus Christ and in the Spirit of our God.[65]

There is a strong contrast in this passage between the unrighteous (*adikaios*: the prefix *a* is the negation of *dikaios*) in verses 9–10 who are unclean and those who are "washed," "sanctified," and "justified" in verse 11.

Another passage of Paul's that helps us to understand the meaning of *hagios* is seen in his letter to the Ephesian church.

---

64. The nouns righteousness and justification, including their associated parts of speech, are both translations of the one Greek word, *dikaios,* in the same way that sanctification and holiness are both translations of the same Greek word, *hagios.*

65. 1 Cor 6:9–11.

> Husbands, love your wives, just as Christ loved the church and gave himself up for her to make her holy, cleansing her by the washing with water through the word,[66]

In verse 26, "cleansing her by the washing of water" (an obvious allusion to baptism) cannot be separated from "make her holy" ("sanctify her"). They are concurrent actions. Because there has been confusion in the translation and interpretation of this verse, a closer technical analysis will be presented in the "Excursus on Eph 5:26" at the end of this chapter.

It would be tempting at this point to veer off to look at other words in the New Testament that are also akin to *hagios*, such as *teleios*, *hieros* and *katharos*, which also point to being made complete, perfect, and clean. However, the focus of this project is to establish significance of holiness and sanctification to baptism.

The Use of Holiness and Sanctification in the New Testament

When we see how *hagnos* and *hagios* (and their various parts of speech) are used in the New Testament, it becomes obvious that sanctification plays a vital role in what happened on the Cross of Christ. We will first look at *hagnos* to see how it is used since it is less complicated than *hagios* and has fewer occurrences.

Concerning the Corinthian Church, Paul said that he presented her (the Corinthian congregation) for marriage to Christ and called the church a pure virgin.

> For I am jealous for you with a godly jealousy; for I betrothed you to one husband, so that to Christ I might present you as a pure [*hagnos*] virgin.[67]

Standing before God to present the congregation for marriage to his Son, Paul was passionate that they be found as a pure virgin, fit for marriage to the King. In like manner, James uses the verb *hagnidzo* when referring to the cleansing of hands in parallel with the purifying of the heart.

---

66. Eph 5:25-26, (New International Version).
67. 2 Cor 11:2.

> Draw near to God and he will draw near to you. Cleanse [*katharidzo*] your hands, you sinners; and purify [*hagnidzo*] your hearts, you double-minded.[68]

By placing *hagnos* in parallel with *katharidzo*, James emphasizes the cleansing action of both verbs. Since *hagnos* and *hagnedzo* universally refer to cleansing and washing, and since they share the same root (*hag*) as *hagios*, with its other parts of speech, it is logical to conclude that this whole family of words is concerned with purification.

When we look at the word *hagios*, we have a higher volume of passages to work with. As with *qadosh* in the Old Testament, we will look at enough of these passages to establish the way the word *hagios* is used in the New Testament.

Paul made the statement, "For God has not called us for the purpose of impurity [*akatharsia*[69]], but in sanctification [*hagiasmos* (noun)]."[70] In this passage, Paul places impurity in contrast to sanctification. It is also clear in this passage that the purpose for God's calling is our sanctification. In another statement by Paul, the word "sanctification" is placed alongside the words "righteousness" and "redemption." All three of these words are inseparable from Jesus' sacrifice for us on the Cross.

> But by his [God's] doing you are in Christ Jesus, who became to us wisdom from God, and righteousness and sanctification, and redemption [*apolutrosis*: pardon, release, deliverance].[71]

The phrase "But by his doing you are in Christ Jesus" is a clear reference to what God did on the Cross. The wisdom of God, righteousness, sanctification, and redemption are all directly related to the Cross.

Emphasizing *hagios* as a purifying action does not diminish the importance of a person's life being "set apart" from the uncleanness of the world. Our life in Christ is very unique and lofty; it is a life that requires a way of living that is distinct from the ways of the world. Like the Old Testament, the New Testament has several words that communicate the idea of being distinct.

---

68. Jas 4:8.

69. As noted above, the verb *katharidzo* and the noun *katharismos* refer to cleansing and purification. The negative of that meaning is expressed by *akatharsia*: "uncleanness" or "impurity."

70. 1 Thess 4:7.

71. 1 Cor 1:30.

> While they were ministering to the Lord and fasting, the Holy Spirit said, "Set apart [*aphoridzo*] for me Barnabas and Saul for the work to which I have called them."[72]
>
>> *aphoridzo*: to separate, divide, sever.
>
> Paul, a bond-servant of Christ Jesus, called as an apostle, set apart [*aphoridzo*] for the gospel of God.[73]
>
> Remember that you were at that time separate from [*choris*] Christ, excluded from [*apallotrioo*] the commonwealth of Israel, and strangers [*xenos*] to the covenants of promise, having no hope and without God in the world.[74]
>
>> *choris*: apart from, outside, without.
>> *apallotrioo*: estranged, alienated.
>> *xenos*: foreigner, alien.
>
> But are you willing to recognize, you foolish fellow, that faith without [*choris*: apart from] works is useless?[75]

The words *aphoridzo*, *choris*, *apallotrioo*, and *xenos* all refer to marking a distinction. These words when they stand by themselves are insufficient; they do not identify that which causes the distinction, and without *hagios*, they are meaningless.

Summary

Everyone, especially God, puts great emphasis on purity. Without it, we are destined to go through life with our hand over our mouth and like the leper declare, "Unclean, unclean."

> As for the leper who has the infection, his clothes shall be torn, and the hair of his head shall be uncovered, and he shall cover his mustache and cry, "Unclean! Unclean!" he shall remain unclean all the days during which he has the infection; he is unclean. He shall live alone; his dwelling shall be outside the camp.[76]

Without the purifying work of Jesus on the Cross, we are left unclean and considered aliens to God, banished to a life outside the camp of the

---

72. Acts 13:2.
73. Rom 1:1.
74. Eph 2:12.
75. Jas 2:20.
76. Lev 13:45–46.

faithful. Without purity, there is no way we can hope to enter that *holy* city of heaven where there is only absolute purity. *Qadosh* and *hagios* are the words God chose to express his gracious love for us. He chose them to communicate to us the essence of our salvation. Let us with great care hold them in the high regard that is due to them.

In the following chapters, we will explore several New Testament passages about baptism as the sanctifying event in which God's grace imparts cleansing (forgiveness) from sin, initiation into union with Christ, and assurance of the glorious hope of a home that he has gone to prepare for us.

Excursus 1

Ephesians 5:25–26

Husbands, love your wives, just as Christ also loved the church and gave himself up for her, so that he might sanctify her, having cleansed her by the washing of water with the word.

Hoi andres, agapate tas gunaikas, kathos kai ho Christos eigapeisen tein ekkleisian kai eauton paredoken huper auteis, hina autein hagiasei katharisas to loutro tou hudatos en hreimati.

THE PRIMARY QUESTION THAT we are concerned with in these verses is the chronological relationship between the verbs *hagiasei* (he sanctified) and *katharisas* (cleansing). We want to determine whether the cleansing is an action that takes place antecedent to (before) sanctification or if it is the cleansing action that takes place *in* sanctification. The relationship between the verbs in these two verses and their grammatical construction will help us see that *hagiasei* and *katharisas* are inseparable.

If the cleansing takes place before sanctification (as suggested in the NASU, RSV, and ESV: "having cleansed"), then the action of cleansing must necessarily be completed before sanctification. This understanding would force us to define sanctification as an event that is different than and subsequent to cleansing. This would clear the way for the translation of *hagiadzo* as "set apart." However, as noted earlier in this chapter, "set apart" is what happens after the cleansing of sanctification. On the other hand, if these two verbs are concurrent, referring to the same event, then the concept "set apart" is something Paul did not deal with in these two verses.

How are we to decide whether these two verbs are two separate actions or if they refer to the same action? For the solution to this question, we need to look at the language Paul used when he wrote it—the Greek. The four verbs we are concerned with in these two verses are:

eigapeisen	aorist, active, indicative	"He [Christ] loved."
paredoken	aorist, active, indicative	"He [Christ] gave."
hagiasei	aorist, active, subjunctive	"He [Christ] might sanctify."
katharisas	aorist, active, participle	"cleansing her" [the church]

It is quite obvious that the first two verbs, *eigapeisen* and *paredoken*, refer to the death of Christ on the Cross. *Eigapeisen* and *paredoken* are aorist active verbs and indicate the specific event being dealt with by Paul. The subjunctive *hagiasei* describes the purpose of *eigapeisen* and *paredoken*. The reason that "Christ also loved the church and gave himself up for her" was *in order that* (*hina*) he might sanctify her.

As a participle, *katharisas* serves in an adjectival relationship to *hagiasei*, describing what takes place in *hagiasei*. A participle does not carry any connotation of time of its own but owes its timing to its leading verb, which, in this case, is *hagiasei*.

> The participle is a verbal adjective, sharing in part the characteristics of both the verb and the adjective; it describes its subject as a doer of the action denoted by the verb . . . The tenses of the participle, like those of the other dependent moods, do not, in general, in themselves denote time.[1]

The timing of the action in an event (in this case, the Cross and its purifying action) is not determined by the participle, but by the participle's leading verb (*hagiasei*). When both the participle and its leading verb are in the aorist tense, the element of time is absent from the participle, and both the participle and its verb are concurrent.[2]

Since all four verbs under consideration in verses 25 and 26 are in the aorist tense, they each represent a simple event, lending to the idea that they are chronologically concurrent and each indicates a different perspective of the same event. This analysis of the Greek text would lead

---

1. Burton, *Syntax*, 53–54.
2. Blass and Debrunner, *Greek Grammar*, 339.

to the conclusion that the NIV most accurately renders verse 26 into the English language:

> . . . to make her holy, cleansing her by the washing with water through the word.

5

The Baptism of John the Baptist

JOHN THE BAPTIST SHOWED up abruptly on the stage of history, living a radical lifestyle and preaching an even more radical message. The sudden appearance of this wilderness preacher is vividly captured by Mark's Gospel. Unlike the other three Gospel writers, Mark began his Gospel with no introduction other than . . .

> John the Baptist appeared in the wilderness preaching a baptism of repentance for the forgiveness of sins. And all the country of Judea was going out to him, and all the people of Jerusalem; and they were being baptized by him in the Jordan River, confessing their sins. John was clothed with camel's hair and wore a leather belt around his waist, and his diet was locusts and wild honey. And he was preaching, and saying, "After me One is coming who is mightier than I, and I am not fit to stoop down and untie the thong of his sandals. I baptized you with water; but he will baptize you with the Holy Spirit."[1]

John came out of the Judean wilderness to the banks of the Jordan River with the demand in his preaching, "Repent, for the kingdom of heaven is at hand."[2] Jesus came from Galilee to the Jordan River to be baptized by his cousin John, and then he also began preaching, "Repent, for the kingdom of heaven is at hand."[3] Later, with the same message,

1. Mark 1:4–8.
2. Matt 3:1–2.
3. Matt 4:17.

Jesus commissioned his disciples, "And as you go, preach, saying, 'The kingdom of heaven is at hand.'"[4]

This message struck a very sensitive chord with the Jewish people. In this simple phrase, the long history of the Jewish messianic hope was revived. The coming of the Messiah—a revival of the old Davidic dynasty—to redeem Israel's rightful place among the nations of the world was the dream that gave the Jews their identity. Even though at that time they were dominated by a foreign pagan nation, they knew that they, of all the people on the Earth, were still God's chosen people! That the ungodly Roman rulers could enforce their pagan way of life on them was an unbearable insult to their pride, especially since they were being forced to pay income taxes from their hard-earned money to support their hated oppressors. Into this tinderbox came John the Baptist, and the people were eager to hear the words, "The Kingdom of Heaven is at hand." The long tradition of messianic hope that God would restore the Kingdom of Israel brought throngs of people to the banks of the Jordan River to hear John's preaching.

John's life was as radical and bold as the message he preached. Living a hermit's life with locust and wild honey for a diet and wearing rough clothing made from camel's hair[5] added to the aura of this wilderness preacher. Large crowds of Jews from Jerusalem and other areas of Judea and Galilee came daily to witness this strange phenomenon. They gathered on the banks of the Jordan and waited expectantly for the wilderness preacher to appear. Striding down out of the desert hills he came; he looked over the crowd; and he then commenced to preach a message the like of which had not been heard since the days of the prophets of old. Many hearers whose hearts were touched by his preaching were baptized by him; thus, the name John the Baptist became attached to him.

The Originality of John's Baptism

Where John got the idea that he should baptize his disciples has been the subject of considerable speculation. Some suggest that it was the result of his association with the Essene sect of the Qumran Community. Others feel that the washings of the Law of Moses were his primary blueprint. Some see in John's baptism a version of the Jewish practice of proselyte

4. Matt 10:7.
5. Matt 3:4.

baptism. Was John merely propagating a baptism already in vogue, or was it independent of all previous ablutions? In order to clarify this matter, it is advantageous to look at the purpose of these other baptisms.

Qumran

The hermits of Qumran lived in an austere desert community, making use of caves dug into the cliffs overlooking the Jordan River valley as their habitation. It is from the scrolls they kept stored in those caves that we learn the nature of their lifestyle and their religious teachings. The Qumran community emphasized that their ablutions must be accompanied by both purity of heart and purity of body. No one was allowed to enter "the community" who walks

> in the stubbornness of his heart, for his soul detests the wise teaching of just laws . . . He shall not be reckoned among the perfect; he shall neither be purified by atonement, nor cleansed by purifying waters, nor sanctified by seas and rivers, nor washed clean with any ablution. Unclean, unclean shall he be. For as long as he despises the precepts of God he shall receive no instruction in the Community of his counsel.[6]

> *Concerning purification by water.* No man shall bathe in dirty water or in an amount too shallow to cover a man. He shall not purify himself with water contained in a vessel.[7]

Because these desert ascetics had a healthy respect for cleanness of both body and soul, it was common for them to practice baptismal ablutions frequently, even multiple times a day. Illnesses (especially leprosy), body emissions, touching of a corpse (animal or human), and even such things as impure thoughts called for cleansing rituals. They had strict laws concerning the numerous things that could render a person unclean and the rituals necessary to absolve them. Some of their cleansing rituals appear to have required living (running) water, while other ablutions did not. The nearest running water to their community was the Jordan River, which was about seven miles away. One can readily see why the lesser impurities that required frequent baptisms in their lives did not require running water. Their daily "washings" (to call them "baptisms" stretches the meaning of baptism) could be something as simple as a washing of

---

6. Vermes, "Manual of Discipline," 74–75.
7. Vermes, "Damascus Rule," 111–12.

the hands to the complete submersion of their body in cisterns made especially for that purpose.

Like their fellow Jewish contemporaries, the Qumran community saw water as a crucial element in these ablutions. Unlike pagan religions that also emphasized the role of water, the Qumran community placed significant emphasis on the fact that it was not the water of the ablutions that cleansed a person's soul but the condition of a heart in obedience to God and to the *Rule for the Community*.

Whether or not John the Baptist was influenced in any way by the Qumran Community is unclear. Since he lived in that same area,[8] he could hardly have failed to at least know about them. Both John and the Community associated a strong concern for cleansing with their baptismal practices, and both strongly insisted on a high level of moral conduct.

When we read the Qumran literature and the Gospels, it becomes apparent that there were several significant differences between the ablutions of the Qumran disciples and the baptism of John's disciples. It is obvious that John's baptism was a one-time event, whereas the Qumran disciples practiced their baptisms on a frequent basis.[9] Also, John's baptism was a passive act administered by John himself, whereas in the Qumran community the disciples typically baptized themselves. In their strict observance of the community's many regulations, their diligent pursuit for moral perfection and purity, and their repetitive ablutions, the Qumran devotees sought to purify themselves from the contaminations of the world. Noble as these virtues are, we find an absence of a humble and contrite bowing before the Lord appealing for his mercy. Rather, we find a rigid lifestyle by which they sought to obtain approval from God and their community through strict ascetic rituals. Yet, there was recognition of the grace of God and the need for divine mercy found in their hymns. Whether God's mercy was associated with their baptismal rituals is not clear.

> Righteousness, I know is not of man,
> nor is perfection of way of the son of man:
> to the Most High God belong all righteous deeds.
> The way of man is not established
> except by the spirit which God created for him

---

8. Matt (3:1, 5), Mark (1:4–5), and Luke (3:2–3) identified the area of John's ministry as the wilderness of Judea and that he was baptizing his disciples in the Jordan River.

9. Beasley-Murray, *Baptism*, 18–31.

> to make perfect a way for the children of men,
> that all his creatures might know
> the might of his power,
> and the abundance of his mercies
> towards all the sons of his grace . . .
> I lean on Thy grace
> and on the multitude of Thy mercies,
> for Thou wilt pardon iniquity
> and through Thy righteousness
> [Thou wilt purify man] of his sin.[10]

John's baptism was clearly for the cleansing of the soul and induction into a relationship with God. The community's various ablutions were concerned more with acceptance and continued favor in the community.[11] Missing in the community's teaching and practice of baptism was its connection with the grace of God, and in its place, the emphasis was placed on keeping themselves pure.

Law of Moses

Another suggested influence on John's practice of baptism was the many purification rites associated with the Law of Moses. There are many references in the Law, especially in Leviticus, concerning things that can bring about physical, moral, and spiritual impurity, all of which required a cleansing ritual. The cleansing of contaminated garments, cleansing of the priestly garments, washings associated with the sacrifices, bathing of the body after various bodily emissions, etc., make it obvious that the Jewish Law, like the Qumran Community and the old pagan practices, considered holiness important and associated it with cleansing rituals. These cleansing ablutions lack the emphasis on conversion we see in John's baptism. The frequent repetition of these ablutions sets them apart

---

10. Vermes, "Hymns," 163–64.

11. Most theological historians do not think that the Qumran Community associated their baptisms with God's grace. While they did put a strong emphasis on both spiritual and physical purity and believed that the ablutions associated with water had a purifying aspect, the absence of an appeal to God for forgiveness of sins was not a dominant theme in their teachings. However, Beasley-Murray (*Baptism*, 15–16) disagrees with this, " . . . it is essential that we do not under-estimate the genuinely sacramental nature of these lustrations." Later in that same paragraph he acknowledges that "Unfortunately our documents are vague at the point where we could have wished for clarity."

from John's baptism. These rituals were focused more on moral cleanness than the washing away the contamination of sin that we see in John's baptism.

> Accordingly both gifts and sacrifices [of the first covenant] are offered which cannot make the worshiper perfect in conscience, since they relate only to food and drink and various washings, regulations for the body imposed until a time of reformation.[12]

Jewish Proselytes

The question of whether the Jews had begun the practice of baptizing those who converted from paganism[13] to Judaism prior to the last decades of the first century AD is still an ongoing investigation.[14] Even if John was acquainted with Jewish proselyte baptisms, and even though there are similarities between the two practices, there are still too many differences to assume that John (and later the Christian church) got their baptismal origins from proselyte baptisms. Besides the lack of evidence for the early practice of proselyte baptism, there is a significant difference between the Gentile's baptism as an induction into the Jewish faith and the role of conversion in John's baptism. Circumcision was the crucial act that initiated the non-Jew into the Jewish faith. The baptism of the proselyte followed later as a ritual bath. Unlike John's baptism, the proselyte's baptism was a practice that took place after their conversion.

Divine Origin

While it is interesting to explore these baptismal practices that may have had some influence on the purpose of John's baptism, it is obvious that he came preaching a message that was unique in many ways. Luke declared, "the word of God came to John, the son of Zacharias, in the wilderness." His ministry was ordained of God and was the fulfillment of prophecy— "as it is written in the book of the words of Isaiah the prophet."[15] Whether or not John's message was influenced by the Qumran sect, the Law of

---

12. Heb 9:9–11.
13. The Jews considered anyone who was not of Jewish descent as a pagan, or heathen.
14. Beasley-Murray, *Baptism*, 18.
15. Luke 3:2, 4.

Moses, Jewish proselyte initiation, or any other ablutionary practices becomes irrelevant in light of the fact that "the word of God came to John." There can be no doubt that John was convinced that his preaching and practice of baptism were of God, not man.[16] Jesus clearly recognized this divine origin when he challenged the chief priests and elders.

> When he [Jesus] entered the temple, the chief priests and the elders of the people came to him while he was teaching, and said, "By what authority are you doing these things, and who gave you this authority?" Jesus said to them, "I will also ask you one thing, which if you tell me, I will also tell you by what authority I do these things. The baptism of John was from what source, from heaven or from men?" And they began reasoning among themselves, saying, "If we say, 'From heaven,' he will say to us, 'Then why did you not believe him?' But if we say, 'From men,' we fear the people; for they all regard John as a prophet." And answering Jesus, they said, "We do not know."[17]

Purpose of John's Baptism

John's message and baptism focused on three main themes: 1). he called the people to a conversion (repentance) baptism; 2). he heralded the immediate coming of the Kingdom of God; and 3). he called the people to live a high moral lifestyle. When the people came to hear him preach, they were amazed that their genealogy had not already automatically secured their salvation. He made it clear to the crowds who flocked out to hear,

> . . . and do not say to yourselves, "We have Abraham for our father," for I say to you that God is able from these stones to raise up children to Abraham.[18]

John's baptism was not a matter of national or ethnic identity; rather, it had to do with the individual's status in their relationship to God. In it, "a transition was sought from the condition and destiny of the unrighteous to that of the righteous."[19]

---

16. John 1:33.
17. Matt 21:23–27. See also Mark 11:27–33 and Luke 20:1–7.
18. Matt 3:9.
19. Beasley-Murray, *Baptism*, 33.

The significance and purpose of John's baptism becomes clear with a closer and more technical look at the relevant passages in Matthew, Mark, Luke, and Acts. There are five passages that describe the purpose of John's baptism:

> As for me, I baptize you with water for repentance . . .[20]

> John the Baptist appeared in the wilderness preaching a baptism of repentance for the forgiveness of sins.[21]

> And he [John] came into all the district around the Jordan, preaching a baptism of repentance for the forgiveness of sins.[22]

> . . . after John had proclaimed before his [Jesus] coming a baptism of repentance to all the people of Israel.[23]

> And Paul said, "John baptized with the baptism of repentance . . ."[24]

In these texts, repentance and forgiveness of sins are intimately associated with John's baptism. Any serious treatment of the doctrine of baptism as it is presented in the New Testament would be remiss without diligent examination of these passages.

Baptism of/into Repentance

"Repent, for the kingdom of heaven is at hand."[25] It is impossible to read the Gospel accounts about John the Baptist without recognizing that repentance was central to his message. Repentance is mentioned in connection with baptism in all five of the above passages. Matthew is different in that he uses the phrase "baptism for repentance" rather than the phrase "baptism of repentance."

Because John placed baptism in such an intimate relationship with repentance, we need to take a closer look at the meaning of repentance and its relationship to baptism. What is repentance? The answer to this question may seem obvious to some people, but since repentance is so

20. Matt 3:11.
21. Mark 1:4.
22. Luke 3:3.
23. Acts 13:24.
24. Acts 19:4.
25. Matt 3:2.

central to our salvation and there are so many definitions that have been put forth, it is important to make sure we are clear what we mean by it. For this endeavor, we turn to how it is used in the Old and New Testaments.

The primary Hebrew word for repent is *shub*. It occurs in the Old Testament over 1,050 times. It is found in Jeremiah 111 times, in the Psalms seventy-one times, in Genesis sixty-eight times, in Ezekiel sixty-two times, in 1 Kings sixty-two times, in 2 Chronicles sixty-one times, in 2 Kings fifty-five times, in Isaiah fifty-one times, and 509 times throughout the remaining Old Testament books.

Shub is sometimes used to refer to physical motion (e.g., "return"),[26] and sometimes to indicate repetition (e.g., "again").[27] But the more common use of *shub* describes a conversion, a change from alienation to fellowship with God. This is especially its intent in the prophets. The following verses from Ezekiel are a good example.

> And the word of the Lord came to me, saying, "Son of man, these men have set up their idols in their hearts and have put right before their faces the stumbling block of their iniquity . . . Therefore say to the house of Israel, 'Thus says the Lord God, "Repent [*shub*] and turn away [*shub*] from your idols and turn [*shub*] your faces away from all your abominations."'"[28]

These three occurrences of *shub* in such a short space clearly reflect the emphatic urgency to convert.[29]

Another Hebrew word, *nacham*, is often translated "repent." The origin of the root seems to reflect the idea of "breathing deeply," hence the physical display of one's feelings, usually sorrow, compassion, or comfort. It is primarily used to refer to God, not men.[30]

> The Lord was sorry [*nacham*] that he had made man on the earth, and he was grieved [*ahtsab*: displease, hurt] in his heart. The Lord said, "I will blot out man whom I have created from the face of the land, from man to animals to creeping things and to birds of the sky; for I am sorry [*nacham*] that I have made them."[31]

---

26. See Gen 18:14.
27. See Gen 26:18.
28. Ezek 14:2–3, 6.
29. Keil, *Ezekiel-Daniel*, 103.
30. Wilson, "*nacham*," 570–71.
31. Gen 6:6–7.

The use of the word *nacham* does not refer to "sorry" as we often use to it express apology for some wrong word or behavior. Rather, it indicates a feeling of injury or violation. The verb *ahtsab* in this passage can refer to physical pain as well as emotional and spiritual distress.[32]

The primary New Testament Greek verb for "repent" is *metanoeo* (*meta-no-e-o*). It occurs in the New Testament thirty-three times (fifteen times in Matt, Mark, and Luke; five times in Acts; once in Paul's letters; and twelve times in Rev). The noun, *metanoia* (repentance), occurs twenty-four times in the New Testament (ten times in Matthew, Mark, and Luke; six times in Acts; seven times in the letters of Paul and Hebrews; and once in Peter's letters).

In the New Testament, *metanoia*, like *shub* in the Old Testament, means "conversion." It refers to the act of being converted from "dead works" to a "faith toward God."[33] This conversion is a life-changing event. It is more than merely a cognitive recognition of sorrow for sin; it involves one's whole self. The intellect, the emotion, and the will are transformed in the conversion event.

In the Mark, Luke, and Acts passages above, baptism is described as a "baptism of repentance" (*baptisma metanoias*). The genitive of description, *metanoias*, is a noun that describes the nature of the baptism. John did not practice just any baptism, but specifically a baptism in which repentance occurred. In his baptism was an appeal to God for a radical change, a transformation from the condemnation of the unrighteous to the blessedness of the righteous. It was a baptism of change from unclean to clean, from profane to sanctified, and consequently, from being out of favor with God to being in his favor. Though metanoia is most often translated with the word "repentance," it is more accurately understood by using the word "conversion." John practiced a conversion baptism.

Matthew's wording, though a little different, also integrates repentance (conversion) into the act of baptism. According to Matthew, John the Baptist was baptizing people "for [*eis*] repentance." Since the preposition *eis* conveys the concept of purpose, John's baptism was the place where his disciples were converted. Matthew's use of the preposition *eis* expresses the purpose (i.e., repentance) of the action in the verb

---

32. Allen, "*ahtsab*," 687–88.
33. Heb 6:1.

(baptize). John was preaching a baptism "into," or "for the purpose of," conversion.[34]

Much hinges on how the preposition *eis* is translated in these verses. It is frequently presumed that in certain passages of the Bible, the preposition *eis* can be translated as causal. That is, instead of treating the preposition as purposive ("for the purpose of"), they prefer to render *eis* as casual ("because of"), especially in verses where baptism is mentioned alongside repentance and forgiveness of sins. Thus, they translate such phrases as Matt 3:11 as causal—"I baptize you with water because of repentance"—where repentance is seen as something that occurs antecedent to baptism. If this causal use of *eis* were legitimate, then baptism would be an act that occurs subsequent to repentance rather than concurrent with repentance. For further discussion on the meaning of *eis*, see the "Excursus on *Eis*" at the end of this chapter.

The radical transformation John called for in *baptisma metanoias* was more than a change in moral behavior; it was a radical conversion in one's relationship with God. A change in their moral behavior was the necessary result of such a baptism, not the purpose for their baptism. John preached with great fervor, saying that once they were transformed from being alienated from God to citizenship in the Kingdom of God in their baptism, they could no longer live by their old desires. Now, whatever they did in word or deed, it had to be according to the will of God for his glory.

Many of the Jews stumbled over the idea of a need for conversion. After all, they were already children of Abraham; they were already God's people. So why was John preaching to them the need to be converted? The Pharisees and Sadducees addressed this same issue with Jesus,

> We are Abraham's descendants and have never yet been enslaved to anyone; how is it that you say, "You will become free?"[35]

They failed to recognize that it was not their national identity that needed changing but their relationship to God. John was calling them to a baptism in which occurred a conversion from self-lordship to the lordship of God.

---

34. Beasley-Murray, *Baptism*, 34.
35. John 8:33.

Josephus on the Purpose of John's Baptism

Herod Antipas married Phasaelis of Nabatae, daughter of Aretas, king of Arabia, but later he fell in love with Herodias, his brother's wife. He secretly made plans to divorce Phasaelis and marry Herodias. However, Phasaelis learned of it and returned to her father in Arabia. Enmity already existed between Herod and Aretas over border disputes and now, with the unethical treatment of his daughter, he made war with Herod. Herod was defeated and among the Jews some were convinced that he lost the battle because God was displeased over his execution of John the Baptist. In writing about these events, Josephus gave his opinion on the purpose of John's baptism.

> Now some of the Jews thought that the destruction of Herod's army came from God, and that very justly, as a punishment of what he did against John, that was called the Baptist; for Herod slew him, who was a good man, and commanded the Jews to exercise virtue, both as to righteousness towards one another, and piety towards God, and so to come to baptism; for that the washing [with water] would be acceptable to him, if they made use of it, not in order to the putting away [or the remission] of some sins [only], but for the purification of the body; supposing still that the soul was thoroughly purified beforehand by righteousness. Now when [many] others came in crowds about him, for they were very greatly moved [or pleased] by hearing his words, Herod, who feared lest the great influence John had over the people might put it into his power and inclination to raise a rebellion (for they seemed ready to do any thing he should advise), thought it best, by putting him to death, to prevent any mischief he might cause, and not bring himself into difficulties, by sparing a man who might make him repent of it when it would be too late. Accordingly he was sent a prisoner, out of Herod's suspicious temper, to Macherus, the castle I before mentioned, and was there put to death. Now the Jews had an opinion that the destruction of this army was sent as a punishment upon Herod, and a mark of God's displeasure to him. (Words in brackets by translator)[36]

Whereas Mark and Luke describe the purpose of John's baptism as a "baptism of repentance for the forgiveness of sins" (*baptisma metanoias*

---

36. Josephus, *Antiquities of the Jews* 18.5.2 (18.24).

eis aphesin hamartion),[37] and Peter made the point that baptism is "not the removal of dirt from the flesh" (*ou sarkos apotheosis hrupou*),[38] Josephus, in contradiction to these biblical authors, declared that the baptism of John was "not in order to the putting away [or the remission] of some sins [only], but for the purification of the body" (brackets by translator). Josephus further emphasized his opinion of John's baptism by stating "that the soul was thoroughly purified beforehand by righteousness."

Sin, Sorrow, and Repentance

There have been many attempts to equate repentance with sorrow. Some have assumed that repentance means simply an intellectual (and perhaps emotional) regret for the sins in their life, that it merely means "to be sorry for sin." This would require that repentance be understood as a prerequisite to baptism. We do not at all wish to diminish the importance of sorrow or its relationship to repentance. A healthy sin-awareness is vital to understanding repentance; it is a very biblical concept. Sorrow is the attitude that brings a person to the repentance (conversion) found in baptism. Repentance cannot be both conversion and the catalyst that brings about conversion. Paul gave us a clear understanding of the nature of repentance and of its relationship with sorrow and regret.

2 Corinthians 7:8–11

> For though I caused you sorrow [*lupeo*] by my letter, I do not regret [*metamelomai*] it; though I did regret [*metamelomai*] it for—I see that that letter caused you sorrow [*lupeo*], though only for a while—I now rejoice, not that you were made sorrowful [*lupeo*], but that you were made sorrowful [*lupeo*] to the point of [*eis*] repentance [*metanoia*]; for you were made sorrowful [*lupeo*] according to the will of God, so that you might not suffer loss in anything through us. For the sorrow [*lupei*] that is according to the will of God produces a repentance [*metanoia*] without regret, leading to [*eis*] salvation, but the sorrow [*lupei*] of the world produces death. For behold what earnestness this very thing, this godly sorrow [*lupeo*], has produced in you: what vindication of yourselves, what indignation, what fear, what

---

37. Mark 1:4 and Luke 3:3.
38. 1 Pet 3:21.

longing, what zeal, what avenging of wrong! In everything you demonstrated yourselves to be innocent in the matter.[39]

In this passage, the words sorrow (*lupeo*) and regret (*metamelomai*) were used by Paul to express a concept quite different from repentance (*metanoia*). The experience of grief (*lupeo*) and the hurt of regret (*metamelomai*) are internal attitudes only, whereas repentance is a restoration of a broken relationship. Thomas Brents clearly explained the difference between sorrow for sin and repentance:

> When used in the New Testament as a command to the alien [non-Christian] in order to the remission of sins, it [*metanoeo*] always indicates such a change of mind as produces a change or reformation of life under circumstances warranting the conclusion that sorrow for the past would or had preceded it. When so used it is invariably a translation of the Greek word *metanoia*; and when used to indicate sorrow or regret it is always from *metamelomai*—a different word, though improperly rendered the same in English. Had these words been properly translated we think it likely that much of the confusion on the subject of repentance would have been prevented. Regret is certainly a much more fitting representative of *metamelomai* than repentance. And why it has not been so translated is more than we can tell . . . The words *repentance*, in the commission Luke xxiv:47, and *repent*, as used by Peter, Acts ii:38 and iii:19, are from the Greek *metanoia*, and not from *metamelomai*, and hence means *more* than sorrow for past sins.[40]

This same distinction between remorse and repentance is also noted by Otto Michel in his article on *metamelomai* in the *Theological Dictionary of the New Testament*:

> When "remorse" is ascribed to man, there is an obvious difference from repentance (*metanoein*) . . . *metamelesthai* is not equivalent to *metanoein*. When Judas saw that Jesus was condemned, he was filled with remorse (*metameleisthei*) and brought back the thirty pieces of silver.[41]

39. 2 Cor 7:8–11.

40. Brents, *Plan of Salvation*, 236. Thomas Wesley Brents (1823–1905) published his first edition in 1874. He was a medical doctor, college president, businessman and preacher. For more details about him see http://www.therestorationmovement.com/books/BSOpdf, 204–7.

41. Michel, "*metamelomai, ametameleitos*," Theological Dictinary of the New Testament, 627–28.

Remorse (*metamelomai* and *lupeo*) without conversion (*metanoeo*) "does not have the power to overcome the destructive operation of sin."[42] In like manner, *metanoeo* without *metamelomai* is an empty and meaningless ritual.

Sorrow (the cause) cannot be the same thing as repentance (the result). In his commentary on Acts 2:38, Frederick Brunner remarked, "Repentance is not adequately defined as regret; this the hearers [in Acts 2] already had."[43] Without the prerequisite of sorrow, repentance has no meaning. Mere sorrow may or may not result in appropriate repentant action. Intellectual conversion ("change of mind") without surrender of the heart and body to the lordship of God is not *metanoia*. When "conversion" is recognized as the essence of the meaning of *metanoia*, it gives it a new and deeper insight than merely meaning "sorrow for sin."

Sorrow is a word that is used to express the effect of pain. There are as many shades of sorrow as there are types and levels of pain. Things happen in life that hurt; some hurt more than others. Whether it be physical, emotional, social, or spiritual pain, sorrow is the natural reaction. Pain is common to everyone and causes each of us to react in our own unique way. Tears come in many different facets and with a whole plethora of emotions.

The greatest and deepest pain is caused by sin. Sin hurts! It hurts the sinner; it hurts those around the sinner; *but most of all, sin hurts God!* What concerned king David the most about his sin with Bathsheba was the pain it caused his beloved God.

> For I know my transgressions,
> And my sin is ever before me.
> Against you, you only, I have sinned
> And done what is evil in your sight,
> So that you are justified when you speak
> And blameless when you judge.[44]

The Bible treats sin as a serious matter. Sin contaminates. And, consequently, sin is the great alienator between God and people. The consequence of sin is death, not merely death of the body, but eternal death of the soul as well.

---

42. Michel, "metamelomai, ametameleitos," 628.
43. Bruner, *A Theology*, 166.
44. Ps 51:3–4.

This is why the intimate association of *metanoia* with holiness/sanctification (*qadosh* and *hagios*) must be maintained, as we saw in the last chapter. The conversion (*metanoia*) that takes place in baptism transforms/converts a person from a defiled and condemned soul to a sanctified and redeemed soul, fit for the Kingdom of God. Herein also is the heart of justification—a broken relationship made right and restored.

Repentance is not something we must do as a step toward salvation. That is, it is not a work that the one coming to baptism—the baptizand—must do in order to be saved. *Metanoia* is the conversion that is accomplished by God's work of sanctification in the waters of baptism. While there must be a willingness on the part of the convert to submit to the conversion, the blessings that are accomplished in conversion are all wholly acts of God. The part to be performed in *baptisma metanoias* by the baptizand is to be a willing, passive recipient. *For John the Baptist, repentance was not something the convert had to do as a precursor that led them to baptism; rather, they came to baptism to receive it.*[45]

Baptism for the Forgiveness of Sins

When John baptized his disciples, they were, in that baptism, inducted into a new relationship with God. In that new life, their new Lord endowed them with all the blessings heaven has to offer.[46] In that moment they were transferred from being strangers to God's Kingdom to full citizenship in God's Kingdom. In order for that transformation to take place, something had to be done about their guilt of sin. There could be no admittance into that Kingdom if there was any uncleanness in the converts. Mark and John reported[47] that John's baptism was not only a *baptisma metanoias*; it was also a *baptisma metanoias eis aphesin hamartiown* (baptism of repentance for the forgiveness of sins), where the *eis* expresses the purpose of the baptism. In one wonderful event, John's disciples were both cleansed of the guilt of their sins and inducted into the Kingdom.

This dual purpose of repentance and forgiveness in baptism must not be overlooked or made light of. Jesus clearly united repentance and forgiveness as inseparable when he said,

---

45. Beasley-Murray, *Baptism*, 34.
46. Eph 1:3–14.
47. Mark 1:4; John 3:3.

> Thus it is written, that the Christ would suffer and rise again from the dead the third day, and that repentance for forgiveness of sins [*metanoian eis aphesin hamartion*] would be proclaimed in his name to all the nations, beginning from Jerusalem.[48]

Though the word "baptism" was not used in this passage by Jesus, it is the same grammatical construction as seen in the above references to John's baptism. In Mark 1:4 and Acts 2:38, forgiveness is so bound to repentance and baptism that it would be a gross violation of Scripture to separate them. *Therefore, John's baptism for forgiveness of sins was a purification ritual, an act of God in which he sanctified the sinner; it was an act that resulted in the transformation/conversion of their relationship with God.*

"Objection!" some say. The forgiveness of sins could not have been accomplished in John's baptism because it says in Hebrews that the death of Jesus holds the exclusive power of the forgiveness of sins for all people for all time. How could John's disciples receive forgiveness when Christ's blood had not yet been shed?

> but through his own blood, he entered the holy place once for all, having obtained eternal redemption.[49]

> By this will [of God] we have been sanctified through the offering of the body of Jesus Christ once for all. Every priest stands daily ministering and offering time after time the same sacrifices, which can never take away sins; but he, having offered one sacrifice for sins for all time, SAT DOWN AT THE RIGHT HAND OF GOD, waiting from that time onward UNTIL HIS ENEMIES BE MADE A FOOTSTOOL FOR HIS FEET. For by one offering he has perfected for all time those who are sanctified.[50]

> for the death that he died, he died to sin once for all . . . [51]

In light of these verses, many have concluded that since, in the days of John the Baptist, the Cross was not yet a reality, all of the sins of those who lived prior to the Cross were not forgiven but were somehow "rolled forward," "held in limbo," or in some sense "suspended" until Jesus died on the Cross. Then, in his great sacrifice, Jesus brought all of those ancient

---

48. Luke 24:46–47.
49. Heb 9:12.
50. Heb 10:10–14.
51. Rom 6:10.

sins forward and cleansed all the faithful who had died previous to his death. In support of this view, appeal is made to a passage in Hebrews where it says,

> For the Law, since it has only a shadow of the good things to come and not the very form of things, can never, by the same sacrifices which they offer continually year by year, make perfect those who draw near. Otherwise, would they not have ceased to be offered, because the worshipers, having once been cleansed, would no longer have had consciousness of sins? But in those sacrifices there is a reminder of sins year by year.[52]

There is no reference in this passage to the timing of the forgiveness of sin, nor is there any indication that the guilt of their sins was "rolled forward." The point in verse 1 simply indicates that the sacrifices of the Old Law were impotent to pardon sin. Heb 10:3 explains that the purpose of the yearly sacrifices was to serve as *reminders* to the people of their sinful nature. The sacrifices kept their sinful nature in their conscious awareness for the need of God's grace.

Leviticus 4:20 is a typical example of several Old Testament passages that refer to forgiveness in relation to the sacrifice of the sin offering.

> He shall also do with the bull just as he did with the bull of the sin offering; thus he shall do with it. So the priest shall make atonement for them, and they will be forgiven.[53]

Other similar verses include Lev 4:26, 31, 35, 5:10, 13, 16, 18, 6:7, 19:22; Num 15:25, 26, 28; and Deut 21:8. Because most translations, such as the NIV, ESV, NASU, RSV, KJV, and NKJV, translate the perfect verb "forgiven" prefixed by "shall" or "will" ("will be forgiven"), it has been assumed that the actual forgiveness is to be a future event that looks forward to a future date such as the death of Christ. However, a closer look at the grammar in these verses gives us a clearer understanding of the timing of the sacrifices and forgiveness.

Both "atonement" and "forgiven" are in the perfect tense. The Hebrew language has two tenses, whereas the English has three tenses. In English, we primarily use our verb tenses to describe action in the past, the present, or the future. The two Hebrew tenses, the perfect and the imperfect, are not so concerned with the timing of the action as the status

---

52. Heb 10:1–3.
53. Lev 4:20.

of the action.[54] The perfect tense verb identifies action that is completed, and the imperfect tense verb identifies action that is in progress, or continuous. Because the perfect refers to action that is bounded by a start and a finish, it is often translated as past tense. In the above passages "atonement" and "forgiven," therefore, are represented as a completed action—"are forgiven" rather than "shall/will be forgiven."

In the Mosaic Law (Exodus–Deuteronomy), the Israelites received instructions from God as to how they should conduct their lives as his people. In the above verses, the instructions concerning sacrifices were to be performed at given times by the priests for the people. The sacrifices themselves did not accomplish the forgiveness of their sins. As was noted above, there are several New Testament passages that make it clear that there is no forgiveness apart from the Cross of Christ.

> But in those sacrifices there is a reminder of sins year by year. For it is impossible for the blood of bulls and goats to take away sins.[55]

As long as the Israelites were practicing the sacrifices as prescribed in the Law, God was in the process of extending his mercy upon them, cleansing them of their sins. If they stopped the sacrifices, his forgiveness also stopped. As baptism does not itself forgive sins, but is the condition God chose for it, so the sacrifices did not take away the sins, but was the condition God chose to remind them of their sins and his mercy. Therefore, these verses are not addressing the absence of the forgiveness of sin in the period of the Old Testament; rather, they give the people the assurance that when they practice the Law, they have forgiveness of their sins.

However, the above objection to forgiveness in John's baptism is an astute issue worthy of our consideration. We cannot ignore the fact that apart from the blood of Christ there is no forgiveness. Nor can we ignore the fact that sins were forgiven by God prior to the Cross. In the Old Testament, there are too many passages that specifically state that God forgave (completed action) the people of their sin, which necessitates the

---

54. Weingreen, *Practical Grammar*, 56.
    In Hebrew thinking, an action is regarded as being either completed or incomplete. Hebrew, therefore, knows of no past, present, or future tenses, but has instead a Perfect and an Imperfect (which, in a context, lend themselves to a variety of shades in meaning).
55. Heb 10:3–4.

fact that before Jesus died on the Cross God was actively forgiving the sins of his people.

> "Pardon, I [Moses] pray, the iniquity of this people according to the greatness of your lovingkindness, just as you also have forgiven [past tense] this people, from Egypt even until now." So the Lord said, "I have pardoned [past tense] them according to your word."[56]

David spoke of the removal of guilt as a present reality in his day, not a future event to come many centuries later.

> How blessed is he whose transgression is forgiven,
> Whose sin is covered!
> How blessed is the man to whom the Lord does not impute iniquity,
> And in whose spirit there is no deceit!
> I acknowledged my sin to you,
> And my iniquity I did not hide;
> I said, "I will confess my transgressions to the Lord";
> And you forgave the guilt of my sin.[57]

As participles, the verbs "forgiven" and "covered" in verse one indicate continuous, ongoing action in progress.[58] David's words radiate his passion as he recognized that God was always there to keep all who acknowledge their sins to him pure and sanctified. This, to David, was always a present reality in his life! With the perfect verb, "you forgave," in verse five David expressed confidence that God's forgiveness was a completed reality.[59] In the same way, Isaiah's guilt of "unclean of lips" was taken away and purged as a present reality at the time of his vision:

> Then I said,
> "Woe is me, for I am ruined!
> Because I am a man of unclean lips,
> And I live among a people of unclean lips;
> For my eyes have seen the King, the Lord of hosts."
> Then one of the seraphim flew to me with a burning coal in his hand, which he had taken from the altar with tongs. He touched my mouth

---

56. Num 14:19–20.
57. Ps 32:1, 2, 5.
58. Lambdin, *Introduction to Biblical Hebrew*, 19.
59. Weingreen, *Practical Grammar*, 56.

with it and said, "Behold, this has touched your lips; and your iniquity is taken away and your sin is forgiven."[60]

On his blog, Kevin Cauley tried to find evidence for his conviction that there was no forgiveness of sins under the old covenant.

> In Heb 10:1, the writer of that book as inspired of the Holy Spirit makes the case that the sins under the Old Covenant were not actually forgiven.[61]

Later in this same article, Cauley attempted to explain the problem of forgiveness of sin under the Old Covenant and to reconcile it with the timing of Jesus' death.

> If we recognize Christ as the one and only sacrifice to forgive sin for all times, then the offering of sacrifice under that Old Law represented *potential* forgiveness. That is, they would be potentially forgiven of their sins until Christ came and shed his blood on the cross. Then they could have *actual* forgiveness.[62]

We must object to his unauthorized splitting of forgiveness into *potential* forgiveness and *actual* forgiveness. The identification of two types of forgiveness is nowhere to be found in Scripture! Potential forgiveness? What is that? As we have seen, the Old Testament text says in the above verses (Num 14:19–20; Ps 32:1; and Isa 6:5–7)[63] that the cleansing action of forgiveness was a done deal, not a potential future event; it was a completed action accomplished by God at that time. Is there, then, an error in such an important doctrine in the Bible? Doesn't the Bible say that the only sacrifice for sin is the death of Jesus which was an event that was once for all? But yet, does not the Bible also refer to sins in the Old Testament that were forgiven long before the incarnation and death of Jesus?

At first glance, this may *appear* to be an inconsistency between the Old and New Testaments. If the Bible does, in fact, contradict itself on this vital topic, then we have a grave problem. If this is indeed an error, it brings into question the reliability of the entire Bible. If the Bible errs in one place, especially on such a critical topic, how can it be trusted in other places? It is *not* our purpose here to give an extended defense for the authority and accuracy of the Bible. The question we are faced with

---

60. Isa 6:5–7.
61. Cauley, "Rolled Forward?"
62. Cauley, "Rolled Forward?"
63. See also Ps 85:2.

is whether there are any other credible options to resolve this particular *supposed* error that does not destroy the integrity of the Bible.

One plausible solution is to realize that we are looking at this matter with temporal human eyes, while God sees it with eternal divine eyes. If we were to look at the reality of the Cross from God's *eternal perspective*, we would recognize that, for God, the Cross was a reality from before the beginning of time. Since God is omniscient and knows everything there is to be known in the past, the present, and the future, he knew intimately every detail of the Cross event from before the beginning of time. He knew the pain and agony of the death of his Son from before Gen 1:1. God – the Father, the Son, and the Holy Spirit – was, from eternity, fully aware of the agony brought upon him by the sins of his beloved creatures, and the cost for him to redeem his children. Therefore, since the fullness of the suffering of Christ's death has always been a reality for him, the blood-price for man's sin was, *in God's reality*, shed from before the foundation of the world! If this explanation of the forgiveness of sins is real, then the forgiveness of sins in the Old Testament and in John's baptisms makes very good sense and is in keeping with other biblical passages.

Differences Between John's Practice of Baptism and Jesus'

John made it clear that he was not the Messiah, and that there was a difference between the baptism he practiced and the baptism that would be taught by Jesus. He said,

> As for me, I baptize you with water for repentance, but he who is coming after me is mightier than I, and I am not fit to remove his sandals; he will baptize you with the Holy Spirit and fire.[64]

> The people were in a state of expectation and all were wondering in their hearts about John, as to whether he was the Christ. John answered and said to them all, "As for me, I baptize you with water; but One is coming who is mightier than I, and I am not fit to untie the thong of his sandals; he will baptize you with the Holy Spirit and fire."[65]

> Gathering them together, he [Jesus] commanded them not to leave Jerusalem, but to wait for what the Father had promised, "Which," he said, "you heard of from me; for John baptized with

---

64. Matt 3:11.
65. Luke 3:15–16.

water, but you will be baptized with the Holy Spirit not many days from now."[66]

It is beyond the scope of this project to explore the significance of the Holy Spirit and fire in connection with the practice of Jesus' baptism. There have been many who have offered a wide variety of opinions on this. What John meant by the difference between his baptism and Jesus' baptism, he did not clearly define, nor is this difference clearly explained by any other writer of the New Testament. The authors of this study recognize that there was a difference between John's baptism and the baptism practiced later by the church. The connection of the Holy Spirit and fire with baptism may be the reason why John's disciples were re-baptized when they became followers of Jesus in the book of Acts.

> It happened that while Apollos was at Corinth, Paul passed through the upper country and came to Ephesus, and found some disciples. He said to them, "Did you receive the Holy Spirit when you believed?" And they said to him, "No, we have not even heard whether there is a Holy Spirit." And he said, "Into what then were you baptized?" And they said, "Into John's baptism." Paul said, "John baptized with the baptism of repentance, telling the people to believe in him who was coming after him, that is, in Jesus." When they heard this, they were baptized in the name of the Lord Jesus. And when Paul had laid his hands upon them, the Holy Spirit came on them, and they began speaking with tongues and prophesying.[67]

Luke does mention that they received the Holy Spirit when Paul laid his hands on them. However, Paul identifies the reason for their need to be rebaptized had more to do with their need to be "baptized in [*eis*: into] the name of the Lord Jesus." Given that there was a difference in the work of the Holy Spirit among God's people before and after the Day of Pentecost as described in Acts 2, we want to be careful to not draw inferences that cannot be found in the Bible.

Significance of John's Baptism

It had been over four hundred years since Israel had heard the voices of her great prophets. The years between the last of the Old Testament

---

66. Acts 1:4–5.
67. Acts 19:1–6.

prophets and the birth of Jesus were filled with political strife, social upheaval, and much spiritual darkness. Into that void came John the Baptist. A fresh voice from God once again rang through the land. John reconnected the people to the redeeming preaching of the prophets, calling them to return to an old theme that, in John's day, had been largely forgotten:

> Now then, if you will indeed obey my voice and keep my covenant, then you shall be my own possession among all the peoples, for all the earth is mine; ⁶ and you shall be to me a kingdom of priests and a holy nation.[68]

After 400 years of silence, God once again made a dramatic entrance into human history as John came preaching the same demand that God had made of the Israelites from the days of Moses, "For I am the Lord your God. Consecrate yourselves therefore, and *be holy, for I am holy.*"[69] Malachi, the last of the Old Testament prophets, ended his preaching by predicting this day of restoration and the preaching of John the Baptist:

> Behold, I am going to send you Elijah the prophet before the coming of the great and terrible day of the Lord. He will restore the hearts of the fathers to their children and the hearts of the children to their fathers, so that I will not come and smite the land with a curse.[70]

It was John, Jesus said, who was this new Elijah.[71] It was in John's preaching and baptism that the people found *forgiveness*, the cleansing that made them a holy people. Once again, they heard in John the call of the old redeeming message of holiness; they heard the call to experience anew the joy of being a cleansed people before God and therefore fit to enter the Kingdom of God. This *conversion* was the essence of the baptism preached by John. This baptism was more than a call for a moral conversion, though that was expected of John's converts. This was a call for something far greater, a transformation in one's relationship to God, the Holy One, who alone could convert them from unrighteous sinners to sanctified citizens of his Holy Nation—the Kingdom of God!

---

68. Exod 19:5–6.
69. Lev 11:44.
70. Mal 4:5–6.
71. Matt 11:14; 17:1–13; Mark 9:11–13.

Excursus 2

On the Meaning of Eis in the New Testament

Prepositions are words that show a relationship between nouns
or pronouns and other words or phrases in a sentence.[1]

THE GREEK PREPOSITION *EIS* (pronounced "ace") is a common preposition in the New Testament (used about 1750 times). Prepositions are little words that, though they are easily overlooked, give illumination to a sentence. An English teacher once wisely commented, "Prepositions are pesky little words. Chew them slowly and dissect them carefully, for they are exasperating but immeasurably useful little words."

In many New Testament passages, a preposition can make a significant difference in the meaning of the text and the doctrines taught therein. Though they are basically simple, these little fragments of the sentence offer the serious Bible student an extensive depth and wealth of understanding. This is especially true of the preposition *eis*. In this Excursus, we will explore how the word *eis* enlightens the relationship between its verbs and nouns, specifically regarding faith, baptism, repentance, and forgiveness.

Many prepositions, such as "in," "on," or "beside," indicate location (e.g., "I am riding *in* my car"), while others, such as "into," "through," or "out of," describe motion (e.g., "The boy ran *through* the room"). Some prepositions have both a physical and a non-physical sense, which is determined by the root meaning of the preposition. *Eis* is an example of such a preposition. In the physical sense, it indicates the purpose of

---

1. "Confused Prepositions."

the subject's movement from outside to inside a place (such as a room). In the phrase, "Bill walked into the house," the word "into" shows the purpose of the movement: to get from outside to inside the house. In a metaphysical sense, *eis* is also used where there is no physical motion, but the idea of purpose ("in order to") is still expressed. For example, in the sentence "The defendant spoke boldly *in order to* convince the jury," the purpose for speaking boldly was to convince the jury.

The preposition *eis* is used exclusively with an objective noun, pronoun, adjective, or participle in a sentence. In New Testament Greek, it is easy to know whether a noun, pronoun, adjective, or participle is the subject (nominative case), the object (accusative case), or the indirect object (dative case) in a sentence by the ending letters of the word. For example, *anthropos* ("a man") is always the subject in a sentence because of the last two letters; in the same way, *anthropon* will always be the object in a sentence. *Eis* will always be followed by an accusative case word. As the recipient of the action of the transitive verb that precedes it, the accusative case with an *eis* in front of it indicates the purpose of the verbal action. Because *eis* is used in this way, it is referred to as a purposive preposition.

Different prepositions, such as *dia*, when used with the accusative case show the cause of the verbal action (e.g., "because of," "on account of," "as the result of") and are referred to as causal prepositions. For example, Jesus said, "You are already clean because of (*dia*) the word which I have spoken to you."[2] There has been much debate whether *eis* can also be used in a causal sense like *dia* or if *eis* is used exclusively as a purposive preposition. The causal preposition puts the timing of its objective (accusative) noun as occurring before the action of the verb, whereas the purposive preposition puts the timing of its objective noun as concurrent with the action of the verb, thus enhancing and defining the meaning of the verbal action.

This debate about whether *eis* can be used in a causative manner has frequently centered on Acts 2:38.

> Peter said to them, "Repent, and each of you be baptized in the name of Jesus Christ for (*eis*) the forgiveness of your sins; and you will receive the gift of the Holy Spirit."

At the crux of this debate is the relationship between baptism and forgiveness. If, on the one hand, *eis* can be translated as purposive, then

---

2. John 15:3.

forgiveness of sins is what takes place in baptism as the purpose of baptism. On the other hand, if *eis* is causative (because of forgiveness), then baptism is an event that occurs after conversion because the sins have already been forgiven.

It is the purpose of this excursus to demonstrate that *eis*, as it is used in the New Testament, is exclusively purposive in regard to the relationship between baptism and salvation. Greek language scholars have universally recognized that there is no evidence to support the translation of *eis* as causal. Even those who advocate that *eis* can be used as a causal preposition in some passages recognize that there is no lexical evidence to support such a use. In 1951–52, Drs. J. R. Mantey and Ralph Marcus held a running debate through four articles in the *Journal of Biblical Literature* concerning whether there are any passages where *eis* could be translated causally.[3] At the beginning of the series of articles, in which he proposed that *eis* can be translated as causal in some verses, Prof. Mantey wrote,

> NONE of the Greek lexicons translate *eis* as causal . . . Since *usage rather than lexicons establishes the meanings of words*, we shall present inductive evidence by citing several passages in which the contexts *seem to demand* a causal translation for *eis*. However, we have to admit at the outset that *this type of usage is infrequent and rare*.[4] (emphasis added)

There are three things of note in this quote: (1) Prof. Mantey stated that none of the Greek lexicons render *eis* in a causative sense, (2) usage and inductive reasoning, rather than lexicons, establishes the meaning of words such as *eis*, and (3) the causal usage of *eis* "is infrequent and rare."

In his first point, he was correct concerning the lexical use of *eis* (as we shall see below). Based on lexical research, the evidence is overwhelmingly against the use of *eis* as a causal preposition in the New Testament. At the request of Julius Mantey, Wilbur Gingrich inserted a mini-note in his translation and revision of Walter Baur's monumental *Greek-English Lexicon* in which he indicated that some linguists have advocated for a causal use of *eis*:

> 6. Other uses of *eis*—a. at, in the face of *metyanoein eis to keirugma* repent at the proclamation Mt 12:41; Lk 11:32; cf. Ro 4:20 and perh. Mt 3:11. JR Mantey, JBL, 70, '51, 45–8, 309–11

---

3. Mantey, "Causal Use of *Eis*," 45–48; Marcus, "On Causal *Eis*," 129–30; Mantey, "On Causal *Eis* Again," 309–11; Marcus, "The Elusive Causal *Eis*," 43–44.

4. Mantey, "Causal Use of *Eis*," 45.

argues for a causal use here *because of the proclaim.*, with ref.; against him R Marcus, ibid. 129f; 71, 52, 43f.[5]

In Gingrich's "Other uses of *eis*," there is a tone of reluctance to acknowledge the causal use of *eis* in that he makes a point to credit Julius Mantey rather than himself with that view and points out that Ralph Marcus was in disagreement with Mantey.

In his second point above, Prof. Mantey made a dangerous assumption by subjecting lexical evidence to "usage," where the way a reader thinks a word should be used usurps the lexical evidence. With such subjective determination of what a word means, anyone can define a word based on their own personal understanding in any passage. When a translator advocates for a usage that is contrary to a long history of lexical definition, they must give convincing evidence for their conclusion. They cannot draw their conclusion based on their preconceived theology and with no regard for the meaning of the word as it was intended by the author.

In his third point, Prof. Mantey admitted that the causal use of *eis* "is infrequent and rare." Even if it could be admitted that there are "infrequent and rare" cases in the New Testament where *eis* can be translated as causative, it must be conclusively proven that a purposive usage would, without a doubt, be impossible. It is a basic rule when translating from one language into another that the translator should use the normal meaning of a word first unless that meaning cannot apply in the context. As we shall see later in this study, there are far more than a few "infrequent and rare" occurrences of *eis* in regard to its relationship to baptism, repentance, and forgiveness. In order to be consistent, causal *eis* advocates would have to translate *eis* as causal, not in a few "infrequent and rare" passages, but in every passage that relates *eis* to baptism.

In his article where he said, "usage rather than lexicons establishes the meanings of words," Prof. Mantey put forth the false presupposition that a person's (or church's) theology should take precedence over the actual grammar of the text. That same reasoning was used by Dr. A. T. Robertson when he advocated that theology should take precedence over careful grammatical exegesis of the text of the New Testament.

> Hence a case like Acts 2:38 *eis aphesin ton hamartion* [*into forgiveness of sins*] can mean either *on the basis of forgiveness of sins* (cf. Mk. 1:4f) or *with a view to forgiveness of sins*. There is

---

5. Baur, *A Greek-English Lexicon*, 230.

> nothing in *eis* to compel either result. One will interpret according to his theology.[6]
>
> After all is done, instances remain where *syntax* [grammatical structure] *cannot say the last word, where theological bias will inevitably determine how one interprets the Greek idiom* . . . So in Ac. 2:38 *eis* does not of itself express design (see Mt. 10:41), but it may be so used. *When the grammarian has finished, the theologian steps in, and sometimes before the grammarian is through.*[7] (emphasis added)
>
> 5. *Aim or Purpose.* Sometimes indeed *eis* appears in an atmosphere where aim or purpose is manifestly the resultant idea . . . But it by no means follows that the same idea is expressed by *eis aphesin* in Mk 1:4 and Ac. 2:38 (cf. Mt. 10:41), though that may in abstract be true. *It remains a matter for the interpreter to decide.*[8] (Emphasis added.)

Using this line of reasoning, Prof. Robertson interpreted baptism in Acts 2:38 as a post-conversion experience simply on the basis of what the interpreter decides rather than on what the text says. In line with such illogic he concludes,

> The first thing to do is make a radical and complete change of heart and life. Then let each one be baptized *after* this change has taken place, and the act of baptism be performed "in the name of Jesus Christ"[9] (emphasis added)

Theology has thus trumped exegesis! First, the theologian determines what a doctrine should be, and then the linguist is forced to make the biblical text conform to it.

Such opinions as stressed by Drs. Mantey and Robertson, which separate baptism from forgiveness, would fall on the ears of the first

---

6. Robertson and Davis, *Short Grammar*, 256. Dr. A. T. Robertson (1863–1934) was a Southern Baptist preacher and Greek language scholar. His monumental *A Grammar of the Greek New Testament in the light of Historical Research* and his *Word Pictures of the New Testament* continue to be important tools for the serious New Testament student.

7. Robertson, *A Grammar*, 389.

8. Robertson, *A Grammar*, 594–95. It is interesting to note that in his *A New Short Grammar*, on page 256 (see footnote 182 above), Dr. Robertson associated *eis* in Mark 1:4 with a purposive usage, while in his larger *Grammar*, on page 595 (see this footnote above), he associated *eis* in Mark 1:4 with a causal usage.

9. Robertson, "Acts 2:38."

century Christians as strange doctrine. In fact, they would find it to be a radical false doctrine. One might wonder why, on the Day of Pentecost, if Peter meant to express a causal relationship between baptism and forgiveness (e.g., "baptism . . . because of forgiveness"), he didn't use the stronger causal preposition *dia* (e.g., *dia aphesin ton harmartion*) instead of the purposive preposition *eis* (*eis aphesin ton harmartion*). Knowing that *eis* would fall on the ears of his hearers as purposive, Peter used the preposition that he knew they would understand to indicate that the forgiveness of their sins was the purpose of their baptism.

The question of whether *eis* can also be translated "because of" rather than "for the purpose of" becomes of significance in other New Testament passages besides Acts 2:38, such as Mark 1:4, Luke 3:3, Gal 3:27, and Rom 6:3–4. These and other baptismal passages will be looked at in subsequent chapters. The debate is still ongoing between proponents of the purposive use of *eis* and the proponents of the causal use of *eis*. Innumerable online articles testify to the seriousness of this issue. Many books have been written about baptism in which authors have argued for one view or the other. We will now look at the evidence wherein a purposive translation of *eis* is the only acceptable rendering of the relationship between baptism and salvation.

How *Eis* is Used in the New Testament

From the earliest English translations of the Bible down to our current time, Bible translators have consistently rendered *eis* in a purposive sense. In all of the translations in *The New Testament From 26 Translations*, the phrase *baptistheito . . . eis aphesin ton harmartion humon* ("be baptized . . . for the forgiveness of your sins") in Acts 2:38 was translated with the purposive sense of *eis*. The first complete Bible in the English language was John Wycliffe's translation, which was published in 1382.[10] The quotations below from Wycliffe's Bible illustrate that, even at this early date in the history of translating the Bible into English, *eis* was commonly understood in a purposive sense.

> And Peter said to them, Do ye penance (Penance, he said, do ye), and each of you be baptized in the name of Jesus Christ,

---

10. Bruce, *The English Bible*, 12.

> into [*eis*] remission of your sins; and ye shall take the gift of the Holy Ghost.[11]
>
> I [John] wash you in water (Soothly I christen you in water), into [*eis*] penance...[12]
>
> John was in desert baptizing and preaching the baptism of penance into [*eis*] remission of sins.[13]
>
> And he came into all the country of Jordan, and preached (preaching) baptism of penance into [*eis*] remission of sins.[14]

From the time of Wycliffe to the present, the multitude of Bible translations into English have consistently translated *eis* as purposive. Dr. Jack Lewis, a professor well versed in the history of translations, summed it up well,

> It is doubtful that any English translation can be turned up which understood the verse [Acts 2:38] in any other way.[15]

In the four articles by Drs. Mantey and Marcus mentioned above, Dr. Mantey led off in the first of the four articles, saying,

> NONE of the Greek lexicons translate *eis* as causal... However, a few modern speech *translations* have pioneered the way in doing so. For instance, in Matt 3:11, "I indeed baptize you in water because of repentance," where the R.V. translates *eis* "unto" and the R.S.V. as "for," Weymouth has "on profession of," Goodspeed has "in token of," and Williams has "to picture"— all three are causal in effect.[16] (emphasis added)

All of the three *paraphrases* Dr. Mantey listed (to call them "translations" stretches the meaning beyond its definition), do indeed translate *eis* as causal in Matt 3:11. It is interesting that he had to rely on spurious modern language paraphrases and could find no regular English translations to support his causal *eis* thesis. He failed to mention that these same three paraphrases translate *eis* as purposive in Acts 2:38:

---

11. Acts 2:38.
12. Matthew 3:11.
13. Mark 1:4.
14. Luke 3:3
15. Lewis, "*EIS*."
16. Mantey, "Causal Use of *Eis*," 45.

Weymouth	"be baptized . . . with a view to the remission of your sins."
Goodspeed	"be baptized . . . in order to have your sins forgiven."
Williams	"be baptized . . . that you may have your sins forgiven."

Modern English translations of *baptistheito . . . eis aphesin ton hamartion* in Acts 2:38 are unanimous and demonstrate the universal practice of translating *eis* as purposive:

"be baptized . . . for the remission of sins"	King James Version
"be baptized . . . unto the remission of your sins"	American Standard Version
"be baptized . . . for the remission of sins"	New King James Version
"be baptized . . . for the forgiveness of your sins"	English Standard Version
"be baptized . . . to remission of sins"	Young's Literal Translation
"be baptized . . . for the forgiveness of your sins"	New American Standard
"be baptized . . . for the forgiveness of your sins"	New International Version
"be baptized . . . unto the remission of your sins"	Revised Standard Version
"be baptized . . . for the remission of your sins"	James Moffatt Translation
"be baptized . . . for the remission of your sins"	Douay/Rheims Version

This plethora of modern translations "represents the best understanding of the most capable contemporary scholarship—Catholic, Evangelical, and Protestant."[17]

In their attempt to find a causal use of *eis* in a few New Testament passages, especially in Acts 2:38, some commentators and grammarians refer to other passages, such as Matt 10:40–42 and 12:41, in which they advocate for the causal usage of *eis*. Julius Mantey and A. T. Robertson made reference to these two Matthean passages as justification for transferring a causal meaning of *eis* to other passages, such as Acts 2:38. According to Prof. Robertson,

> It is seen in Matt 10:41 in three examples *ei(s) onoma propheitou, dikaiou, matheitou* where it cannot be purpose or aim, but rather the basis or ground, on the basis of the name of a prophet, righteous man, disciple, because one is, etc. It is seen again in Matt 12:41 about the preaching of Jonah [*ei(s) to khrugma Iwna*]. They repented because of (or at) the preaching of Jonah.

17. Lewis, "*EIS*."

The illustrations of both usages are numerous in the N.T. and the koine ["common"] generally.[18]

Because this conclusion by Prof. Robertson is based on the assumption that the only possible translation of *eis* in Matt 10:40–42 and 12:41 is "because of" or "on the basis of," he then assumes that same usage can apply to Acts 2:38. The fallacy of such a position requires that we take a closer look at these two passages.

Matthew 10:40–42

> He who receives you receives me, and he who receives me receives him who sent me. He who receives a prophet in the name of a prophet (*eis onoma propheitou*) shall receive a prophet's reward; and he who receives a righteous man in the name of a righteous man (*eis onoma dikaiou*) shall receive a righteous man's reward. And whoever in the name of a disciple (*eis onoma matheitou*) gives to one of these little ones even a cup of cold water to drink, truly I say to you, he shall not lose his reward.[19]

Rendering *eis* as causative in these verses is quite understandable. *If* there are any grounds for "infrequent and rare" causal uses of *eis* in the New Testament, these verses come close to justifying such a conclusion. Sometimes it is hard in texts such as this to distinguish between the causal and the purposive. If, however, Jesus wished to emphasize a causal usage in this passage, why did he choose the purposive preposition *eis* rather than a causal preposition such as *dia*?

Concerning Matt 10:40–42, our aim is to show that the phrase "*eis onoma . . .*" indicates the purpose for the verb "receive" (*dexomai*). Matt 10:40–42 comes at the conclusion of a discourse by Jesus (vs. 5–42) to his twelve apostles to prepare them to be sent out to preach the Gospel in various cities. The message they were to preach was, "Repent, for the kingdom of heaven is at hand" (vs.7), which was the same message preached by John the Baptist and Jesus (Matt 3:2; 4:17; Mark 1:14–15). If anyone rejected these preachers, it was also a rejection of their message (vs. 14), and by extension, it was a rejection of both Jesus who sent them out, and the Father (v. 25). He who received these preachers along with their message received both Jesus and the Father (vv. 32–33, 40); and,

---

18. Robertson, "Acts 2:38."
19. Matt 10:40–42.

conversely, those who rejected the messengers and their message rejected both Jesus and the Father. In vss. 41 and 42, *eis* expresses the purpose for receiving these emissaries of Jesus. To receive the "prophet," "righteous man," or "disciple" was to receive Jesus himself and his message from the Father. If these men were welcomed, shown hospitality, and given support so that they could be successful in their preaching, their host would receive a reward—a "blessing of peace" (v. 13)—that accompanied the message that was being preached. *Dexomai* ("receive") was a special and honored practice of hospitality shown to travelers in ancient times, especially roaming priests, prophets, etc.[20] As such, *dexomai* was seen as an act of faith in the one received.[21] This use of *dexomai* was described by Donald Hagner in his commentary on the passage.

> This verse [40] reveals the close relationship between the disciples and Jesus, on the one hand, and Jesus and God, on the other. *Dexetai*, "receives," means here not merely to welcome, e.g., into one's home, but to receive in a deeper sense (cf. v 13-14). It is to accept the message of the disciples and thus the message of Jesus and his person, which is inseparable from the disciples' message (cf. 18:5; John 12:44; 13:20; for a negative statement of the same point, see Luke 10:16) . . . This verse [41] too concerns the receiving of God's messengers, now described under the title of "prophet" *propheiteis* and "righteous person" *dikaios*.[22]

Jesus made it clear in verse 40 that the authority for their message rested upon himself and the Father. By receiving his messengers, the people would be receiving the Son and the Father as well. Those who received (*dexomai*) the messengers also received their message. They did so for the purpose of (*eis*) becoming close associates with their names (the name of a "prophet," "righteous man," or "disciple") and thus with their message, so that the preaching of the Gospel might be further enhanced. This purposive approach to the phrase *eis onoma* alongside of *dexomai* enhances the sense of participation by the people with these preachers in their mission. There are numerous passages in the New Testament where the phrase *eis onoma* ("into the name") is used to establish association and submission to the person(s) named.[23] There are even more

20. Buchsel, "*dexomai*," 51.
21. Buchsel, "*dexomai*," 54.
22. Hagner, *Word Biblical Commentary*, 295.
23. For examples of *eis onoma*, see Matt 18:20; 28:19; John 1:12; 3:18; Acts 8:16; 19:5; 1 Cor 1:13, 15; 1 John 5:13.

numerous occurrences of *en onoma* ("in the name") that carry the same meaning.[24] Jesus' emphasis in this passage was not the reception of the men—the prophet, righteous man, and disciple—but the message associated with them. Thus the *eis* in this passage was not to receive these men *because of their name*, but *for the purpose of identifying with* these men and participation in/into what they stood for. Only in this was there assurance of the reward that accompanied that message.

Matthew 12:41 and Luke 11:32

> The men of Nineveh will stand up with this generation at the judgment, and will condemn it because they repented at [*eis*] the preaching of Jonah; and behold, something greater than Jonah is here.

Like Prof. Robertson in the previous section, Prof. J. R. Mantey also referred to these verses in Matthew and Luke as evidence for a causal translation of *eis*. According to Mantey,

> Matt 12:41 and Luke 11:32, "The men of Nineveh will arise in the judgment with this generation and condemn it; for they repented on account of the preaching of Jonah." *Eis* is translated as *at* here by Goodspeed and in the R.V. and R.S.V., but the *contextual coloring* is clearly causal. What occasioned repentance on the part of the Ninevites? The only reason given was that Jonah had preached to them. And God forgave them due to their repentance and showed mercy to them.[25] (emphasis added)

"Contextual coloring?" First of all, Dr. Mantey is assuming that his readers will understand what he means by his nebulous phrase "contextual coloring;" and secondly, he assumes that his "contextual coloring" is solid evidence and authority for translating a causal meaning of *eis*. Mantey asked the wrong question—"What occasioned repentance on the part of the Ninevites?" *He does not take into consideration that Jesus was not talking about what caused the Ninevites to convert, but rather into what they were converted.* In this passage, Jesus' emphasis was on that to which they were converted. The phrase, *metanoeisan eis to keirugma Iona* ("they repented/converted to/into the preaching of Jonah"), with a purposive

---

24. For examples of *en onoma*, see John 10:25; 16:23; Acts 9:27,28; 16:18; 1 Cor 5:4; 6:11; Eph 5:20; Phil 2:1; Col 3:17; 2 Thess 3:6; Jas 5:10.

25. Mantey, "Causal Use of *Eis*," 47.

eis, indicates that into which they were converted (*metanoeisan*)—the message preached by Jonah.[26]

In his commentary on Matthew's Gospel, Prof. Robertson also assumed a causal interpretation. He translated *hoti metanoeisan eis to keirugma Iona* as "They repented because of (or at) the preaching of Jonah."[27] Again we ask, if Jesus wanted to express Jonah's preaching as the cause of the Ninevites' conversion, why would he use the purposive preposition *eis* to express cause instead of the more common causal preposition, *dia*? By using the purposive preposition *eis*, Jesus put less attention on Jonah, the preacher, and more on the message preached! It was not because of or to Jonah himself that the Ninevites were converted, but their response was to/into the message he preached.

Further Thoughts on the Meaning of *Eis*

At the beginning of the Mantey/Marcus four-article debate mentioned above, Dr. Mantey made several unsubstantiated claims, such as, "There are at least nine NT passages in which *eis* could reasonably be translated causal."[28] At the heart of his attempt to disassociate baptism from forgiveness of sins, he assumed that there are a few "infrequent and rare"[29] occurrences of causal *eis* in the New Testament. He then uses that assumption to justify the use for a causative interpretation of *eis* in passages that concern baptism and forgiveness, such as Acts 2:38 and Matt 3:11. If forcing an assumed definition of a word from one context into another context is a legitimate exegetical method of interpretation, then that would justify the exploitation of *eis* in other such passages as well, such as Matt 26:27–28.

> And when he had taken a cup and given thanks, he gave it to them, saying, "Drink from it, all of you; for this is my blood of

---

26. The word *keirux* (noun: "preacher," e.g., 2 Tim 1:11) puts the emphasis on the person who does the preaching; the word *keirusso* (verb: "preach," e.g., Luke 12:3) refers to the act of preaching; and the word *keirugma* (noun: "preaching," "message," "proclamation," e.g., Rom 16:25) applies to the message itself. Paul, in 1 Cor. 2:4, placed *keirugma* in parallel with *logos*.

27. Robertson, *Word Pictures*, "Acts 2:38."

28. Mantey, "Causal Use of *Eis*," 46.

29. Mantey, "Causal Use of *Eis*," 45.
   However, we have to admit at the outset that this type of usage is infrequent and rare.

the covenant, which is poured out for many for forgiveness of sins [*eis aphesin harmartion*]."

A causal use of *eis* in this passage would lead us to the conclusion that the blood of Jesus was poured out *because of* the forgiveness of sin rather than *for the purpose of* the forgiveness of sin. This would necessitate the conclusion that forgiveness of sins occurred before his blood was poured out. Such a translation would certainly have to be rejected as contrary to basic biblical doctrine. A serious student of the Bible cannot arbitrarily pick and choose, without solid reasons, when a word should be translated one way in one text and another way in another text.

The phrase *Eis aphesin harmartion* occurs five times in the New Testament. John preached a baptism of repentance "for the forgiveness of sins" (Mark 1:4; Luke 3:3); Jesus poured out his blood of the covenant "for the forgiveness of sins" (Matt 26:28); the apostles were ordered to preach repentance "for the forgiveness of sin" (Luke 24:47); and Peter commanded both repentance and baptism "for the forgiveness of sins" (Acts 2:38). All five of them consistently demonstrate the importance of rendering *eis* in a purposive sense.

The debate concerning the meaning of *eis* has predominantly centered on Acts 2:38, which will be considered in greater detail in Chapter 7. It is easy to understand how some commentators can perceive *eis* as causal in a few New Testament passages. However, to opt for a causal translation of *eis* where the more common purposive rendering is more in tune with lexical, grammatical, and contextual evidence—as well as parallel passages—is to err. Such illogic forces the exegete to make the biblical text comply to a preconceived theology.

6

Baptism in the Ministry of Jesus

IN THIS CHAPTER, WE will look at four questions concerning the practice of baptism associated with Jesus' ministry: (1) Why did Jesus go down to the Jordan River to be baptized by his cousin?[1] (2) Did Jesus, like John, call for the baptism of his disciples? (3) What did Jesus instruct his disciples to do in the Great Commission? (4) Was Jesus referring to baptism in his conversation with Nicodemus?

Why Was Jesus Baptized by John?

All four of the Gospels mention Jesus' baptism by John the Baptist. Mark and Luke mentioned the fact of his baptism and that it was followed by the appearance of the Holy Spirit in the form of a dove and the voice out of heaven.[2] The only reference to John's baptism of Jesus in John's Gospel is a quote by John the Baptist in which he says, "I have seen the Spirit descending as a dove out of heaven, and he remained upon him," but he makes no mention of the baptism itself or the voice out of heaven.[3] Only Matthew describes the full event and its purpose.

---

1. We do not know just what kin Jesus was to John. When Mary was pregnant with Jesus, she went to see her relative Elizabeth, who was pregnant with John. The word "relative" (*suggeneis*) can refer to a wide variety of relationships. Since Elizabeth was older, she may have been Mary's Aunt, which would make Jesus a cousin of John.

2. Mark 1:9–11; Luke 3:21–22.

3. John 1:32–33.

Of all the people who came to John to be baptized, Jesus stood out as unique. John recognized this and knew Jesus was greater than him. Therefore, he told Jesus that it was he who should be baptized by Jesus.

> Then Jesus arrived from Galilee at the Jordan coming to John, to be baptized by him. But John tried to prevent him, saying, "I have need to be baptized by you, and do you come to me?" But Jesus answering said to him, "Permit it at this time . . ."[4]

John then complied and baptized him. As Jesus ascended from the water, the divine stamp of approval was declared by the descent of the Holy Spirit and the voice out of heaven.

> After being baptized, Jesus came up immediately from the water; and behold, the heavens were opened, and he saw the Spirit of God descending as a dove and lighting on him, and behold, a voice out of the heavens said, "This is my beloved Son, in whom I am well-pleased."[5]

None of the others who were coming to John to be baptized received such divine confirmation, nor were any of John's other disciples identified by name at their baptism. His was not an ordinary baptism! While all others came to John for baptism confessing their sins ("and they were being baptized by him in the Jordan River, confessing their sins"[6]), there is no record of a confession of sin coming from the lips of Jesus.

So, why then did Jesus come to John to be baptized? It has been proposed that though Jesus was a gifted and faithful man in the first three decades of his life, he was, nevertheless, an ordinary man. Consequently, it was not until his baptism that he gained his full messianic consciousness, at which time the Son of God descended upon the man Jesus and inhabited his life.

From the early centuries of the church to the present time, there have been those who have speculated that perhaps Jesus' sinless nature was not a given fact until after his baptism; they posit that because of a sin-awareness in his life he, like all of the other pilgrims to the Jordan,

---

4. Matt 3:13–15.

5. Matt 3:16–17; John 1:32. It has been suggested that the dove and the voice were seen and heard by no one other than Jesus. However, when John said, "I have seen the Spirit descending as a dove out of heaven, and He remained upon him," it would seem logical that the others present would have witnessed the dove and the voice. There is nothing in John's testimony to indicate that he alone heard the voice.

6. Mark 1:5.

needed a baptism for repentance and the forgiveness of sin.[7] An example that demonstrates the ongoing question of whether Jesus committed sin(s) or not can be seen on the blog, *debate.org*.[8] Posts from both sides of the issue are listed side-by-side in pro and con columns, with 53 percent of the responses arguing that Jesus did sin and 47 percent arguing that he did not. None of the New Testament authors acknowledged any sin in the life of Jesus. In fact, all through the New Testament Jesus' sinlessness is plainly proclaimed.

> He made him who knew no sin to be sin on our behalf, so that we might become the righteousness of God in him.[9]
>
> For you have been called for this purpose, since Christ also suffered for you, leaving you an example for you to follow in his steps, WHO COMMITTED NO SIN, NOR WAS ANY DECEIT FOUND IN HIS MOUTH.[10]
>
> For we do not have a high priest who cannot sympathize with our weaknesses, but One who has been tempted in all things as we are, yet without sin.[11]
>
> You know that he appeared in order to take away sins; and in him there is no sin.[12]
>
> ... knowing that you were not redeemed with perishable things like silver or gold from your futile way of life inherited from your forefathers, but with precious blood, as of a lamb unblemished and spotless, the blood of Christ.[13]
>
> ... how much more will the blood of Christ, who through the eternal Spirit offered himself without blemish to God, cleanse your conscience from dead works to serve the living God?[14]

---

7. Oekpe, "*bapto, baptidzo,*" 1:538.
8. "Did Jesus Ever Sin?" Debate.org.
   Debate.org is a free online community where intelligent minds from around the world come to debate their views online and read the opinions of others.
9. 2 Cor 5:21.
10. 1 Pet 2:21–22. (See OT quote: Isa 53:9.)
11. Heb 4:15.
12. 1 John 3:5.
13. 1 Pet 1:18–19.
14. Heb 9:14.

Since Jesus had no sins to bring to John's baptism like all of John's other disciples, again, we ask, "Why was he baptized?" Commentators on this event have come up with numerous explanations why Jesus traveled the ninety-plus miles from his home in Nazareth to the Jordan to be baptized. Perhaps, it has been suggested, Jesus became enamored with John's preaching and the success of his ministry, so he came to John for baptism because he wanted it to be known that he could not hold himself aloof from such a righteous revival. Others have proposed that Jesus' baptism was a precursor of the Cross; while sinless himself, Jesus identified himself alongside sinners and began, even as early as his baptism, to take their sins upon himself. However, it is in his death that redemption is accomplished by his blood; no mention is made in the New Testament that the forgiveness of sins was effected by His baptism.

It has also been proposed that Jesus came to John because he knew that John's baptism was from God, and he simply wanted to be in obedience to his Father.[15] A popular explanation of the purpose of Jesus' baptism can be found in many church doctrinal statements: Jesus was baptized in order to set a good example for us to follow and we, too, should be baptized because Jesus was. Obedience to God was a characteristic of the whole of Jesus' life, wherein he exemplified for us a model to follow.[16] In his baptism, it is argued, he was obviously in conformity to his Father's will, which is seen as the motivation for our baptism since we, too, come to the water of baptism in order to conform to his will. However, being obedient and setting an example, while commendable, are not adequate to explain the purpose that Jesus wished to accomplish in his baptism.

The one problem with each of these suggestions above is that there is no biblical support for such conclusions! They are all based on human supposition and extra-biblical reasoning in their attempt to explain a spiritual reality. The only clue given in the Bible for the reason that Jesus came to John to be baptized was given by Jesus himself when he told John,

> "Permit it at this time; for in this way it is fitting for us to fulfill all righteousness." Then he permitted him.[17]

---

15. Matt 26:39; John 4:34; 5:30; 6:38; 10:18; 12:49–50; 14:30–31; 15:10; Phil 2:8.
16. John 13:15; 1 Cor 11:1; Eph 5:1–2; Col 3:13; 1 Pet 2:20–22; 1 John 2:5–6.
17. Matt 3:15.

While we might wish that Jesus had been more explicit in what he meant, there are two words that give us insight into his meaning.

The word "fulfill" (*pleiroo*:"play-ro-o") means "to make complete," "to bring to an end/conclusion," "to fill up/make full." This makes it obvious that Jesus came to John for a purpose greater than meeting a personal need; it superseded some felt need within himself. His baptism pointed to something that existed before his incarnation, something for which he came to bring to its fullness. Paul expressed this well when he wrote to Timothy:

> It is a trustworthy statement, deserving full acceptance, that Christ Jesus came into the world to save sinners, among whom I am foremost of all.[18]

In the word "fulfill," Jesus was making it known that he had a clear awareness that his mission transcended any self-concern.

The other word that gives us a clue as to the reason for Jesus' baptism is "righteousness," and its twin word, "justification."[19] Righteousness is a relationship word. It concerns making right, or just, that which has been damaged or destroyed in a relationship. Only in God does true righteousness dwell, for there is nothing in him that in any way endangers his relationship with his people. If there is a problem in any relationship between God and a person, it is not because God was guilty of violating the covenant. Sometimes, people in the Bible are referred to as righteous. Noah, Job, Joseph (the husband of Mary), and Joseph (who took care of the body of Jesus) are called righteous, for in their submission to God, there was nothing in their lives that would separate them from their relationship with God.[20]

That which destroys one's relationship with God is sin. Throughout history, sin has been that which profaned and contaminated man's nature. The solution to this universal problem is righteousness (justification). Jesus told John, that in his baptism he was taking on this universal problem of sin. He himself was the fulfillment of the righteousness that would make it possible for contaminated man to be sanctified and thus qualified to stand in holiness before God.

---

18. 1 Tim 1:15.

19. "Righteousness" and "justification" are identical in meaning for they are both English translations from one Old Testament word, *tsedeq* (tse-deek), and from one New Testament Greek word, *dikaiosunei* (dee-kie-o-su-nay).

20. Gen 6:9; Matt 1:19; and Luke 23:50.

Because Jesus was faithful to that mission, holiness became a real possibility among men. Because of his Cross, those who came in faith to God could now be sanctified of all uncleanness and stand before God as righteous. For this magnificent mission of Jesus, heaven opened and the Dove and the Voice came from the throne to sanction and endorse this event.

The Practice of Baptism During the Ministry of Jesus

> After these things Jesus and His disciples came into the land of Judea, and there He was spending time with them and baptizing.[21]

> Therefore when the Lord knew that the Pharisees had heard that Jesus was making and baptizing more disciples than John (although Jesus himself was not baptizing, but His disciples were), He left Judea and went away again into Galilee.[22]

Matthew, Mark, and Luke do not mention the fact that Jesus' preaching ministry included baptizing people. There is only the briefest mention of it in John's Gospel. It strikes our human minds as strange that so much is said in the Gospels concerning John's practice of baptism and so little in Jesus' ministry. In these four verses, John simply informed us (1) that baptism was being practiced in Jesus' ministry; (2) that, at least for a while, the ministries of John and Jesus were concurrent with one another, and they were baptizing in the same region; (3) that more people were now coming to Jesus for baptism than to John; (4) that the Pharisees knew about the popularity of the baptisms being practiced in Jesus' ministry; and (5) that Jesus himself was not actually performing the baptisms, but they were being administered by his disciples.

As Jesus' popularity grew, John's disciples became jealous.[23] However, John assured them of his pleasure at the success of his cousin and reminded them, "I am not the Christ . . . He must increase, but I must decrease."[24] It was not long after this that John was imprisoned by Herod and eventually beheaded. Jesus then returned to Galilee.[25]

21. John 3:22.
22. John 4:1–3.
23. John 3:25.
24. John 3:28, 30.
25. Matt 4:12; Mark 1:14.

While we have very specific information on John's purpose for baptizing his disciples, we are not similarly enlightened about the purpose of baptism in the ministry of Jesus. There are, however, some things we do know. Both John and Jesus preached the same message: "Repent, for the kingdom of heaven is at hand."[26] Also, as one reads Jesus' sermons, it is obvious that, like John, he expected a higher moral lifestyle as a result of conversion. Since repentance, forgiveness, and the kingdom with its high moral standard were all important in the preaching of both of them, it seems plausible that Jesus would have the same purpose for baptizing that John did. It would stand to reason that if Jesus had a different purpose for the practice of baptism in his ministry than John, such a distinction would be necessarily recorded in the Gospel accounts.

The Great Commission

Matthew 28:18–20

> And Jesus came up and spoke to them, saying, "All authority has been given to me in heaven and on earth. Go therefore and make disciples of all the nations, baptizing them in the name of the Father and the Son and the Holy Spirit, teaching them to observe all that I commanded you; and lo, I am with you always, even to the end of the age."[27]

This passage is the one people most often think of when the Great Commission is mentioned. The eleven apostles left Judea and went to a mountain in Galilee as Jesus had instructed them (v. 16). There, he met the eleven, and even still, Matthew noted, there were disciples of his inner circle who had doubts, though we are not told specifically who they were nor what those doubts were. When Jesus joined up with them, he first assured them of his complete authority in heaven and on earth (v. 18).

There are four verbs (one imperative and three participles) in Matthew's account in verses 19 and 20 that are interrelated. The primary leading verb is the imperative (command) to "make disciples" (*matheiteusate*: aorist, active, imperative).[28] The other three verbs are participles that

---

26. Matt 3:2; 4:17; Mark 1:15.

27. Matt 28:18–20.

28. The word "disciple" (*matheiteis*) refers to one who accompanies a teacher as a follower (or apprentice) in order to learn from and be trained by the teacher.

define the leading verb.[29] The command to make disciples is the heart of the action of the Great Commission.

The first of the three participles, *poreuthentes,* is an aorist passive participle,[30] from the lexicon form of the word, *poreuomai* (present passive indicative), which means "I go."[31] Almost every English translation has rendered *poreuthentes* as an imperative verb, "go," rather than as an aorist participle—"having gone." Young's Literal Translation is one of the few that adheres to the literal translation of *poreuthentes* as "having gone." "Having gone" expresses Jesus' foreknowledge that his disciples would disperse from Jerusalem and go to "all nations," and having gone, they would "make disciples." The command in Jesus' Great Commission is not for a disciple to leave where he or she might be and go to another place to make disciples; rather, having gone forth into the world, wherever the disciple might be, they were to make disciples. The participle "having gone," being chronologically dependent on the primary verb, is, therefore, concurrent with "make disciples."

The second participle is *baptidzontes,* from the lexicon form *baptidzo,* "I baptize." As a present active participle (baptizing), this action also occurs simultaneously with the action of the leading verb, "make disciples."[32] The command was not to make disciples and then baptize them; rather, the person was to become a disciple in their baptism. In verse 19 the phrase "baptizing them in (*eis*: into[33]) the name of the Father and the Son and the Holy Spirit" indicates the *purpose* of baptism; it is the incorporation of the one being baptized into the name of the Father, Son, and Holy Spirit. "Into the name of" is a technical phrase that carries the

---

29. Participles are both a verb and an adjective. When translated into English, they are usually easily identified by their "-ing" ending. They are verbs in that they involve action and are like adjectives in that they are descriptive.

30. Burton, *Syntax,* 64.
    139. The Aorist Participle of Identical Action. The Aorist Participle agreeing with the subject of a verb not infrequently denotes the same action that is expressed by the verb.

31. *Poreuomai* is a deponent verb, which means that although its lexical form is passive, it is translated as an active verb.

32. Burton, *Syntax,* 54.
    119. The Present Participle of Simultaneous Action. The Present Participle most frequently denotes an action in progress, simultaneous with the action of the principal verb.

33. For the further explanation of the meaning of *eis,* see the "Excursus on *Eis*" at the end of Chapter 5.

significant idea of becoming identified as one with God. In one's baptism, they are given the privilege to wear that holy Name as their own. In like manner, in a wedding ceremony the bride and groom assume a common life and share a common name; thus, they become united as one.

> For this reason a man shall leave his father and his mother, and be joined to his wife; and they shall become one flesh.[34]

In his commentary on the Gospels, Alford states it in this manner: "Baptism is the contract of espousal (Eph. V. 26) between Christ and his Church."[35]

The third participle, *didaskontes*, is from the lexicon form, *didasko*, "I teach." "Teaching them," like the participle "baptizing them," is a present active participle verb, which indicates that, chronologically, its action is also concurrent with the imperative "make disciples." It would be inconceivable that a person could become a disciple without being taught the Gospel; thus, the teaching must have a concurrent connection with both "going" and "baptizing them." According to Jesus, the actions of these four verbs are intricately woven together, and to rend them asunder would destroy the fabric of the Great Commission. In his book, which surveys the history of the British Baptist recovery of baptismal sacramentalism, Stanley K. Fowler addressed the concurrent connectedness between the verbs in this passage.

> Although many Baptists have assumed a chronological relationship (make disciples, then baptize the disciples, then continue to teach them), this is not a self-evident interpretation. It may well be that the participles are instrumental or modal in force, describing the way in which the nations are to be brought into Christian discipleship (make disciples by baptizing them and teaching them).[36]

In a similar statement written earlier (1962), George Beasley-Murray, another prominent British Baptist theologian, when commenting on the Great Commission, wrote:

> Accordingly it is proposed that the participles describe the manner in which a disciple is made: the church is commissioned to make disciples *by* baptizing men and putting them under

---

34. Gen 2:24.
35. Alford, *The Four Gospels*, 1:291.
36. Fowler, *More Than a Symbol*, 158–59.

> instruction. An explanatory note to this effect has been inserted in the current edition of the Luther Bible, and it has actually governed the translation of the passage . . . From the linguistic point of view, Lindlom has pointed out that when participles in Greek are coordinated with the main verb they are linked by means of a *kai*, or *te* . . . *kai*, or *de*: if they follow one another without any such binding conjunction or particle they must be viewed as depending on one another or depending in differing ways on the chief verb.[37]

Given the concurrent relationship of the three participial verbs with the imperative verb, "make disciples," as an expression of induction into the godhead, it is safe to conclude that Jesus had the very highest regard for the practice of baptism as the event in which his salvation should be bestowed. In baptism the baptizand is made a disciple of Christ rather than testifying that they had already become a disciple.

Mark 16:15–16

> And he said to them, "Go into all the world and preach the gospel to all creation. He who has believed and has been baptized shall be saved; but he who has disbelieved shall be condemned."

Much attention has been given to whether the last twelve verses of Mark's Gospel (16:9–20) were originally written by Mark or if they were added later. Some commentators claim that there seems to be an abrupt break in the narrative between verses 8 and 9; in addition, they say that the writing style of 16:9–20 is different from the rest of the Gospel. If 16:9–20 was added to the end of Mark at a later date, and if Mark's original writing did actually end abruptly with verse 8, it could be conjectured that there might have been more that Mark wrote (or intended to write), leaving us to suppose that the final section of his original manuscript was lost for some reason before it was copied and distributed among the churches. Others have suggested that, given his tendency to brevity in his writing, Mark may have simply ended his work with verse 8.

What we do know is that the earliest known manuscripts of Mark's Gospel (from the second to the fourth centuries) do not contain 16:9–20.[38]

---

37. Beasley-Murray, *Baptism*, 88–89.

38. There were other endings added later to Mark's Gospel after the 4th century that have failed the test of literary critique. Most every Bible from the fourth or fifth century onward contains the traditional ending of Mark as in our modern translations.

Why these twelve verses are absent in the earliest manuscripts is an unsolved mystery.

> Whether Mark's hand was stayed by death or whether the original ending was lost in some way, or whether the abrupt ending represents Mark's deliberate intention to close his record in a fashion agreeable to the style of his narrative, we have no means of knowing.[39]

These verses are usually enclosed in brackets in modern English translations to indicate their questionable origin.

This question about the ending of Mark's Gospel is applicable to our current study about baptism in that if 16:9–20 is part of Mark's original writing, then we must examine it as we would any other New Testament text to determine what he wrote about baptism in 16:16. If they are not original to Mark, then we must ask whether there is any legitimate reason that these verses should be given credence with the rest of Scripture. Given that these twelve verses showed up in manuscripts at such an early date and have remained a part of the Gospel down through the centuries, it is obvious that they have been accepted as authoritative and as reliable doctrine by the church. Even if these twelve verses are not a part of Mark's original manuscript, they still give us insight into the mindset of the church at a very early date in its history. Also, a close look at these twelve verses reveals no doctrinal discrepancy between them and the rest of the New Testament. It is also noteworthy that God, in his omnipotent wisdom, has allowed these verses to persevere in his word.

Based on the weight of the above evidence, whether 16:9–20 was originally written by Mark or added later, the authors of this study assume that these verses should be treated as authoritative and inspired by God. Therefore, we feel it advantageous to take a closer look at the wording of these verses.

By comparing Mark 16:15 and Matt 26:29, we can see a very close parallel, which lends credibility to Mark's ending.

> Mark 16:15–16: And he said to them, "Having gone into all the world preach the Gospel to all the creation. The one who

---

The four earliest known manuscripts do not contain these twelve verses. The late 2nd century Sinaitic Old Syriac manuscript and three 4th century manuscripts (Vaticanus, Sinaiticus, and Armenian) all end Mark's Gospel at 16:8.

39. Harrison, *Introduction*, 92.

believes and is baptized shall be saved; but the person who disbelieves shall be condemned."

Matthew 26:29: "Having gone therefore, make disciples of all nations, baptizing them into the name of the Father and the Son and the Holy Spirit."[40]

In both passages, Jesus began his commission with *poreuthentes* (having gone: aorist, passive deponent, participle). Mark's "preach the Gospel" and Matthew's "make disciples" are both aorist, active, imperative verbs, making them the focal point of their respective passages. Both Gospel writers place baptism in an intimate relation to becoming a disciple and being saved.

In Mark's passage, faith and baptism are set in parallel. Because the word "faith" (*pistis*, noun; *pisteuo*, verb) is used so frequently in the Bible and plays such an important part in the doctrine of salvation, it is essential that we examine how it is used in the New Testament, and to search out its relationship to baptism and redemption.

The New Testament presents faith as the surrender (commitment) of our whole life to the lordship of Christ. In conversion, the mind, heart, and soul are surrendered to his control. The head, the heart, and the hands become his to use as he directs. If any one of these three—knowledge, conviction, and devotion—are shortchanged, faith becomes an empty, meaningless word that undermines our confidence, our hope. Paul recognized the necessity of all three aspects of faith in his very personal statement to Timothy about his faith (belief).

> For this reason I also suffer these things, but I am not ashamed; for *I know* whom I have believed (*pepisteuka*, perfect, active, indicative of *pisteuo*) and *I am convinced* that he is able to guard what *I have entrusted* to him until that day.[41]

In the old stories of knights and kings, the knight came before the king or queen and bowed down before the throne. The king/queen would lay the blade of a sword on the knight's shoulder; thus, they would dub him with knighthood, which initiated the knight into the absolute service

---

40. These verses are the author's translation of:Mark 16:15–16: *Kai eipen autois poreuthentes eis kosmon keiruxate to euaggelion pasei tei ktisei. Ho pisteusas kai baptistheis sotheisetai, ho de apistoteisas katakritheisetai.*

Matt. 28:19: *Poreuthentes oun matheiteusate panta ta ethnei, baptidzontes autous eis to onoma tou patros and the huiou and tou hagiou pneumatos.*

41. 2 Tim 1:12.

of the ruler. The only reason a knight would take such a drastic measure would be if he knew the monarch was worthy of such faith and loyalty. Unless the prospective knight was willing to commit his loyalty to the throne, there could be no knighthood for him. No matter whether the knight was assigned to noble or lowly service, he was bound to his master's will. So it is when a person bows before the throne of Christ. Based on this understanding of faith, Mark 16:16 takes on a deeper and more serious meaning.

In Mark's passage, faith and baptism are connected by the conjunction "and" (*kai*). A common mistake many people make in their study of the Bible is to assume that when two or more things are connected by the word *kai,* they must be understood to occur in chronological order. For example, in the text we are now looking at, the verb "believes" (*pisteuo*) precedes the verb "is baptized" (*baptidzo*). Because they are connected by *kai,* it does not necessarily justify the conclusion that baptism is an action that occurs subsequent to faith. That they are joined by the conjunction *kai* can mean that they are concurrent. According to many popular church doctrines, faith is thought to be a required prerequisite to salvation, and baptism is relegated to an action subsequent to salvation. Upon a closer examination of the grammar of this passage and how these words relate to one another, faith, baptism, and salvation are all three brought into one concurrent event. The concurrent relationship of belief, baptism, and salvation is the natural understanding in the following translations from Mark 16:16.

Ho pisteusas kai baptistheis sotheisetai	Greek
He [the one] who believes and is baptized will be saved	NASU
Whoever believes and is baptized will be saved	ESV
Whoever believes and is baptized will be saved	NIV
He that believeth and is baptized shall be saved	KJV
He who hath believed, and hath been baptized, shall be saved	Youngs Literal Translation

In this passage, *pisteusas* is the aorist active participle of the lexicon form, *pisteuo,* and *baptistheis* is the aorist passive participle of the lexicon form, *baptidzo.* Since participles do not, in general, in themselves denote time, they are dependent on the leading verb, "shall be saved" to denote the time of the action.⁴² This being the case, it is necessary to conclude that the two participles, "believes" and "is baptized," occur simultaneously with "will be saved."

Both participles, *pisteusas*, and *baptistheis* in verse 16 share a common article, *ho* ("the," "the one who"), that also bonds *pisteusas* and *baptistheis* together chronologically. Because the second participle, "is baptized," refers back to the same subject of the sentence (*ho*) as "believes," the *ho*⁴³ stands for both participles.⁴⁴ Though belief and baptism are closely associated in this verse, they are each unique in meaning, but even though different in meaning they are two complementary ingredients; they both are concurrent with "shall be saved."

When we consider the relationship between faith, baptism, and salvation in the ministry of Jesus, there is an obvious close and simultaneous relationship between them. Should any one of these three terms be given a false definition or the concurrency of the triad be broken, it would gravely endanger not only the meaning of the other two, but it would also put a person's salvation in danger.

Luke 24:46-48

> and he said to them, "Thus it is written, that the Christ would suffer and rise again from the dead the third day, and that repentance for forgiveness of sins would be proclaimed [*keirusso*] in his name to all the nations, beginning from Jerusalem. You are witnesses of these things."⁴⁵

While baptism is not specifically mentioned in this passage, it is obvious that Luke was addressing the same commission as Matt 28 and Mark 16. In Luke and Mark, the verb, "to preach" (*keirusso*), is parallel to "make disciples" (*matheiteuo*) in Matthew. Another characteristic all three passages have in common is the universal intent of Jesus' commission. Jesus clearly intended that his commission extend to "all nations" (Matthew and Luke) and "all the world" (Mark). In contrast to the Jewish mindset

---

42. Burton, *Syntax*, 54.

43. Normally, *ho* is simply the article "the." However, when an adjective or participle is a nominative (subject), the article makes it substantive. Thus, it is translated: "the one who . . ." or "whoever . . ."

44. Blass and Debrunner, *Greek Grammar*, 144-45. See also: Robertson, *Grammar of the Greek*, 785-87, par. (d); and Dana and Mantey, *A Manual Grammar*, 146-47.

45. Luke 24:46-48.

of exclusivism, believing that only the Jews are Yahweh's people, Jesus' vision for the Gospel was universal. He meant for it to go out to the whole world.

In Luke's account of the Great Commission, the phrase "for forgiveness of sins" (*eis aphesin hamartion*) is equivalent to the phrase used to describe the purpose of John's baptism in Mark 1:4 and Luke 3:3 (*eis aphesin hamartion*). In Mark 1:4 and Luke 3:3 the purpose of John's baptism was "for the forgiveness of sins; in Luke, the purpose of *metanoia* (repentance, conversion) is also "for the forgiveness of sins." The same forgiveness occurs in baptism that occurs in repentance (conversion). Further, John the Baptist said in Matt 3:11 that he baptized in water for repentance (*eis metanoia*), which tied baptism in an intimate relationship with not only forgiveness, but repentance (conversion) as well.

Keiruxtheinai . . . metanoian eis aphesin hamartion to preach . . . repentance for forgiveness of sins	Luke 24:47
baptisma metanoias eis aphesin hamartion baptism of repentance for the forgiveness of sins	Mark 1:4
baptisma metanoias eis aphesin hamartion baptism of repentance for the forgiveness of sins	Luke 3:3
baptidzo en hudati eis metanoian I baptize in water for repentance	Matt 3:11

Baptism in water for repentance and for forgiveness are so wove together that to remove either one of them from the other would destroy the beauty of redemption.

Acts 1:6–8

> So when they had come together, they were asking him, saying, "Lord, is it at this time You are restoring the kingdom to Israel?" He said to them, "It is not for you to know times or epochs which the Father has fixed by his own authority; but you will receive power when the Holy Spirit has come upon you; and you shall be my witnesses both in Jerusalem, and in all Judea and Samaria, and even to the remotest part of the earth."[46]

There is no mention in this passage concerning baptism, faith, salvation, or repentance. However, the close parallel between the phrase in Acts,

---

46. Acts 1:6–8.

"you shall be my witnesses," to "preach" and "make disciples" in the other Great Commission passages, gives them a common theme. It would be safe to assume that Jesus had this same mission in mind in Acts 1:8. Another factor tying this passage in Acts to Matthew, Mark, and Luke is that Jesus made it clear in all of these accounts that his message was universal. It was for "all nations" (Matthew and Luke); they were told to go "into all the world and . . . to all creation" (Mark), and to take the Gospel "even to the remotest part of the earth" (Acts).

This Great Commission is such an important and large charge that Jesus knew they would need divine power to carry it out. A significant addition that Acts 1:8 brings to the Great Commission is the promise that they would "receive power when the Holy Spirit has come upon you." The Great Commission came at the close of Jesus' three years of ministry, during which time he was training and nurturing his disciples. As this part of the Gospel story came to an end, Jesus' commission pointed his disciples forward. Beginning with the Day of Pentecost, they went forth to fulfill that commission, "even to the remotest part of the earth." To fulfill this commission they were to receive a divine partnership by the participation of the Holy Spirit.

Nicodemus and Jesus

John 3:1-10

Now there was a man of the Pharisees, named Nicodemus, a ruler of the Jews; this man came to Jesus by night and said to him, "Rabbi, we know that you have come from God as a teacher; for no one can do these signs that you do unless God is with him." Jesus answered and said to him, "Truly, truly, I say to you, if anyone is not born again he cannot see the kingdom of God." Nicodemus said to him, "How can a man be born when he is old? He cannot enter a second time into his mother's womb and be born, can he?" Jesus answered, "Truly, truly, I say to you, if anyone is not born of water and the Spirit he cannot enter into the kingdom of God. That which is born of the flesh is flesh, and that which is born of the Spirit Is spirit. Do not be amazed that I said to you, 'You must be born again.' The wind blows where it wishes and you hear the sound of it, but do not know where it comes from and where it is going; so is everyone who is born of the Spirit." Nicodemus said to him, "How can these things be?"

Jesus answered and said to him, "Are you the teacher of Israel and do not understand these things?"[47]

It is striking that Nicodemus, as a "ruler of the Jews,"[48] came to Jesus making the statement, "Rabbi, we know that you have come from God as a teacher; for no one can do these signs that you do unless God is with him." Who is the "we" Nicodemus referred to except the great Sanhedrin itself, the very men who sought so vehemently to destroy Jesus? They knew who he was, and they crucified him! To all Jews in all nations, the men of the Sanhedrin were looked upon as the epitome of righteousness. They had no recognition for the need of a conversion in their lives. After all, they were elite descendants of Abraham! It is to the heart of this elitism that Jesus struck. "Are you the teacher of Israel and do not understand these things?" Jesus asked him.

Jesus had the uncanny ability to see into people's mind. When he spoke, it went to the heart of Nicodemus's soul. Jesus' first response to him was, "Truly, truly, I say to you, unless one is born from above[49] he cannot see the kingdom of God." By making "born from above" and "born of water and the Spirit" a necessary condition to "see" (verse 3) or "enter" (verse 5) "the kingdom of God," Jesus immediately set the need for conversion on a higher and more critical level. The reason Nicodemus recognized that Jesus was "come from God as a teacher" was because of his ability to do what "no man can do." Jesus ignored this superficial logic and cut through the surface issues to the quick where Nicodemus was most vulnerable. He wanted Nicodemus to see a higher spiritual reality than merely being enamored with the signs he did.

> So Jesus said to him, "Unless you people see signs and wonders, you simply will not believe."[50]

By ignoring the comment by Nicodemus, Jesus raised the conversation from the performance of miracles to the matter of entrance into

---

47. Parts of these verses have been altered from the New American Standard Version to comply with a more accurate rendering of the original Greek. "Born again" has been changed to "born from above" in verses 3 and 7, and "unless one is born" has been changed to "if anyone is not born" in verses 3 and 5.

48. As a "ruler of the Jews" Nicodemus was probably a member of that exalted body called the Sanhedrin, which all Jews worldwide looked up to for direction in their lives.

49. We will explore this deviation from the text below.

50. John 4:48.

the kingdom of God—a matter of eternal destiny. Jesus knew that while his miracles got the people's attention, there must be something more substantial than his physical miracles upon which their faith should be based. As with the Samaritan woman at the well (John 4:3–26), Jesus had a way of raising people's vision to see things from above.

Whether "born from above" is the correct translation of *genneithei anothen* rather than the more popular "born again" has a bearing on whether this birth is a reference to baptism or not. If it is merely another birth ("born again") among any number of other births, it lacks the power of origin that is found in the phrase "born from above." Most major translations of this passage render the phrase as "born again." *Anothen* was translated as "again" in The NASB (and the updated edition), the ESV, the KJV, the NKJV, the RSV, and the NIV. The NRSV, the Tyndale Version, Young's Literal Translation, and the New American Bible (revised edition) translate *anothen* as "from above." The phrase "born again" in verses 3 and 7 can have numerous vague connotations of any of a number of births, but there can be no confusion that "born from above" definitely indicates a heavenly origin. This birth "from above," with its origin in heaven, becomes a matter that transcends any physical origins.

To comply with sound exegesis of Scripture, we must look at how *anothen* is used in other contexts. In the other three occurrences of *anothen* in John's Gospel, it is obvious that it means "from above," not "again."

> He who comes from above is above all [*ho anothen erxomeno epano panton estin*][51]
>
> You would have no authority over me, unless it had been given you from above [*ouk eikses exousian kat emou oudemian ei mei ein dedomenon soi anothen*][52]
>
> the tunic was seamless, woven in one piece [literal: from the top woven through the whole]. [*ho xiton araphos, ek ton anothen uphantos di holou*][53]

Besides these verses in John's Gospel, there are eight other passages where *anothen* occurs in the New Testament. In all but one of these verses,

---

51. John 3:31.
52. John 19:11.
53. John 19:23

anothen refers to that which is from above or from a beginning.[54] Paul used *anothen* as "again" his letter to the Galatian churches:

> How is it that you turn back again [*anothen*] to the weak and worthless elemental things?[55]

Nicodemus picked up on the idea of being born, but apparently failed to grasp the spiritual significance of the phrase "from above." He asked Jesus, "How can a man be born when he is old? He cannot enter a second time into his mother's womb and be born, can he?"[56] It is easy to see where Nicodemus's confusion was coming from. While he knew that there were various conversions that were referred to as a birth, such as Gentile proselytes who converted (were born again) to Judaism, he saw no way that this could apply to himself. He was a child of Abraham, already of God's chosen people, so why should he need to experience another birth? In the discourse that followed, Jesus pushed him to rise above a physical frame of reference to see spiritual concepts that came from above. He told Nicodemus,

> That which is born of the flesh is flesh, and that which is born of the Spirit is spirit.[57]

Jesus identified this birth as both a physical act ("of water") and a spiritual act ("of the Spirit").

> Jesus answered, "Truly, truly, I say to you, unless one is born of water and the Spirit he cannot enter into the kingdom of God"[58]

Since we humans have both a body and soul, this birth has a physical and spiritual reality. It was the spiritual reality that Jesus was attempting to get Nicodemus to see. Being a leader of the Jews, Nicodemus knew about John's preaching and baptizing people in the Jordan River. Did he see the connection between John's baptism and this statement by Jesus? The birth from above is more than merely a physical or symbolic act; it is more than just some vague religious experience. In the ministry of both John and Jesus, the converts were being baptized in water for conversion.

---

54. Matt 27:51; Mark 15:38; Luke 1:3; Acts 26:5; Jas 1:17; 3:15, 17.
55. Gal 4:9.
56. John 3:4.
57. John 3:6.
58. John 3:5.

The transformation involved in the birth from above recalls to our minds Paul's description of baptism in Romans 6. While there is much symbolism in the birth from above (John 3) and in baptism (Rom 6), these are events where, by divine activity, real things happen—e.g., entrance into the Kingdom and forgiveness of sin. Both John and Paul refer to baptism as an event in which a significant transformation takes place. We will see this frequently in subsequent chapters that deal with the preaching of the apostles in Acts and the writings of Paul and Peter.

There are no other passages in the New Testament (except perhaps Mark 16:16 and 1 Pet 3:21) that better describes the necessity of baptism than these words of Jesus to Nicodemus,

> Jesus answered and said to him, "Truly, truly, I say to you, unless one is born again he cannot see the kingdom of God."[59]

Most versions of the Bible translate the phrase *Ean mei tis genneithei* as "unless (or except) one is born." This can be seen in the table below:

NASU	"unless one is born"	NIV	"unless he is born"
ESV	"unless one is born"	ASV	"Except one be born"
RSV	"unless one is born"	KJV	"Except a man be born"
NKJV	"unless one is born"	YLT	"If any one may not be born"

Again two verses later Jesus made another statement with similar wording:

> Jesus answered, "Truly, truly, I say to you, unless (or except) one is born (*ean mei tis genneithei*) of water and the Spirit he cannot enter into the kingdom of God."[60]

NASU	"unless one is born"	NIV	"unless he is born"
ESV	"unless one is born"	ASV	"Except one be born"
RSV	"unless one is born"	KJV	"Except a man be born"
NKJV	"unless one is born"	YLT	"If any one may not be born"

While "unless" captures some sense of this phrase, a more literal translation, such as Young's Literal Translation, translates it in the precise words that Jesus actually used—"If anyone is not born." The force of *ean* (if), *tis*

---

59. John 3:3.
60. John 3:5.

(anyone), and *mei* (is not: a strong negative) makes the statement more emphatic than "unless." If Jesus was referring to baptism in these words (and we believe he was), he put the practice of baptism as the place of conversion and in the realm of necessity for anyone who would enter the Kingdom of Heaven.

The significance of this encounter between Jesus and Nicodemus demonstrates the importance and purpose of baptism in the Gospel message. This can be summarized in the following list:

1. Entrance into the Kingdom was not dependent on the recognition of the signs and wonders Jesus performed. Nicodemus opened the dialogue with a statement about Jesus' mighty works, but Jesus completely ignored it and addressed what he knew to be at the heart of Nicodemus's life.
2. It is a traumatic experience when a child is born from their mother's womb. In like manner, the radical transformation from sinner to saint in baptism is a traumatic birth experience.
3. This birth is more than a movement from one religion to another. The new life that comes forth out of the baptismal womb has its origin from above, in heaven.
4. Nicodemus was a Jew, even a leader of the Jews. That was not sufficient to enter the Kingdom of Heaven.
5. Both, to be "born from above" (verse 3) and to be "born of water and the Spirit" (verse 5), describe the moment of induction into the Kingdom.
6. Baptism in water was practiced in Jesus' ministry.

These observations make it hard to imagine anything other than baptism being that moment of birth from above that Jesus was referring to with Nicodemus.

7

Baptism in the Preaching of the Early Church

THROUGHOUT THE NEW TESTAMENT, baptism is referred to as the washing, the cleansing, and the forgiveness from the guilt of sin. *If the action of washing from sin (sanctification) should be separated from the practice of baptism, there would no longer remain a biblical purpose for the practice of baptism.* Granted, there are other gifts of God's grace that are also endowed in baptism, which are all very important, but if the bond between holiness and baptism is maintained, those other wonderful gifts will be there also. If forgiveness of sins is divorced from the act of baptism, there is no washing, and if there is no washing, there is alienation from God. And with that alienation comes severance from all the blessings which are in Christ Jesus.[1] We will be encountering these other gifts of grace as we look at the various New Testament passages concerning baptism.

There was a young married couple in the early 1970s who, upon studying the Bible with the authors of this book, came to the conclusion that they needed to be baptized. They had lived a typical worldly way of life with its lax morals, and right after the baptism, as we were visiting with them in front of the baptistery, the young lady said, "You know, for the first time in my life, I feel clean." In that statement, she confirmed that she understood the meaning of holiness and that baptism is the place where God incorporates us into the cleansing power of the blood of Christ. This is the same joy of baptismal cleansing that was at the heart of the preaching of Jesus' disciples as they went about carrying out the Great Commission.

---

1. Eph 1:3–14.

The message of those early preachers fell upon the ears of a sin-weary world. The people were hungry for freedom from their tradition-bound religions. They longed for freedom from oppressions perpetrated upon them by the multitude of injustices in their societies and the governing powers. But, most of all, they needed deliverance from their enslavement to the guilt of their own "sin which so easily entangles us."[2] In a world full of the muck and mire of life, was there any place where they could find refuge to "escape the defilements of the world?"[3] For those who chose to accept the Gospel message, Christians went forth proclaiming that there was a place of refuge, a place of peace in the midst of turmoil. Their message was Cross-centered, calling people to be converted from the ungodly impurities of the world and to be inducted into citizenship in the Kingdom of God through the washing of sanctification.

> Or do you not know that the unrighteous will not inherit the kingdom of God? Do not be deceived; neither fornicators, nor idolaters, nor adulterers, nor effeminate, nor homosexuals, nor thieves, nor the covetous, nor drunkards, nor revilers, nor swindlers, will inherit the kingdom of God. Such were some of you; but you were *washed*, but you were *sanctified*, but you were *justified* in the name of the Lord Jesus Christ and in the Spirit of our God.[4]

In this chapter, we will take a close look at how the early church taught and practiced baptism as the doorway into God's grace. Acts of the Apostles tells the story of the phenomenal spread of the Gospel to all corners of the world. Wherever the disciples went, they were making disciples, baptizing their converts as their Lord had instructed them.

The Day of Pentecost

Acts 2:38

> Peter said to them, "Repent, and each of you be baptized in the name of Jesus Christ for the forgiveness of your sins; and you will receive the gift of the Holy Spirit."[5]

---

2. Heb 12:1.
3. 2 Pet 2:20.
4. 1 Cor 6:9–11.
5. Acts 2:38.

The Gospel burst forth in Jerusalem on the Day of Pentecost (Acts 2) accompanied by unique miraculous signs (tongues like fire, great noise like a mighty wind, and speaking in languages they did not know). These were definitely attention-grabbing signs, to say the least. On that day there were crowds of people in Jerusalem from all corners of the world to celebrate Pentecost. Of those who witnessed these miracles, many believed and were baptized. The disciples, empowered by the Holy Spirit, began preaching the Gospel with zeal. There was a new power at work in them, a transformation brought about by the Holy Spirit. Hundreds, and even thousands, were being converted and baptized. It was not long before this explosion of the Gospel caught the attention of the Jewish leaders, who launched a strong persecution against them.

> a great persecution began against the church in Jerusalem, and they were all scattered throughout the regions of Judea and Samaria, except the apostles . . . Therefore, those who had been scattered went about preaching the word.[6]

It was not really a new message. God has been in the redemption business from the beginning of time, calling people to repentance. The folks there on that Day of Pentecost who heard Peter's sermon still had fresh memories of John the Baptist, who had come preaching the necessity of repentance and baptism for the forgiveness of sins.

We cannot ignore the similarity of Peter's language in Acts 2:38 to the language John the Baptist used to describe his baptism. Both of them proclaimed a definite call for repentance (*metanoia*)[7] and both preached a baptism for (*eis*)[8] the forgiveness of sins. The difference between them and those baptized by John was that, on the Day of Pentecost, Peter told the people that in their baptism they would "receive the gift of the Holy Spirit" as it had been foretold by John.[9]

Peter's Pentecost sermon began, "Men of Judea and all you who live in Jerusalem."[10] He then confronted them with the starkness of the truth that they had crucified their long-looked-for Messiah, the very

---

6. Acts 8:1, 4.

7. For the meaning of "repentance" as "conversion" in the New Testament, see the "Baptism of/into Repentance" in Chapter 5 above.

8. For the translation of *eis* in the New Testament, see the "Excursus on *Eis*" at the end of Chapter 5.

9. Matt 3:11; Mark 1:8; Luke 3:16.

10. Acts 2:14.

One God had sent into this world for their redemption. Peter's logic was impeccable. The people to whom he was preaching were themselves witnesses of the "miracles and wonders and signs which Jesus did *in your midst.*"[11] And now the news of Jesus' resurrection was being talked about all over the city; it was still fresh in their minds as he declared to them,

> Men of Israel, listen to these words: Jesus the Nazarene, a man attested to you by God with miracles and wonders and signs which God performed through him in your midst, *just as you yourselves know*—this Man, delivered over by the predetermined plan and foreknowledge of God, *you nailed to a cross* by the hands of godless men and put him to death . . . This Jesus God raised up again to which *we are all witnesses.* Therefore having been exalted to the right hand of God, and having received from the Father the promise of the Holy Spirit, he has poured forth this which you both see and hear . . . Therefore let all the house of Israel know for certain that God has made him both Lord and Christ—*this Jesus whom you crucified.*[12]

Twice Peter confronted them, in shocking words, with the fact that they themselves were responsible for the crucifixion of Jesus—their Lord and Messiah. To drive his point home, he used their own Scriptures for support and authority for what he was saying (Joel 2:28–32; Ps 16:8–11; and Ps 110:1). Upon hearing the words of this dramatic sermon, they were cut to the heart.[13]

> Now when they heard this, they were pierced to the heart, and said to Peter and the rest of the apostles, "Brethren, what shall we do?"[14]

Their consciences forced them to face up to their crime against God! What a dawning! What a sense of shame! What fear! If the One they crucified should indeed be The Lord—the Son of God—and he is now alive,

---

11. Acts 2:22.
12. Acts 2:22–23, 32–33, 36.
13. Barnes, "Acts 2:37."
    The word translated "were pricked," *katenugeesan*, is not used elsewhere in the New Testament. It properly denotes "to pierce or penetrate with a needle, lancet, or sharp instrument"; and then "to pierce with grief, or acute pain of any kind." It implies also the idea of sudden as well as acute grief. In this case it means that they were suddenly and deeply affected with anguish and alarm at what Peter had said.
14. Acts 2:37.

then, as Almighty God, what vengeance might his justice rain down upon them for what they did to his Son? No wonder, with trembling hearts, they cried out, "Brethren, what shall we do?" *There was no way they could undo what had been done.*

> What they had done could not be undone. The guilt remained; they could not wash it out. They had imbrued[15] theft hands in the blood of innocence, and the guilt of that oppressed their souls.[16]

Was there any hope for them? How were they to make right such a heinous act? In Peter's imperative answer was a challenge for them to be transformed, not only in their way of thinking, but in their whole outlook on life.

What they needed to hear, and me like them, was the promise that there really is forgiveness of sins, even for this most evil of all crimes. Can I stand aloof and look with disdain on them for what they did? Can I, from twenty centuries away, hurl condemnation on them with the confidence that if I had been there, I would not have been a part of the mob that screamed, "Crucify him?" Do I not turn my back on him every time I decide, "My will, not Thine be done?" I, too, need to hear Peter's assurance that there is hope for even me; there is forgiveness for all who repent, are baptized, and receive the guidance of the Holy Spirit in their lives.

What relief to hear these words of Peter that hold the solution to our guilt, the cleansing power required to make us right with God. The whole verse must be taken as a unit. Repentance, baptism, forgiveness, and the Holy Spirit were wrapped up in that solution, and none of them can be removed without destroying the integrity of the whole statement! Nor can the fact be ignored that there is a close connection between Peter's baptismal command and the baptism *that day* of 3,000 souls.

> So then, those who had received his word were baptized; and that day there were added about three thousand souls.[17]

Down through the centuries, many people have read these words of Peter and, like those folks on the Day of Pentecost, were converted, surrendering to the Lord in baptism so that they too might have the assurance of the forgiveness of their sins. However, in more recent centuries,

---

15. Imbrue: to stain, saturate, permeate; especially with blood.
16. Barnes, "Acts 2:37."
17. Acts 2:41.

there have been many attempts to dissect these words of Peter in such a way as to render baptism an irrelevant parenthetical phrase, disconnected from the rest of the passage. Once baptism has been isolated from repentance, the forgiveness of sin, and the receiving of the Holy Spirit, it becomes a shallow, empty, and meaningless ritual. Our challenge is to search out anew Peter's response as God intended for it to be understood. Because the words of Peter in Acts 2:38 are vital to understanding our deliverance and salvation, we need to take a critical look to see just what this message is that God wants us to hear.

"Repent!"

This imperative was the same as that which had been preached by the prophets; they had heard it again with both John the Baptist and Jesus. John and Jesus had called for repentance as they announced the imminence of the coming of the Kingdom with power.[18] Now, on that memorable day of Pentecost, the Kingdom had come with the power of the Holy Spirit. Thus, there was launched a new movement of even greater proportions than that of John's. In this command to be converted (*metanoeo*) was the call for total loyalty, the surrender of their will to the will of the One they had crucified. Only then could there be hope.

This transformation was not something they could accomplish themselves, some sort of deed by which they could undo their guilt; they were guilty of high crimes against God, and only God could transform them from their darkness to light, from their hopelessness to salvation, and from their impurity to cleanness. The price for the sanctification of their guilt was the blood that was shed by the one they had killed.

"And be baptized for the forgiveness of your sins!"

It is interesting that the command to be baptized did not cause a controversy among Peter's audience. That day 3,000 people understood what he meant, and they obeyed without debating whether baptism and forgiveness of sins belonged together or apart!

In the years since the Reformation, one of the arguments set forth in an effort to sever the intimate relationship between baptism and forgiveness mistakenly presupposes that baptism is a work that a person must

---

18. See chapter 6, "The Baptism of John the Baptist."

perform. The reasoning is that since forgiveness is an act of God's grace and is not accomplished by any works of man, forgiveness cannot be associated with the crude physical act of baptism. Thus, baptism cannot be necessary for salvation. "A crude physical act like baptism," they argue, "cannot be associated with such a lofty spiritual event as forgiveness of sins." If they are right, then we must figure out what to do with baptism; we must come up with some biblical purpose for it. If their presupposition that baptism is an act of human work were true, then their fear of preaching a salvation by works in baptism would be justified, and we would have to search in vain for an alternative way to understand the meaning and purpose of baptism in the New Testament.

However, if it can be shown that *what is accomplished in baptism is God's work of redemption,* not a human work required in order to *obtain* forgiveness, then the whole statement by Peter maintains a beautiful harmony with an integrity that is compatible with the many other New Testament passages on baptism. To illustrate this problem, there were two preachers one Sunday morning in the early 1970s on a Nashville radio station delivering their sermons. One was a Baptist preacher, and the other was a preacher for the Churches of Christ. The main point of the Baptist preacher's sermon was that we are saved by faith alone, not by works. He defined baptism as a work; therefore, as a work of man, it could not be credited with forgiveness of sins resulting in salvation. To avoid the conclusion of salvation by works, he relegated baptism to a post-conversion event that a person must do *after* they have been saved.

Whether the two preachers had pre-arranged to speak on the same topic that morning is unknown. The Church of Christ preacher who followed him also declared that baptism is a work a person must do. However, he insisted that as a work, it was a deed that a person must do in order to get salvation. Since Peter made it clear in Acts 2:38 that baptism is necessary for the forgiveness of sin, we are therefore saved by faith and by works (baptism). Both preachers were wrong! Baptism is not a performance done by humans in order to accomplish the forgiveness of sins. Baptism is indeed a work, but it is God's work, not man's, that attains to salvation! Everything that happens in baptism is the gracious work of God.[19]

Because we are dealing in this passage with a matter that concerns our salvation and eternal destiny, we need to take a closer look at the

---

19. We will take a closer look at the grace available to man in baptism in a later chapter.

grammar in Acts 2:38 to be certain that we stand on the solid rock of Jesus Christ, not on the drifting sand of uncertainty. In doing this, we must remember that we are not merely analyzing Peter's words or his theology. We are looking at the words Peter spoke to us by the power of the Holy Spirit. We can be thankful that no matter how critically we exam the word of God, we can have confidence that we are dealing with the very word of God. Let us, then, take a close look at the words of Peter:

> Peter said to them, "Repent, and each of you be baptized in the name of Jesus Christ for the forgiveness of your sins; and you will receive the gift of the Holy Spirit."

> *Petros de pros autous, "Metanoeisate, kai baptistheito ekastos humon epi to onomati Ieisou Christos eis aphesin ton hamartion humon kai leimpsesthe tein dorean tou hagiou pheumatos."*

In this statement by Peter, there is a mixture of singular and plural words that some have used to try to prove that the association of baptism with forgiveness is a violation of correct grammar. "Repent" (*metanoeisate*) is a *plural* imperative verb; "be baptized" (*baptistheito*) is a *singular* imperative verb; and "your" (*humon*) occurs twice as a *plural* pronoun. It has been pointed out that it is improper grammar for the plural pronoun "your" ("you all") to be conjoined with the singular verb "be baptized" without violating linguistic rules. The conclusion is then drawn that since "your (*humon*) sins" is plural, it cannot be matched up with the singular "be baptized." Rather, the plural "forgiveness" must be conjoined instead with the plural imperative "repent." Acts 2:38 would then have to read, "Repent (plural) for the forgiveness of your (plural) sins and (then later) be baptized." This exegesis of this text, while appearing to solve the issue of baptism, ignores some grammatical considerations that we will take a closer look at below.

In *Bibliotheca Sacra*, a theological journal published by Dallas Theological Seminary, Luther McIntyre set forth this issue with the question:

> "To which verb—*metanoeisate* ('repent') or *baptistheito* ('be baptized'—the only occurrence of this third person imperative in the New Testament)—does the prepositional phrase 'for the remission of your sins' refer?"[20]

McIntyre's concern was that since the pronoun "your" (*humon*) in the phrase "for the forgiveness of your sins" is plural, it must have a plural

20. McIntyre, "Baptism and Forgiveness," 54.

verb to go with it. And therefore, he reasoned, since "you all repent" is a plural verb and "you be baptized" is a singular verb, the phrase, "for the forgiveness of *your* (plural) sins," must be matched up with the "repent" and not with "be baptized." McIntyre thus concluded,

> The plural pronoun "your" points back to some other substantive to which it refers (its antecedent) . . . Concerning concord [agreement] with respect to person, only ignorance would allow one to mix his persons [singular and plural] in the use of the verb.[21] While Robertson notes some exceptions, none of them apply to Acts 2:38. Polhill hints at the basic issue involved when he says, "The usual connection of the forgiveness of sins in Luke-Acts is with repentance and not with baptism at all."[22] *The concord between verb and pronoun requires that the remission of sins be connected with repentance, not with baptism.* However, if one associates forgiveness with baptism, the verse translated into English with due accord to person and number, would read, "let him (third singular) be baptized for the remission of your (second plural) sins." The folly of ignoring concord then is obvious[23] (emphasis added).

If the above grammatical rule, which McIntyre called "concord," applies to Acts 2:38 in the way he suggested, then there is a cumbersome problem of what to do with the imperative verb "be baptized." With such a view, baptism would become some kind of throwaway act, an extraneous, irrelevant, and superfluous imperative that has no connection with anything else in that verse. In the above statement, McIntyre referred to A. T. Robertson, who noted that there are some exceptions to the concord rule, but, in his quote above, McIntyre discounted the exception, saying, "While Robertson does note some exceptions, *none of them apply to Acts 2:38.*" (emphasis added). Such a dismissal is merely his opinion for which he gave no evidence. McIntyre then quoted Dr. John Polhill of Southern Baptist Theological Seminary, who wrote, "The *usual* connection of the forgiveness of sins in Luke-Acts is with repentance and not with baptism at all." What did Polhill mean by "the *usual* connection?" Would not the association of baptism with both forgiveness and repentance in John the Baptist's baptism contradict such a conclusion? Whatever other

---

21. Robertson, *A Grammar*, 402.
22. Polhill, *New American Commentary*, 117.
23. Polhill, *New American Commentary*, 55.

BAPTISM IN THE PREACHING OF THE EARLY CHURCH 109

"*usual* connections" of repentance with forgiveness, to the exclusion of baptism, Polhill had in mind we are not told.

Such confidence in the concord rule is irrelevant to this passage if we consider the role of the word *ekastos* (each one, every one) in the phrase *baptistheito ekastos humon . . . eis aphesin ton hamartion humon*: "be baptized [singular] each one [*ekastos*] of you all [plural] . . . for the forgiveness of your sins." McIntyre changed the entire meaning of this passage when he translated this phrase: "let him [third singular] be baptized for the remission of your [second plural] sins." He completely left out the word *ekastos*! The word *ekastos* identifies a singular person within a collective of persons. *Ekasto* identifies each individual (singularly) within the collective group (*humon*) of Peter's audience. This grammatical construction is called a "Partitive Apposition."[24] "*Humon*" is the whole audience being addressed by Peter, while the command "be baptized" is addressed to each individual within that collective audience. Therefore, the phrases "you all repent" and "each one of you be baptized" are actually addressed to the same audience, whose repentance (conversion) *and* baptism are both to be understood as "for the purpose of [*eis*] the forgiveness of sins."

Another attempt to dissect baptism from Peter's answer in Acts 2:38 has been the ongoing discussion about whether the preposition *eis* should be translated as causal (because of, on account of) or purposive (into, for the purpose of). We looked at this issue in Chapter 5 concerning the practice of baptism by John the Baptist. In this controversy, two leading proponents who maintain that there are a few rare passages where *eis* can be translated "because of" (especially Acts 2:38) are Drs. A. T. Robertson and J. R. Mantey. Evidence, as we have seen in previous passages, has made it clear that *eis* in the New Testament is universally used as a purposive preposition. For a more thorough explanation of the meaning of *eis* in the New Testament, see the Excursus on "The Meaning of *Eis* in the New Testament" at the end of chapter 5.

---

24. When a word is used *alongside of* another word in a sentence that it describes, the two words are said to be *in apposition* to each other. When one of the words in the apposition expresses *part(s) of the other word* it is called a *partitive*; thus, the two words together become a *Partitive Apposition*. In Acts 2:38, *humon* (plural—"you all") is a pronoun that refers to Peter's audience as a whole and sits in *apposition* to *ekastos* ("each one"), each one in the whole assembly. Since "each one of you all" refers to each individual in the whole audience, "be baptized" must be singular. Thus, we have the Partitive Apposition as the solution to the grammatical problem expressed by McIntyre.

Drs. Robertson and Mantey were both Greek language professors and both wrote excellent Greek grammars. However, in regard to the use of *eis* in the New Testament, they abandoned their faith in the accuracy and authority of the biblical text in favor of their theological presuppositions. By advocating for a causal use of *eis* in Acts 2:38 rather than a purposive use, they attempted to divorce baptism from forgiveness of sins. If a Bible reader approached Acts 2:38 afresh without any presuppositions to taint their understanding of baptism, they, like the audience on the Day of Pentecost, would naturally recognize the intimate relationship between "be baptized" and "forgiveness of your sins."

The question about *eis* in this verse concerns whether repentance is directly connected to *eis aphesin ton hamartion humon* (for the forgiveness of your sins) or if repentance stands alone as a prerequisite to baptism. In the examination of the meaning of "repentance" (*metanoeo*) in chapter 5, it was shown that "conversion," not "be sorry," expresses the true meaning of repentance. Since repentance means conversion and baptism is the place where God converts a person from sinner to saint by the washing of sanctification, it would be wrong to chronologically separate "repent" from either "baptism" or "the forgiveness of your sins." Since repentance and baptism refer to two things that occur concurrently, then *eis aphesin ton hamartion humon* should apply to both of them. By translating *metanoeisate* (aorist, active, imperative, 2nd, plural) as "be converted" instead of "repent," Peter's statement would read, "Be converted, and be baptized, each one of you . . ."

"In the name of Jesus Christ"

In the phrase *epi to onomati Ieisou Christos* (in the name of Jesus Christ), the word *epi* is a preposition whose root idea means "resting upon" or "on the basis of."[25] *Onomati* is the neuter, dative, singular of *onoma* (name). When *epi* is associated with the dative noun, it answers the question of authority or origin. *Epi* is used with a dative noun "to introduce the person or thing by reason of whom (or which) something happens."[26] *Epi* with a dative noun is also used in response to the question "where?"[27] In this light, it would seem that *epi to onomati Ieisou Christos* identifies

---

25. Robertson and Davis, *Short Grammar*, 257.
26. Baur, *A Greek–English Lexicon*, 286–87.
27. Blass and Debrunner, *Greek Grammar*, 123.

Jesus as the place or source (origin or authority) for both commands to "repent" and to "be baptized." This would also be in agreement with Jesus' declaration of his authority in heaven and on earth in Matt 28:17.

There is a difference between Peter's statement, "upon the name of Jesus Christ" (*epi to onomati Ieisou Christos*) in Acts 2:38, and the one Jesus made at the end of Matthew's Gospel, "in the name of the Father and the Son and the Holy Spirit" (*eis to onoma tou patros kai the huiou and tou hagiou pneumatos*).[28] Some textual commentators have assumed that because of this difference in the use of two prepositions (*epi* and *eis*), there must have been an older form of baptism (with *eis*) that was practiced before Pentecost in the ministry of Jesus and the form of baptism (with *epi*) that was practiced later by the apostles. In the attempt to reinforce their conclusion, it is also noted that Jesus' commission included the Father and Holy Spirit in his baptismal formula, while Peter omitted the Father and Holy Spirit in his baptismal formula. With these two differences, it has been concluded that the practice of baptism in the Gospels should be excluded as a help to understand the purpose of baptism as it was later preached by the apostles in the early church. Thus, the conclusion has been made that Matthew's text, "make disciples of all the nations, baptizing them," and Mark's text, "He who has believed and has been baptized shall be saved," can have no bearing on trying to understand the meaning of baptism in Acts 2:38.

However, if we realize that the two prepositions, *eis* and *epi*, are not contradictory but complementary, the harmony of Matthew's text with Peter's is easily seen. In Matthew, the preposition *eis* indicates the goal, direction, and purpose of baptism, while in Acts, the preposition *epi* expresses the authority and origin of the call to repentance and baptism. While *epi* looks behind the baptism for its source or authority, *eis* looks forward into that which the one being baptized is introduced. Concerning the divine names, it must be realized that whether a person's baptism is associated with the name of Jesus only or with the whole Trinity, to call upon one is to call upon all three. Jesus said, " . . . whatever the Father does, these things the Son also does in like manner."[29] The divine triad are one in purpose and work. Where one is, the other two are there also.

---

28. Matt 28:19.
29. John 5:19.

"and you will receive the gift of the Holy Spirit"

John the Baptist made it clear that he was not the Messiah and prophesied that when the Messiah came, he would "baptize you with the Holy Spirit."[30] Acts 2:38 marks the fulfillment of that prophecy about the Holy Spirit's role in baptism. Just a few days before Pentecost, Jesus again foretold the receiving of the Holy Spirit in connection with baptism when he told his disciples,

> . . . for John baptized with water, but you will be baptized with [*en*: in, by] the Holy Spirit not many days from now.[31]

Beasley-Murray said it well: " . . . in the Acts and Epistles baptism is the supreme moment of the impartation of the Spirit and of the work of the Spirit in the believer."[32] The New Testament knows of no situation where a person is in Christ without also being in the Spirit.

> However, you are not in the flesh but in the *Spirit*, if indeed the *Spirit* of *God* dwells in you. But if anyone does not have the *Spirit* of *Christ*, he does not belong to him . . . For all who are being led by the *Spirit* of *God*, these are sons of *God*.[33]

The unity of the Trinity in the lives of the faithful permeates this passage. Those who belong to Jesus are "sons of God" and are "in the Spirit" and are "being led by the Spirit." This incorporation of the Holy Spirit into the life of the believer at baptism is the assurance of God's presence. The initiation of a convert into the Spirit as a gift of God is said by Peter to be accomplished in one's baptism. It would be a gross violation of the word of God to divorce the receiving of the Holy Spirit from baptism. The use of the future tense of the verb "will receive" (*leimpsesthe*) in this passage indicates that when they respond to the command to "be baptized" (*baptistheito*), at that time they would receive not only the forgiveness of their sins but the Holy Spirit as well.[34]

---

30. Mark 1:8 and John 1:33 mention the Holy Spirit only, while Matt 3:11 and Luke 3:16 expand it to say, "He will baptize you with the Holy Spirit and fire."

31. Acts 1:5.

32. Beasley-Murray, *Baptism*, 275.

33. Rom 8:9, 14.

34. Bruner, *A Theology*, 167–68.

The Samaritans

Acts 8:12-17

> But when they believed Philip preaching the good news about the kingdom of God and the name of Jesus Christ, they were being baptized, men and women alike. Even Simon himself believed; and after being baptized, he continued on with Philip, and as he observed signs and great miracles taking place, he was constantly amazed. Now when the apostles in Jerusalem heard that Samaria had received the word of God, they sent them Peter and John, who came down and prayed for them that they might receive the Holy Spirit. For he had not yet fallen upon any of them; they had simply been baptized in the name of the Lord Jesus. Then they began laying their hands on them, and they were receiving the Holy Spirit.[35]

Philip the Evangelist first showed up on the stage of Bible history[36] as one of the seven men chosen by the church and commissioned by the apostles to "serve tables." These men were also busy going about preaching the Gospel. In Acts 8:5 we find Philip in Samaria "preaching the good news about the kingdom of God and the name of Jesus Christ." Apparently, the people were receiving his preaching quite favorably, for "when [*hote*] they believed Philip preaching the good news about the kingdom of God and the name of Jesus Christ, they were being baptized, men and women alike." (8:12).

Writing about this event, Luke used the Greek word *hote* (when) in verse 12 to describe the relationship between the Samaritan's belief and their baptism—"when [*hote*] they believed . . . they were being baptized, men and women alike." The chronological relationship between when they believed and when they were baptized is dependent on two factors. The first concerns the meaning of *hote*. All of the major English translations render *hote* as "when" in this passage. The adverb *hote* is commonly used with verbs in the indicative mood (occasionally with the subjunctive mood). As a verb modifier, it expresses the conjunction of time between verbs. *Hote* indicates the point in time when one event occurs that is simultaneous with another event.[37] An example that demonstrates the

---

35. Acts 8:12–17.
36. Acts 6:5.
37. Louw and Nida, *Greek-English Lexicon*, 67.30.

concurrence of two events occurring simultaneously because they share a common *hote* is Matt 7:28:

> When [*hote*] Jesus had finished these words, the crowds were amazed at his teaching;

The amazement of the crowd was simultaneous with Jesus speaking. The *hote* of Acts 8:12 likewise requires the conclusion that the point of time that the Samaritans believed is the same time as their baptism.

The second factor that helps determine the timing of the Samaritans' belief in relation to their baptism is the meaning of the word faith. Obviously, mere knowledge of God is not sufficient grounds for a person to assume that they are pleasing to God. There are numerous people who know a lot about God, but they have not submitted their will to his. Nor is heart-felt emotion sufficient. Paul had great zeal in his persecution of Christians, but he was certainly not pleasing to God in that devotion of the heart. *Only when knowledge of God unites with strong convictions and results in the surrender of their will to God's will can a person say they have biblical faith and are thus pleasing to God.* God chose baptism as the time and place for the surrender of faith to occur. To separate faith from baptism chronologically would be to render them both impotent and futile.

Cornelius and his Household

Acts 10:43

> To him [Jesus] all the prophets bear witness that forgiveness of sins is to be received through his name to all who believe in him.[38]

In the case of the Samaritans in the previous passage with Philip, we noted that their faith was concurrent with their baptism. In this story, Peter, explaining the Gospel to Cornelius and his household, also indicated that faith and forgiveness of sins are concurrent. There are two verbs of interest in this verse: (1) the word for "received" (*labein*) is an aorist active infinite, and (2) the word "believe" (*pisteuonta*) is a present active participle. The main leading verb, "received," is the primary action of the sentence. Since the present participle, "those who believe," denotes

---

38. Acts 10:43. Author's translation of *touto pantes hoi propheitai marturousin aphesin hamartion lambein dia tou onomatos autou panta ton pisteuonta eis auton.*

action that occurred at the same time as the action of the leading verb (received), believing and receiving forgiveness of sins are simultaneous actions.[39]

Since faith is concurrent with baptism in the case of the Samaritans and faith is also concurrent with forgiveness in the story of Cornelius, then faith and forgiveness must both occur simultaneously in baptism. While faith and forgiveness have different meanings, they converge together in the waters of baptism. Faith, forgiveness, and repentance are all vital aspects of God's salvation in baptism.

Baptism of the Ephesian Disciples of John

Acts 19:5-6

While on his last missionary journey, Paul encountered in Ephesus a group of disciples who had been baptized with the baptism of John the Baptist. When Paul informed them of Jesus' ministry,

> ... they were baptized in (*eis*) the name of the Lord Jesus. And when Paul had laid his hands upon them, the Holy Spirit came on them, and they began speaking with tongues and prophesying.[40]

Again, in this short account, we encounter that little preposition, *eis*. If it were true, as advocated by Professors J. R. Mantey and A. T. Robertson above, that there are "rare" passages where *eis* can be translated as causal (because of), such as Acts 2:38, then to be consistent, their same policy must be made to apply to this passage as well. If these two professors were correct, we are finding that their *rare* usage of *eis* as a causal preposition is actually becoming quite *common* as we discover more and more passages of this same construction with the use of *eis*.

If they applied their same causal principle to all the passages where *eis* is in juxtaposition with baptism, they would be hard-pressed to defend

---

39. Burton, *Syntax*, 54–55.
   119. The Present Participle of Simultaneous Actions. The Present Participle most frequently denotes an action in progress, simultaneous with the action of the principal verb ... 122. A Present Participle of Identical Action, since it denotes action in progress, most naturally accompanies a verb denoting action in progress. Sometimes, however, a Present Participle accompanies an Aorist verb denoting the same action.

40. Acts 19:5–6.

their view that the causal use of *eis* is rare. John the Baptist baptized into (*eis*) both forgiveness of sins and repentance.[41] Jesus commanded his disciples to baptize into (*eis*) the name of the Father, the Son, and the Holy Spirit. Jesus told his disciples that repentance for (*eis*) forgiveness of sins would be proclaimed in his name.[42] The Samaritans were baptized into (*eis*) the name of the Lord Jesus.[43] Paul baptized the Ephesian disciples of John into (*eis*) the name of the Lord Jesus.[44] Three times Paul used *eis* to describe the purpose of baptism as inducting people into (*eis*) Christ and into (*eis*) his death.[45] To the Galatian churches, Paul described his readers as those who were baptized into (*eis*) Christ.[46] To the Corinthians, Paul stated that "we were all baptized into (*eis*) one body."[47] Why didn't Professors Mantey and Robertson apply their "rare" causal use of *eis* to all these other passages as they tried to do with Acts 2:38? But then, of course, if they did, the causal use of *eis* would no longer be rare, and that would destroy their thesis! How can they justify changing their rules of grammar and translation in a text of God's Word just to make it conform to their theology? Rather, shouldn't theology be made to conform to all these texts?

Saul's (Paul's) Conversion

Acts 9:17–18; 22:16

So Ananias departed and entered the house, and after laying his hands on him said, "Brother Saul, the Lord Jesus, who appeared to you on the road by which you were coming, has sent me so that you may regain your sight and be filled with the Holy Spirit." And immediately there fell from his eyes something like scales, and he regained his sight, and he got up and was baptized.

[Ananias to Paul] Now why do you delay? Get up and be baptized, and wash away your sins, calling on his name.[48]

---

41. Mark 1:4; Luke 3:3.
42. Luke 24:47.
43. Acts 8:16.
44. Acts 19:5.
45. Rom 6:3–4.
46. Gal 3:27.
47. 1 Cor 12:13.
48. Acts 9:17–18; 22:16.

It appears obvious that when Ananias came to Paul and spoke to him, somewhere in the visit he explained the purpose and need for Paul to be baptized. Otherwise, how would Paul know that he needed to be baptized? Several years later, when Paul was defending his conversion before a crowd of angry Jews in Acts 22:16, he told them that Ananias asked him why he delayed and told him, "Arising, be baptized and wash away your sins, calling on his name."[49] There are four verbs in this quote:

"Arising": aorist active participle
"Be baptized": aorist middle imperative
"Wash away": aorist middle imperative
"Calling": aorist middle participle

All four verbs are in the aorist tense. The aorist tense identifies action as a point-action event (punctiliar), presenting the action as a completed event in contrast to action that is ongoing or progressive (present tense). Of the four verbs, the first and fourth are in the participle mood, and the second and third are in the imperative mood. An imperative mood verb presents the action as a command. The participle mood indicates the action of the verb in its relationship to the principal verb(s) which, in this case, are "be baptized" and "wash away." A participle has no indication of timing in itself but is dependent on the timing of the principal verb(s).

In Paul's quotation of Ananias (22:16), the two leading verbs are the imperatives, "be baptized" and "wash away," which are packaged between the two Participles, "arising" and "calling." It would be difficult to separate the respective actions of these verbs chronologically without destroying their structure and mutual interrelationship. If one were inclined to attempt to treat them as a progression of action, it would result in placing baptism chronologically before the washing, a conclusion that would become a very difficult and cumbersome translation.

According to Ananias's statement, up to the time he spoke with Paul, Paul's sins had not yet been washed away. Paul's encounter with Jesus on the road as he approached Damascus was not his saving event. Later in Damascus, the instructions to Paul by Ananias indicate that the washing of his sins was something that Paul had not yet experienced. If Paul was saved when the light appeared on the Damascus road, before his

---

49. This is the author's translation. There is only one "and" in this verse, and it falls between "be baptized" and "wash away." The first verb is translated as "Get up" in the NASU and NIV, while the ESV, RSV, and KJV translate it as "Rise" or "Arise." All of them translate the word as an imperative instead of a participle.

encounter with Ananias, why did Ananias instruct him to "be baptized and wash away your sins?" It seems obvious that up to the point of his encounter with Ananias and his baptism, Paul's sins were still unforgiven. If he were saved at the time of the bright light, he would have had no need to be baptized to wash away his sins.

To speculate what would have happened if Paul had died between his vision and his baptism is a game many have played in an attempt to discredit the importance of the role of baptism. A story has been passed around—fictional or otherwise is unknown—about a man who was about to be baptized. When he and the one baptizing him stepped into the flood-swollen river, they were both swept away and drowned. Was the man who came to the river to be baptized saved since he was "providentially hindered" within moments of his baptism? We humans seem to delight in speculating on things that we know very little about rather than in obeying the things we do know.

In both of the phrases, *anastas ebaptisthei* (9:18) and *anastas baptisai* (22:16), *anastas* is an aorist, active, participle, and should, therefore, be literally translated as "standing up" (*ana*: "up," and *stasis*: "stand"). It can also be translated by other synonyms such as "arising," "lifting up," "getting up," and "raising up." In neither of these verses is *anastas* an imperative, but it is translated in 22:16 as an imperative in the NASU, NIV, ESV, RSV, KJV, and NKJV. Being a participle, the action in *anastas* assumes the timing of the primary verbs—*ebaptisthei* in 9:18 and *baptisai* in 22:16. Also, in both 9:18 and 22:16, there is no *kai* ("and") after *anastas* which makes Paul's arising and his baptism even more concurrent. There is a *kai* between "be baptized" and "wash away" connecting these two imperatives. To try to arrange these two verbs so as to make baptism an event subsequent to the washing would require a complete rearranging of this comment by Annanias.

Receiving of the Holy Spirit in the Acts of the Apostles

The receiving of the Holy Spirit in the conversion stories of Acts has given rise to several difficult questions. According to Jesus in the Great Commission, the baptizands were to be inducted into a relationship with the Trinity as a part of their baptismal experience, "baptizing them into the name of the Father, the Son, and the Holy Spirit."[50] Peter told his Pen-

---

50. Matt 28:19.

tecost audience that in their baptism they would not only be forgiven of their sins, but they would receive the Holy Spirit as well.[51] In the account of the conversion of the Samaritans, Philip preached to them and they were baptized, but the Holy Spirit "had not yet fallen upon any of them." It was *at a later time*, when Peter and John came down to Samaria from Jerusalem, that they "received the Holy Spirit" when the apostles prayed and laid hands on them.[52] In this story of the conversion of Cornelius and his household, there is yet another scenario. While Peter was teaching them, "the Holy Spirit fell upon all those who were listening to the message" *before* they were baptized.[53] When Paul encountered the disciples of John the Baptist in Ephesus who had been baptized with John's baptism but did not have any knowledge of the Holy Spirit, he baptized them in the name of the Lord Jesus, *after which* Paul laid hands on them and "the Holy Spirit came upon them."[54] To simplify all these situations, we can compare the stories in the following chart:

Matt 28:19	Great Commission	Baptized into (*eis*) the name of the Father and the Son and the Holy Spirit	Holy Spirit received *in* baptism
Acts 2:38	Peter's audience	Baptized in (*epi*) the name of Jesus Christ and received the Holy Spirit	Holy Spirit received *in* baptism
Acts 8:12–17	Samaritans	Baptized in (*eis*) the name of the Lord Jesus (v. 16)	Holy Spirit received *after* baptism (v. 17)
Acts 10:44–48	Cornelius	Baptized in (*en*) the name of Jesus Christ (48)	Holy Spirit fell upon them *before* baptism (v. 44)
Acts 19:5–6	Paul and the Ephesians	Baptized in (*eis*) the name of the Lord Jesus (v. 5)	Holy Spirit came upon them *after* baptism (v. 6)

In light of these baptismal events in Acts, there has been much discussion among Bible scholars down through the centuries about the

---

51. Acts 2:38.
52. Acts 8:12–17.
53. Acts 10:44–48.
54. Acts 19:1–7.

relationship between baptism and the receiving of the Holy Spirit. Paul made it quite clear in Romans 8 that a person must have the Spirit dwelling in them in order to be a child of God.

> However, you are not in the flesh but in the Spirit, if indeed the Spirit of God dwells in you. *But if anyone does not have the Spirit of Christ, he does not belong to him* . . . For all who are being led by the Spirit of God, these are sons of God . . . The Spirit himself testifies with our spirit that we are children of God.[55]

Wherever Jesus is, there too is the Holy Spirit and the Father. The Bible makes it clear that the Divine Three are inseparable. If any One of Them dwells in a person, the other Two are there also. Therefore, we have to recognize the fact that in baptism, a person is united with all Three. The normal, direct, and immediate association of the Father, the Son, and the Spirit with the baptismal event is made clear by the authors of the New Testament. Concerning the unity of the godhead in connection with baptism, Stanley Fowler recognized that

> The connection could hardly be denied, for if baptism unites the individual to Christ and thus to the benefits of Christ's redemptive work, and if the gift of the Holy Spirit is central to the benefits of the Messianic salvation (as envisioned by the Hebrew prophets and John the Baptist), then any act which accomplishes union with Christ must be presumed to mediate the presence of the Spirit.[56]

Those situations in Acts where the Spirit fell upon people before or after their baptism are presented by Luke as exceptional situations. Luke's descriptions of these baptismal stories make it difficult to miss the fact that they were unusual.

So, how are we to understand the receiving of the Holy Spirit in these three unusual passages in Acts 8, 10, and 19? The uniqueness of the above passages where the Holy Spirit came upon them before or after baptism has given rise to much confusion and numerous opinions. One proposed solution is that God intervened in these three situations in unusual ways to get the church's attention and to convince them that they must accept a broader vision of his commission. Would the Jewish church have accepted Samaritans and Gentiles without these extraordinary measures? While this understanding has some plausibility to it, the fact remains that

---

55. Rom 8:9, 14.
56. Fowler, *More Than a Symbol*, 219.

this solution is not mentioned in the Acts narrative. We must be careful about drawing conclusions not found in the text.

There are two facts we know about the conversion stories in Acts concerning the Holy Spirit. One is that everyone who was baptized into Christ received the indwelling of the Holy Spirit in their lives at the time of their baptism. The other fact is that we are not told why in these three unusual cases God saw fit that the Holy Spirit should come upon them before or after their baptism. G. R. Beasley-Murray made mention of this confusion in his discussion of baptism and the Holy Spirit.

> Here we must exercise patience as we consider the evidence of the Acts on this issue . . . To account for these divergencies of practice and harmonize the theology (or theologies) presumed by them gives room for the exercise of ingenuity, and it cannot be said that it has been wanting in the explanations provided. Some of the difficulties are attributable to the meagerness of the descriptions; *the needful information for their satisfactory solution has not been provided* . . . Much energy has been expended on trying to recover traditions which Luke has utilized in writing his narratives . . . but the subjective element in these reconstructions makes them at best tentative and leaves one with a feeling of disquiet.[57] (emphasis added)

After his thorough discussion of the issues raised by these unusual baptismal stories, Beasley-Murray concluded:

> Our review of the evidence in Acts relating to the gift of the Spirit and baptism should have made one important lesson plain: while baptism and the Spirit are set in close relation, allowances must always be made for the freedom of God in bestowing the Spirit.[58]

Because these biblical stories do not give complete information about these events, it is difficult for us to refrain from trying to fill in the blanks. Unlike Paul Harvey, we cannot say, "Now you know the rest of the story." One thing we do know is how little we know about the Holy Spirit. As the old hymn by William Cowper ("Cooper") goes, "God moves in a mysterious way, his wonders to perform."[59] It reminds us that the ways of God are not our ways, and our ways must always bow to his.

---

57. Beasley-Murray, *Baptism*, 104–6.
58. Beasley-Murray, *Baptism*, 120.
59. "God Moves in a Mysterious Way" is thought to be the last hymn Cowper ever

> "For my thoughts are not your thoughts, nor are your ways my ways," declares the Lord. "For as the heavens are higher than the earth, so are my ways higher than your ways and my thoughts than your thoughts."[60]

Perhaps the following admonition by Frederick Bruner is the wisest path for all of us to follow when trying to figure out such works of God.

> . . . and where the text is silent, especially about a matter as important as the evidence of the Holy Spirit, perhaps it is best for the interpreter to remain silent too.[61]

While Luke did not explain why these three unusual actions concerning the Holy Spirit occurred, there may be a possible clue in the story of Paul and the Ephesians. Immediately after the Ephesian disciples of John were baptized, "Paul laid his hands upon them, the Holy Spirit came on them, and they began speaking with tongues and prophesying." (19:6). This close association of the Holy Spirit coming upon them in connection with their speaking in tongues and prophesying *may* suggest that this coming of the Holy Spirit was not related to the *indwelling* of the Spirit, but rather to a *unique working* of the Holy Spirit. In all three of these cases—the Samaritans, the Cornelius household, and the Ephesian disciples of John—everyone received the indwelling of the Holy Spirit when they were baptized; the uniqueness of these events *may* be found in the special imparting of certain gifts by the Holy Spirit.

When addressing this issue and in response to those who hold that in those special situations the people did not receive the Holy Spirit at baptism, Beasley-Murray wrote,

> The major difficulty of this view is to know how to conceive of a church consisting of believers baptized in the name of the Lord Jesus yet not possessing the Spirit sent by the Risen Lord. It seems to be a theologically impossible abstraction. To Paul the idea would have been a contradiction in terms, for the Spirit is the Mediator of the life of Christ to the Christian, as he is the soul of the Body which is the Church . . . Can it be, therefore, that he [Luke] regarded these Christians as *not without the Spirit, but without the spiritual gifts that characterized*

---

wrote in 1773. It was published in the 1779 *Olney Hymns* along with numerous other hymns by John Newton and William Cowper.

60. Isa 55:8–9.
61. Bruner, *A Theology*, 179.

> *the common life of the Christian communities? . . .* Paul clearly distinguished between the charismata and the possession of the Spirit as such; all Christians possess the Spirit but not all possess the same gifts . . . It is freely admitted that this interpretation can only tentatively be put forward, but it does seem to make sense of an otherwise incomprehensible situation without resorting to drastic emendation of Luke's narrative. (italics in original)[62]

We know the diversity of the many gifts that were given by the Spirit and the unusual ways they are received. As Paul explained to the Corinthian church:

> But to each one is given the manifestation of the Spirit for the common good. For to one is given the word of wisdom through the Spirit, and to another the word of knowledge according to the same Spirit; to another faith by the same Spirit, and to another gifts of healing by the one Spirit, and to another the effecting of miracles, and to another prophecy, and to another the distinguishing of spirits, to another various kinds of tongues, and to another the interpretation of tongues. But one and the same Spirit works all these things, distributing to each one individually *just as He wills.*[63]

Some have assumed that since there were supernatural gifts bestowed upon the Christians in the first century church, the same must be true for our day. While it is obvious that God is quite able to bestow such *charismata* (plural of *charisma,* translated "gifts" throughout 1 Corinthians 12) at any time or place he wishes, there are certain observations that the supernatural *charismata* exhibit all through Scripture:

1. Regardless of whether supernatural events were performed by God or by people he chose to empower to do such, they were always in the open, widely known, and verified by large numbers of people, even the enemies of God.[64]

2. The *charismata* were not performed for the recipient's personal well-being, but for the glory of God. While many people, especially

---

62. Beasley-Murray, *Baptism,* 118–20.

63. 1 Cor 12:7–11.

64. When Nicodemus came to Jesus one night (John 3:1–21) he said, "Rabbi, *we know* that you have come from God as a teacher; for no one can do these signs that you do unless God is with him" (verse 2). John introduced him to his readers as a man of the Pharisees, named Nicodemus, a ruler of the Jews, who admitted "we know," presumably the "we" was in reference the Sanhedrin Pharisees.

those healed by Jesus, received benefit from these *charismata*, John said, at the end of his Gospel, that these things were done by Jesus, "so that you may believe that Jesus is the Christ, the Son of God; and that believing you may have life in his name."[65]

3. It is strikingly profound there is no record that those who were chosen to perform these *charismata* did anything special in seeking the ability to do them; they somehow knew when and what to do without any special seeking other than to simply to be available to God for whatever he needed them to do. There is no mention that those who performed the *charismata* worked themselves into any emotional fervor in order to perform them.

4. In the first century church, it was the Holy Spirit who assigned the ability to perform various *charismata* (1 Corinthians 12) as he willed; it was bestowed according to the need of the church rather than the desire of the individual or by the discretion of church leaders.

These, and other such reasons, lead us to believe that if the Holy Spirit decided to endow any of the faithful of our day with the ability to perform *charismata*, it would be done under these same evidences.

The Samaritan story in Acts 8 also gives rise to numerous questions concerning the falling of the Holy Spirit upon them and how that relates to their being baptized in the name of Jesus.

> For he [Holy Spirit] had not yet [*oudepo*] fallen upon any of them; they had simply [*monon*,[66]] been baptized in the name of the Lord Jesus. Then they began laying their hands on them, and they were receiving (*elambanon*) the Holy Spirit. [67]

Did this receiving of the Holy Spirit, which had "not yet fallen (*epipeptokos*[68]) upon any of them," refer to the indwelling of the Spirit, or was it some post-baptismal manifestation of the operations of the Spirit? As noted above, all Christians receive the indwelling of the Holy Spirit at baptism. In this case, there was a significant lapse of time between their baptism and the arrival of the apostles. Since it was not until the apostles Peter and John laid hands on them that the Spirit "fell upon" them, what

---

65. John 20:31.

66. Translated as "only" in ESV, RSV and KJV, and as "simply" in NASU and NIV.

67. Acts 8:16–17.

68. *Epipeptokos* is the combination of the preposition *epi* ("upon") and the verb *pipto* (to "fall").

was their relationship to the Spirit during that interval of time? During that time lapse, before the coming of Peter and John, had the Spirit not been received by them as promised in Acts 2:38? If they had not received the indwelling of the Spirit at the time of their baptism, and without the indwelling of the Spirit they could not be children of God, what was their spiritual condition between the time of their baptism and the arrival of the apostles? Apparently, this laying on of the hands was something special that Philip did not have the authority to do. What the Samaritans received from Peter and John appears to be something that only the apostles could bestow. If this occasion of receiving (falling upon) means that the Spirit had not yet come to indwell them at baptism, we must assume that during that interval they were not children of God.

The word *oudepo*, "not yet," is an adverb indicating that what was expected had not yet happened but that it was expected to come about. It would seem that, like all the other conversions, the Spirit was given at baptism and some further action of the Spirit had "not yet" happened as it had happened to other Christians in other places.[69] The silence of Scripture concerning the details of this story behooves us to take great care lest more is supposed than the text has intended.

The phrase "they had only [*monon*] been baptized in the name of the Lord Jesus" is not to be construed as an indication that in baptism a person is merely or simply baptized in the name of Jesus—as if baptism "in the name of Jesus" is somehow inferior to or lower than the experience of receiving the Holy Spirit. The translation of *monon* as "only" indicates that there is another object that normally applies to the situation without giving reference to its higher or lower priority. It does not suggest that the receiving of the Holy Spirit is something higher than being baptized into the name of Jesus. To suggest that there is something greater and more significant than baptism into Jesus for the forgiveness of sins makes the Cross something less than the central doctrine in the Gospel message.

> Now I make known to you, brethren, the gospel which I preached to you, which also you received, in which also you stand, by which also you are saved, if you hold fast the word which I preached to you, unless you believed in vain. For I delivered to you as of *first importance* what I also received, that Christ died for our sins according to the Scriptures, and that he

---

69. Ferguson, *Baptism*, 171.

was buried, and that he was raised on the third day according to the Scriptures,[70]

Conclusion

It is obvious, even to a casual reader of Luke's record of the early church, that baptism played a crucial role in the preaching of the early church. The apostles and the early church considered baptism an ordinance given by God to serve as a person's initiatory event into the new life with Christ. The intimate association of the receiving the indwelling of the Holy Spirit with baptism permeates the Acts conversion stories. Baptism into the divine name perfected a unity between the Father, the Son, the Holy Spirit, and the disciple. The divine name gives baptism its authority and saving power. In the Lukan stories in Acts, baptism is inseparable from repentance, faith, and forgiveness. Baptism was that point where they were converted from sinner to saint, where they surrendered their will to the lordship of Christ.

The role of baptism as the place God has designed for a person to be initiated into the cleansing of sanctification is absolutely vital to being in Christ. Without that purification, there is no hope for his glory in our lives, but rather a terrifying expectation of total alienation from God and its dreaded eternal consequences. "You shall be holy, for I am holy!"

---

70. 1 Cor 15:1–4.

8

Baptism in the Letters to the Churches

Pauline Theology

WHEN WE LOOK AT the Christian doctrines in the letters of Paul, there are two things we need to keep in mind. First, we need to be aware that Paul did not write mere theological treatises. As a missionary and preacher, he wrote inspired letters to his churches that reflected the passion and fondness he had toward them, and the desire to aid them in their Christian walk. Whether to correct or to encourage, his letters reflected his intimate relationship with them. Second, it is difficult to separate one doctrine from another in his correspondence. Each doctrine he addressed was intertwined with other aspects of the Gospel. We must look at his writings as we would a painting, observing the blending of the various colors (doctrines) to see the beauty of the whole painting of the Gospel. As we delve into Paul's teaching about baptism, we need to keep these two observations in mind.

Paul's baptism following his vision on the road to Damascus was a significant turning point in the spread of the Gospel. With his conversion, a wildfire roared forth over land and sea, fanned by the power of the Holy Spirit. In his extensive travels, his preaching and teaching were so astounding that large numbers of both Jews and Gentiles were converted. They marveled at his logic and insight. While conversion to Christianity for many people may be a quiet and sincere transformation of life, Paul's conversion from Judaism to Christianity was quite dramatic, exploding on the world with the fullness of his great intellect and communication skills. New congregations sprang up in most of the major cities in the Roman Empire. Cities were shaken and converted from their pagan temples and Jewish synagogues. He proclaimed Christ to all who would hear—the great and the small; the rich and the poor; the healthy and the weak. He spoke with boldness before kings and reached out with tender hands to the poor and infirm. Because of his impact on these cities, there were those among both the Gentiles and the Jews who rebelled, causing him and his coworkers much harm—but that did not slow them down.

Paul had previously been a Pharisee, a man of influence and ambition, a leader among the Jews. As such, he was determined to eradicate the blasphemous followers of Jesus. In his devotion to the Law, he saw Jesus as a treasonable threat to the traditional Hebrew way of life. His zeal in persecuting Christians was rampant, even bringing about death to those of the fanatic sect called "The Way."[1] Such was his conviction and devotion to God, misguided though it was.

His conversion in Damascus changed everything about him. It was a moment that he would always remember with fondness as his special, life-altering event. His letters sometimes reflected how special that baptismal event with Ananias was in his life. After his conversion, Paul did not consult with any of the other apostles or church leaders but left Damascus and went away into the wilderness of Arabia, where Jesus revealed his Gospel to him. Paul was emphatic that his new Gospel came from God and that, because of its divine origin, it was capable of standing in the face of all criticisms. He was meticulous as he delved into the many facets of the Gospel. No detail was small enough to escape examination by his critical mind.

> For am I now seeking the favor of men, or of God? Or am I striving to please men? If I were still trying to please men, I would not be a bond-servant of Christ. For I would have you know, brethren, that the gospel which was preached by me is not according to man. For I neither received it from man, nor was I taught it, but I received it through a revelation of Jesus Christ.[2]

Through his letters to the churches, we have a better grasp of the great themes of salvation, such as grace, hope, atonement, faith, conversion, sanctification, justification, and baptism. At the heart of Paul's message was the Cross. Any doctrine that supplanted or stood in precedence over the death of Jesus he called anathema. His stern words to the Galatian and Corinthian churches demonstrated the fervor of his devotion to the preservation of the Cross as the heart of the Gospel.

---

1. Acts 9:1–2; 19:9, 23; 24:14, 22.
2. Gal 1:11–12.

> I am amazed that you are so quickly deserting him who called you by the grace of Christ, for a different gospel; which is really not another; only there are some who are disturbing you and want to distort the gospel of Christ. But even if we, or an angel from heaven, should preach to you a gospel contrary to what we have preached to you, *he is to be accursed*! As we have said before, so I say again now, if any man is preaching to you a gospel contrary to what you received, *he is to be accursed*! [3]
>
> Now I make known to you, brethren, the gospel which I preached to you, which also you received, in which also you stand, by which also you are saved, if you hold fast the word which I preached to you, unless you believed in vain. For I delivered to you as of *first importance* what I also received, that Christ died for our sins according to the Scriptures, and that he was buried, and that he was raised on the third day according to the Scriptures, and that he appeared to Cephas, then to the twelve. After that he appeared to more than five hundred brethren at one time, most of whom remain until now, but some have fallen asleep; then he appeared to James, then to all the apostles; and last of all, as to one untimely born, he appeared to me also.[4]

Blood, Cross, Atonement

Without the cleansing power of the blood of Christ, the whole foundation of the New Testament crumbles. In the same way, when baptism is torn from this mooring in the blood of the Cross, it becomes a meaningless ritual. This sanctification of sinners by the power of his blood is initiated by God in the waters of baptism.

There are those to whom the blood of Christ as a cleansing agent is offensive. It is contrary to their aesthetic tastes of culture and civilization. Blood is to be appreciated as a life-sustaining fluid inside the body, but it becomes a source of ugliness and is unsanitary outside the body, something to be thoroughly cleaned up using disinfectants and protective gear. The ignominy of Christ's Cross and Blood conjures up images of disgrace, shame, humiliation, and dishonor. They find it cheap and crude. For this reason, the New Testament's focus on death and blood is repulsive to them. This attitude is not limited to such sophistic people. It is said by many "Christians" that Christianity is a religion of victory and honor,

3. Gal 1:6–9.
4. 1 Cor 15:1–8.

while the Cross belongs to a religion couched in defeat and humiliation. J. Vernon McGee expressed the haughtiness of those who have this kind of mindset:

> The objection to the idea that the blood of Christ was presented in heaven is that it offends the sensibilities of folk. It is contrary to the highest aesthetic tastes of culture and civilization. To this we would affirm that the whole Bible doctrine of blood atonement is offensive to the natural man ... The liberal theologian discounts the blood with this sneering remark, "I do not care for a religion of the shambles; there shall be no slaughterhouse religion for me." [5]

In their cavalier, optimistic humanism, they fail to recognize that what is truly crude, offensive, and humiliating is the ugliness of sin.

The Hebrews and Christians were not the only ones to recognize the importance of blood to both physical and spiritual life. Even primitive religions recognized the connection between sacrifice, blood, deliverance, and cleansing. Even though they did not know much about the circulation of blood through the body as a life-giving stream, they knew the significance of blood to life. When the body lost its blood or the blood lost its cleanness, death was the result. Consequently, blood came to play a significant role in their rituals and ceremonies, even in their spiritual healings. Could it be that somehow, even in their primitive existence, God was at work making known basic spiritual truths to them? For the faithful, the concept of the power and majesty of the death of Christ and the shedding of his blood is the redeeming power undergirding our salvation. In heaven, the Cross with its bloodshed is received with divine honor and praise. What is precious to God ought not to be treated with disdain among men.

> When he had taken the book, the four living creatures and the twenty-four elders fell down before the Lamb, each one holding a harp and golden bowls full of incense, which are the prayers of the saints. And they sang a new song, saying, "Worthy are you to take the book and to break its seals; for you were slain, and purchased for God *with your blood* men from every tribe and tongue and people and nation."[6]

---

5. McGee, *The Tabernacle*, 27.
6. Rev 5:8–9.

On the other hand, the death of Christ on the Cross and the shedding of his blood is an ignoble historical fact. The reality of the physical body and blood of Jesus on the Cross was an audacious judgment upon God by man; the innocent God was proclaimed guilty by guilty man. With trials that were unjust and illegal, even according to their own laws, their leaders condemned deity—even though they knew who He was![7] What travesty! But in spite of its crude and unjust reality, when the Bible speaks of the redemption of the saints by the blood of the Lamb, there is a transcendence that restores glory and dignity to his flesh and blood in the crucifixion story.

> After these things I looked, and behold, a great multitude which no one could count, from every nation and all tribes and peoples and tongues, standing before the throne and before the Lamb, clothed in white robes, and palm branches were in their hands . . . And he said to me, "These are the ones who come out of the great tribulation, and *they have washed their robes and made them white in the blood of the Lamb.*"[8]

How can something so disgusting and physical as a Roman crucifixion result in such a glorious spiritual redemption? Can a physical event such as the Cross have spiritual consequences? The death of Christ on the Cross was a physical reality in a specific place and time, yet it was an event with eternal and spiritual ramifications. Even still, in our present time, his sanctifying blood is effectual in the cleansing of sin. How can the blood of Christ, which he shed as a past event, continue to be a current reality? Is there a continual fountain of Christ's blood that transcends the historical Cross? The physical body of Jesus perished on the Cross, and therefore, being physical, it cannot exist in the spiritual heaven. Yet, the death and blood of Jesus is a present, continual cleansing of sin.

> If we say that we have fellowship with him and yet walk in the darkness, we lie and do not practice the truth; but if we walk in the Light as he himself is in the Light, we have fellowship with one another, and the blood of Jesus his Son cleanses (present, active, indicative verb: "is continually cleansing") us from all sin.[9]

---

7. John 3:2. Nicodemus, speaking as one of the rulers of the Jews said, "Rabbi, *we know* that you have come from God as a teacher; for no one can do these signs that you do unless God is with him."

8. Rev 7:9, 14.

9. 1 John 1:6–7.

The real cleansing of the blood of Jesus transcends that of his earthly execution. This in no way invalidates that long-ago historical event, nor does it make it irrelevant. If Jesus did not hang on the Roman Cross in real physical time, it would cease to be a real, present, and spiritual event in heaven as well.

Paul went to quite some lengths in 1 Corinthians 15 to make it clear that when the physical body of a saint dies, the old mortal body ceases to exist; it is transformed into a spiritual and immortal body that is fit for a heavenly existence. Since the human body can be transformed into a spiritual body, why would it not be so with Jesus? Could the Cross be as real, or really even more real, in heaven than it was in Jerusalem in the first century? It would be foolish to assume that physical blood could wash heavenly robes and make them white as snow, especially blood from a death that occurred many centuries ago. Could it be that the real and powerful blood of Christ on the Cross became transformed into an even more powerful spiritual cleansing blood in a heavenly sense?

> What can wash away my sins? Nothing but the blood of Jesus.
> What can make me whole again? Nothing but the blood of Jesus.
> For my pardon this I see—Nothing but the blood of Jesus.
> For my pardon this my plea—Nothing but the blood of Jesus.
> Nothing can for sin atone—Nothing but the blood of Jesus.
> Naught of good that I have done—Nothing but the blood of Jesus.
> O precious is the flow that makes me white as snow;
> No other fount I know, Nothing but the blood of Jesus.[10]

> ... through his own blood, he entered the holy place once for all, having obtained eternal redemption ... how much more will the blood of Christ, who through the eternal Spirit offered himself without blemish to God, cleanse your conscience from dead works to serve the living God?[11]

The blood of Jesus shed on the Cross gives the two great themes of Paul's theology—sanctification and justification—their substance. While sanctification and justification each have their own identity, they are inseparably linked to each other by the blood of Jesus. Doctrines such

---

10. Hawn, "History of Hymns." Words and music were written by Robert Lowry (1826–1899) in 1876 based on the quotation "Without the shedding of blood there is no remission of sin" (Heb. 9:22). Many of his over 500 hymns are still popular today. In the 1950s and 1960s, this song was among the five most sung hymns in the churches.

11. Heb 9:12, 14.

as conversion, faith, and baptism are intimately bound up in these two doctrines. They all work together as vital ingredients in the salvation event as we shall see as we look at the various baptismal passages in Paul's writings.

When we look at the doctrine of baptism in the writings of Paul, we recognize its importance to salvation and its depth of meaning. As we examine the following passages about baptism, three things stand out: 1). the idea of being in Christ apart from the waters of baptism was a concept foreign to Paul and the Christians to whom he wrote; 2). Paul so wove the purpose of baptism into the salvation event that its removal as the place of conversion would destroy the Gospel's integrity; and 3). baptism was a significant and commonly practiced event in their lives that united them all in Christ.

Romans 6:1-11

> What shall we say then? Are we to continue in sin so that grace may increase? May it never be! How shall we who died to sin still live in it? Or do you not know that all of us who have been baptized into Christ Jesus have been baptized into his death? Therefore we have been buried with him through baptism into death, so that as Christ was raised from the dead through the glory of the Father, so we too might walk in newness of life. For if we have become united with him in the likeness of his death, certainly we shall also be in the likeness of his resurrection, knowing this, that our old self [*anthropos*: man, person] was crucified with him, in order that our body of sin might be done away with, so that we would no longer be slaves to sin; for he who has died is freed from sin. Now if we have died with Christ, we believe that we shall also live with him, knowing that Christ, having been raised from the dead, is never to die again; death no longer is master over him. For the death that he died, he died to sin once for all; but the life that he lives, he lives to God. Even so consider yourselves to be dead to sin, but alive to God in Christ Jesus.

There is much to learn about baptism in these verses. In chapter 5, Paul reminded the Roman Christians of the grandeur of the grace by which they were justified on the basis of faith.[12] In that chapter's last few verses, he contrasted the volume of man's transgressions against God's

---

12. Rom 5:1.

grace. Grace, he wrote, is more abundant and powerful than the whole of sin. Therefore, because of sin, how great is the demonstration of the magnitude of the grace of God![13] Might it be that more sin is a good thing since the practice of sinning results in more grace? Continuing that same line of thought into chapter 6, he exclaimed,

> What shall we say then? Are we to continue in sin so that grace may increase? May it never be! How shall we who died to sin still live in it?[14]

In the next several verses, he proceeded to address these questions by reminding his readers that their "sin-full" way of life died when they were baptized into Christ and into his death (verses 3–4). Consequently, it is impossible to cling to the old self with its sinful ways and walk in the new life in Christ.

> ... our old self was crucified *with* him, in order that our body of sin might be done away with, so that we would no longer be slaves to sin.[15]

The tenor of Paul's answer implies that his Roman audience was familiar with the practice of conversion-baptism and that they had all, like himself, been so baptized. As he wrote these words, perhaps Paul was reflecting on his baptism as well as the baptisms of all the people he had brought to his Lord. Paul used the first-person plural pronouns "we," "us," and "our" fourteen times in verses 1–7, making this passage more than a doctrinal treatise; it was a reminder of the personal relationship between them, himself, and God. In his book about the life and teachings of the apostle Paul, F. F. Bruce recognized this personal nature of Paul's words.

> That Paul himself at his conversion was baptized and so had his sins washed away is the testimony of Acts 22:16 (cf. 9:18). When in his letters he reminds his Christian readers of the meaning of their baptism he associates his own baptism with theirs: "all of us who were baptized into Christ Jesus were baptized into his death" (Rom 6:3); "in one Spirit we were all baptized into one body" (1 Cor 12:13). At the same time, he gives baptism—theirs and his—a new depth of meaning. Baptism, in Paul's teaching, initiates believers into their state of being "in Christ", so that his historical death and resurrection become part of their spiritual

---

13. Rom 5:21–22.
14. Rom 5:1–2.
15. Rom 6:6.

> experience; the baptism in the Spirit which the risen Lord then effects incorporates them into one body with him—or, as Paul puts it to the Galatians, "as many of you as were baptized into Christ have put on Christ . . . you are all one in Christ Jesus" (Gal 3:27f) . . . It is unlikely that they dissociated the washing from their baptism in water, but it was the divine action in their lives that gave their baptism effective meaning and caused Paul to use what has been called the language of sacramental realism.[16]

By calling them back to their baptism, he prompted them to recall that their baptism was a special moment to remember and cherish. Their baptism was of momentous significance, for there, in that moment, the blood of Christ became a cleansing flood; it was a sanctification in which their lives were transformed to the core of their nature. Holiness became a reality when they submitted to the death of their old unclean self and were resurrected into the new sanctified life. To rob baptism of such importance and power would leave the baptismal event an empty shell. It would be a travesty to divest that moment of its glory by allocating some vague meaning to baptism for which there is no biblical evidence.

In Rom 6:3–4, the little preposition *eis* again appears in association with baptism. In the three phrases, "baptized into (*eis*) Christ," "baptized into (*eis*) his death," and "baptism into (*eis*) death," *eis* shows the same bonding of baptism to salvation as Jesus did in Matt 28:19—"baptizing them in (*eis*) the name of the Father and the Son and the Holy Spirit." There are some who are willing to accept that *eis* could have a purposive meaning rather than a causative meaning in Romans 6, but they qualify that by claiming that baptism in Romans 6 is a metaphorical or symbolic baptism—a "spiritual baptism only." As a waterless immersion into Christ it must later be followed by a baptism in water. As one preacher put it to me (Jim) many years ago, "Baptism in Romans 6 does not refer to a physical event in water at all but is a symbolic burial into Christ." In this view, "spiritual" baptism is set in contrast to "physical" baptism. Water baptism is looked upon as crude and worldly; therefore, a high spiritual event such as the salvation of a person's soul cannot be associated with such a lowly physical act as water baptism.

> Many baptistic interpreters argue that the language of baptism "into Christ" (*eis Christon*) is too strong to be referred

---

16. F. F. Bruce, *Paul*, 281.

to water-baptism, their assumption being that such language would teach baptismal regeneration, which is believed to be impossible.[17]

This strong aversion to associating any physical activity with a spiritual reality strips baptism of its power. If baptism in Romans 6 is merely a symbolic commitment of the inner man that must then be followed by water baptism for some other purpose, then a predicament arises as to which of these two baptisms is the "one baptism" affirmed by Paul.

> There is one body and one Spirit, just as also you were called in one hope of your calling; one Lord, one faith, *one baptism*, one God and Father of all who is over all and through all and in all.[18]

When we look throughout biblical history, we can find numerous examples where spiritual realities are associated with physical practices. For example, the physical tabernacle (and later the temple) was known as the designated place where God's name resided. In Solomon's dedication of the new temple, he prayed,

> But will God indeed dwell on the earth? Behold, heaven and the highest heaven cannot contain you, how much less this house which I have built! Yet have regard to the prayer of your servant and to his supplication, O Lord my God, to listen to the cry and to the prayer which your servant prays before you today; that your eyes may be open toward this house night and day, toward the place of which you have said, "*My name shall be there*," to listen to the prayer which your servant shall pray toward this place."[19]

In like manner, the physical act of circumcision was designated by God as the spiritual identity of the people's covenant with God.

> This is my covenant, which you shall keep, between me and you and your descendants after you: every male among you shall be circumcised. And you shall be circumcised in the flesh of your foreskin, and it shall be the sign of the covenant between me and you.[20]

---

17. Fowler, *More Than a Symbol*, 170–74.
18. Eph 4:4–6.
19. 1 Kgs 8:27–29.
20. Gen 17:10–11.

The New Testament is also witness to spiritual realities that occur in physical activities. When Jesus initiated the Lord's Supper with its physical bread and drink, he told his disciples that this physical meal was to serve as a sacred memorial of his death.

> And when he had taken a cup and given thanks, he said, "Take this and share it among yourselves; for I say to you, I will not drink of the fruit of the vine from now on until the kingdom of God comes." And when he had taken some bread and given thanks, he broke it and gave it to them, saying, "This is my body which is given for you; do this in remembrance of me."[21]

If circumcision, the tabernacle/temple, the Lord's Supper, and even the Cross itself, all being physical events, have spiritual realities attached to them, why would it seem so objectionable to recognize that the same would apply to the physical practice of water baptism? It is not that any of these physical things have some magical or mystical significance in themselves. As Solomon said, "Behold, heaven and the highest heaven cannot contain you, how much less this house which I have built!"[22] Just as the waters of the Jordan River did not take away Naaman's leprosy,[23] so the waters of baptism do not remove sin. It was God who removed Naaman's leprosy when he submitted to the waters of the Jordan River. It is God who forgives sins in the waters of baptism. *Baptism is a highly symbolic event, but it is much more than a symbol.*

While the water of baptism itself has no cleansing power to remove sin, it does have significant symbolic associations. As we saw in Chapter 3, to place confidence in the water itself as a redeeming agent would be to revert to a paganization of the practice of baptism. The physical lowering of the baptizand into the water and raising them up symbolizes their death, burial, and resurrection with Christ. As water washes filth from the flesh, so the blood of Christ cleanses the soul of guilt. The significance of the water in a baptismal event is that it is the God-ordained meeting place where Deity cleanses the soul (sanctification), unites man with himself (justification), and bestows upon the baptizand "every spiritual blessing."[24]

---

21. Luke 22:17–19.
22. 1 Kgs 8:27.
23. See 2 Kgs 5:1–14.
24. Eph 1:3.

We must not lose sight of the fact that baptism is a real spiritual experience; real things happen in baptism. It is a real crucifixion of one's old, sinful, unclean self, a real resurrection into a new, sanctified (cleansed) life. It is a real incorporation of the sinner into the death, burial, and resurrection of Jesus. Baptism is, indeed, a highly symbolic event. However, baptism is more than merely a symbolic act; it is a real event involving the whole person (mind, heart, body, and soul) who is buried into Christ and raised into a transformed life. That baptismal moment, like the wedding,[25] should be looked back upon throughout the years as a reminder of their life-altering event.

In Rom 6:3–7, there are four passive verbs that refer to what happens to a person in baptism. In verse 3, *ebaptistheimen* (aorist, passive, indicative: "we have been baptized") occurs twice; in verse 4, the third verb is *sunetapheimen* (2nd aorist, passive, indicative: "we have been buried"); and in verse 6, the fourth verb is *sunestaurothei* (aorist, passive, indicative: "It [the old self] was crucified with him"). There is no virtue ascribed to the action of the baptizand other than that they submit to baptism as a passive participant. It is not a meritorious work accomplished by the person baptized. The passive "we have been baptized" is not a work that a person must do to secure eternal life. The baptizand is the passive recipient upon whom God bestows his gracious work. Even the physical action of lowering the baptizand into the water is passive; it is an action done by another person. Through and through, baptism is a passive event. Baptism is submission to the gracious work of God in which the participant has no active part, only passive. On the other hand, the Lord's Supper, prayer, singing of hymns, deeds of love, worship, etc., are all post-conversion events that require Christians to have an active part.

An analogy of the passive nature of baptism can be seen when a person goes to see their doctor because of a stomachache. Upon examination, the patient is informed by the doctor that they have a tumor and that the only way to resolve the medical malady is through abdominal surgery to remove it. The patient may ask if such surgery is really necessary, but the doctor explains that if there is no surgery, the tumor will continue to grow with increased pain, and will eventually result in death. Even though the patient may agree to have the surgery, the tumor is still

---

25. The wedding ceremony itself does not make a marriage. It is the *place* where the bride and groom come together to end a life of singleness and bond themselves together in a covenant union. Marriage is something that happens between the two of them in the ceremony.

there; it is still growing with increased pain and impending certainty of death. Mere mental assent to the procedure does not remove the tumor. Even when the patient arrives at the hospital and is prepped for surgery, the tumor is still violating the patient's body. It is not until the anesthesiologist "puts the patient under" (making the patient a passive subject) and the doctor removes the tumor that healing can be said to take place. The patient is completely passive throughout this cleansing ordeal. It is true the patient must agree to and submit to the procedure, but who would say that such a procedure is the work of the patient? Who would say that the patient removed the tumor? Who can argue that mental assent and submission to such a procedure is a "work"?

The other two passive verbs—"was crucified" (verse 6) and "been buried" (verse 4)—likewise, put the action of the baptismal event in the hand of God. In the death, burial, and resurrection experienced by the baptizand, it is God who strips away the old body of sin; it is God who raises up a new self that is sanctified by the blood of the Lamb. In verses 4 and 5, although Paul did not use passive voice verbs for the resurrection from baptism, the passive import is obvious—"For if we have become united with him in the likeness of his death, certainly we shall also be in the likeness of his resurrection" (v. 5). It is God who, in baptism, abrogates the old self enslaved to sin and inaugurates a new existence that is free from the condemnation of sin. We have no authority and are powerless to accomplish such ourselves. This is the impact of the passive verbs of this passage.

In verse 3 the phrase "baptized into Christ Jesus" is the fulfillment of the meaning of Immanuel—God with us. To be baptized "into Christ" is to be united in intimate oneness with him.

> Therefore the Lord himself will give you a sign: Behold, a virgin will be with child and bear a son, and she will call his name Immanuel.[26]
>
> Now all this took place to fulfill what was spoken by the Lord through the prophet: "BEHOLD, THE VIRGIN SHALL BE WITH CHILD AND SHALL BEAR A SON, AND THEY SHALL CALL HIS NAME IMMANUEL," which translated means, "GOD WITH US."[27]

---

26. Isa 7:14.
27. Matt 1:22-23.

In the phrase "God with us" (*meth heimon ho Theos*), the word *heimon* is the genitive pronoun "us" and the preposition *meth* (a contraction of *meta*), when it occurs with a genitive, indicates "among," "in the midst."[28] *Meta* carries the strong connotation of *identity with*; it is more intimate than merely *association with*. It is not Jesus alongside us; it is Jesus in us. This is the impact of Paul's reminder to the Romans that baptism means to be absorbed into Christ including his death, burial, and resurrection.

> that is, the mystery which has been hidden from the past ages and generations, but has now been manifested to his saints, to whom God willed to make known what is the riches of the glory of this mystery among the Gentiles, *which is Christ in you*, the hope of glory.[29]

How do we explain this phenomenon? How do we grasp the reality of God with us? Or, more accurately, God in us? God in me? Though the mystery is great, this oneness with God is our confidence. The fact that we do not understand all about it does not negate the fact that we are in fact bonded with God. Jesus told his disciples to baptize "them into (*eis*) the name of the Father and the Son and the Holy Spirit." In our baptism, we become one with (united with) the Father, the Son, and the Holy Spirit!

His was a physical death by crucifixion. It was extremely dramatic, cruel, and bloody. Yet, as sensational as his death was, many others have similarly suffered death by crucifixion. But, his was not merely one among many deaths. The death of Jesus was more than a physical agony; it was a spiritual death: "MY GOD, MY GOD, WHY HAVE YOU FORSAKEN ME?"[30] Jesus went to the Cross with a load to bear that would bring eternal condemnation to any mere man. His was a death accompanied with more than intense physical suffering in torment and humiliation; it was a death in which he took upon himself the horror of the hideous burden of sin. The full weight of the putrid guilt of man was on his shoulders on the Cross. If we had to die a death *like* his, we would be crushed, ruined, even destroyed by it. We would not survive. But he did! This is why we recognize with Paul that it is not our death that is center stage in baptism, as if, in baptism, we accomplish something. Rather, everything in baptism focuses on being "crucified *with* him," being "buried *with* him,"

---

28. Grundmann, "On the Use of," 766–97.
29. Col 1:26–27.
30. Matt 27:46; Mark 15:34.

and consequently, being "raised *with* him." In our baptismal "death," we experience his death.

> Baptism is of decisive significance here. Rom 6:1 ff. and 5:12–21 are related not merely in the warding off of misunderstanding, 5:20–21; 6:1. Paul has contrasted Christ as the second Adam with the first Adam … The union of the individual with the corporate person of Adam is effected by the nexus of begetting and birth, while the union with Christ is brought about by baptism. Whereas the crucifixion of Jesus points beyond itself to the men for whom it takes place, baptism leads us back to this beginning and unites "us" with the "Christ for us." For Paul baptism is acknowledgment of the proclaimed dominion of Jesus Christ which he gained in the cross and resurrection. The personal link between Christ and those he represents is an act of substitution. The Christ who died for men has won them to himself by blotting out their sins and reconciling them to God. *He takes them up into his death.* In baptism they are appropriated to him, and this in such a way that they are united to his death which he died for sin (Rom 6:10: *tei hamartia apethanen*, dat. incommodi) and which is their reconciliation with God (Rom 5:10–11; 6:3).[31] (emphasis added)

Only by participation in his death can the body of sin be done away so that we should no longer be slaves to sin (6:6). What mystery! What majesty! Woe to him who robs baptism of its glory!

In Romans 6 we see the heart of the meaning of repentance. Therein is the conversion that occurs in baptism. The baptizand is no longer alienated from God (justification). In the reconciling power of the Cross, the condemned is yanked from the depth of despair and transplanted into the safety and comfort of oneness with God. *Only by placing the Cross at the center of the meaning of baptism as the cleansing power of God's mercy can holiness become a reality and union be accomplished.*

Baptism is not a crucifixion in which the baptizand merely sets aside a former lifestyle. Being baptized is more than making a pledge or commitment to a new standard of moral behavior. While moral transformation cannot be dismissed or made of little importance, moral conversion is the consequence of one's baptism, not its purpose. The death of the old self and resurrection into a new life through baptism comes with a new Lord. This renewal inaugurates a transformation in behavior. This new

---

31. Grundmann, "On the Use of," 789–90.

morality was preached by John the Baptist as the natural result of the conversion experienced in baptism. So it is with the Christian's baptism.

> Even so consider yourselves to be dead to sin, but alive to God in Christ Jesus. Therefore do not let sin reign in your mortal body so that you obey its lusts, and do not go on presenting the members of your body to sin as instruments of unrighteousness; but present yourselves to God as those alive from the dead, and your members as instruments of righteousness to God. For sin shall not be master over you, for you are not under law but under grace.[32]

In Rom 6:1–11, the sublime beauty of baptism makes it impossible, and even dangerous, to divorce it from sanctification and justification. All of the authors of the New Testament saw this work of Jesus on the Cross as of central importance, but it was Paul, especially in Rom 6, who brought to focus the connection between baptism and the Cross. Prof. Beasley-Murray rightly recognized that it is in this baptismal union with Christ and his Cross that we find a power strong enough to cleanse lives as filthy with sin as our own.

> It was Paul's task to deepen the understanding of the association with Christ in baptism, the manner of cleansing and the nature of the new life. In achieving this end his doctrine was both old and new . . . Christ and his dying, Christ and his rising give the rite all its meaning.[33]

The tomb was empty! Death and sin could not hold him in its grasp! He conquered death. In our union with him in baptism, we too experience *his* triumph, and consequently, we no longer live according to our own will, but according to his. It is a new life with a new Lord. No longer living by the world's status quo, but setting our eyes above where Jesus reigns, we have a born-from-above transformation.

Galatians 3:25–27

> But now that faith has come, we are no longer under a tutor. For you are all sons of God through faith in Christ Jesus. For all of you who were baptized into Christ have clothed yourselves with Christ.

---

32. Rom 6:11–14.
33. Beasley-Murray, *Baptism*, 128, 133.

In Galatians, as in all his writings, the Cross is the heart of Paul's Gospel message. This Gospel was especially crucial in this correspondence because the Galatians took the Law, not as a tutor to bring them to Christ, but as an end in itself. They repudiated the power of the Gospel by believing Law-keeping to be the source of their salvation. As a tutor, the Mosaic Law is a good servant of God (1 Tim 1:5–11). The big lesson taught by the Law is just how insufficient even the best of human efforts are when it comes to living up to the Law's demands. A legalistic mindset requires that Law be kept in its entirety for one to acquire salvation. This distortion of the Gospel and the return to the legalism of Pharisaic doctrines and traditions was the reason for Paul's harsh words to the Galatian churches.

> I am amazed that you are so quickly deserting him who called you by the grace of Christ, for a different gospel; which is really not another; only there are some who are disturbing you and want to distort the gospel of Christ. But even if we, or an angel from heaven, should preach to you a gospel contrary to what we have preached to you, he is to be accursed! As we have said before, so I say again now, if any man is preaching to you a gospel contrary to what you received, he is to be accursed![34]

And again, later in the same letter he wrote,

> Are you so foolish? Having begun by the Spirit, are you now being perfected by the flesh?[35]

Is the Law, then, contrary to the grace of God? May it never be! God created the Law, and because he is the author of only that which is good (Gen 1:31), the Law is good (Psalm 19). If anyone had a reason to be defensive of Law-keeping, it was Paul. In his former life, he devoted himself to the Law along with the profusion of rabbinic traditions attached to it. But in his conversion, he came to realize that keeping Law could not be an end in itself; it was a way doomed to failure. After his conversion, he realized that to fail in the least of the commandments requires a sentence of condemnation. However, rather than cast the Law aside, Paul came to see that it has value as a call to wake men up to their need for redemption in Christ. The big lesson learned from the Law is the need for grace. In his sermon on the mount, Jesus informed his listeners, "Do not think that I came to abolish the Law or the Prophets; I did not come to abolish but to

---

34. Gal 1:6–9.
35. Gal 3:3.

fulfill."³⁶ On the Cross, Jesus took the burden of Law-keeping and placed it on himself. In his death, he took upon himself the guilt of our failure.

> For you are all sons of God through faith in Christ Jesus. For all of you who were baptized into Christ have clothed yourselves with Christ.³⁷

By taking verses 26 and 27 together, Paul clearly understood the intimate connection between faith and baptism. In verse 26 he said, "you are all sons of God through faith in Christ Jesus;" in verse 27 he said, "all of you who were baptized into Christ have clothed yourselves with Christ." The sons of God in verse 26 are the same persons as those who are clothed with Christ in verse 27. Being sons of God is dependent on the presence of faith, and being clothed with Christ is dependent on baptism. Since being sons of God and clothed with Christ are two complementary ways of expressing the same salvation, then that which happens when a person believes (has faith) in Christ is the same thing that happens when a person is baptized into Christ. Therefore, believing and being baptized occur simultaneously in one majestic saving event. Faith cannot be exalted at the expense of baptism, and baptism cannot be exalted at the expense of faith. *Faith and baptism are two facets of the same salvation.* As faith is the surrender of a person's will to God, so baptism is the place where that surrender takes place.

This simultaneous occurrence of faith and baptism is reinforced by the use of "for" at the beginning of verses 26 and 27. Grammatically, that which follows the conjunction *gar* ("for") affirms or explains the result of that which precedes it. To sever this parallel between faith and baptism would destroy the essence of both of them. Dr. Beasley-Murray captured the close relationship between faith and baptism in the following quote:

> But if faith is to be taken seriously, so is baptism . . . The experience of baptism is the experience of faith . . . faith therefore receives Christ in baptism . . . faith is experienced in baptism.³⁸

In like manner Stanley Fowler, in his extensive review of the purpose of baptism in his history of the British baptismal doctrine, wrote,

> This passage [Gal 3:26–27] serves to illustrate the general New Testament truth that the effects ascribed to faith and those

---

36. Matt 5:17.
37. Gal 3:24–27.
38. Beasley-Murray, *Baptism*, 151.

ascribed to baptism are the same. A statement about the reader's faith (vs. 26) is explained in terms of their baptism (vs. 27) . . . The fact that Paul can so naturally shift from faith in 3:26 to baptism in 3:27 should warn us not to drive a wedge between them.[39]

Attempts have been made to mark a distinction between the phrase "in Christ" (*en Christo*) in verse 26 and the phrase "into Christ" (*eis Christon*) in verse 27 in order to divorce faith from baptism and make them separate events. It would be a cumbersome task to explain how one can be "in Christ" without coming "into Christ." The preposition *en* expresses being in a location and the preposition *eis* expresses movement into a location. To go into a place is to no longer be outside of it but in it.

Once again, in verse 27 we find baptism associated with the preposition *eis* in the phrase, "baptized into (*eis*) Christ." We have already noted a large number of passages where *eis* has been consistently used by the writers of the New Testament to express the purpose of baptism as the place where God has chosen to confer upon the baptizand his gracious salvation.[40] As a preposition, *eis* is used to explain the purpose of movement from outside of a location to the inside. To get from outside the house, one passes through the door for the purpose (*eis*) of getting inside the house. To get from outside of Christ, one must pass through baptism to be in Christ. While there may be more than one door that gives access into a house, the New Testament presents baptism as the only access into Christ.

The word "clothed" (*enduo*) usually means the donning of clothing on a body. It is frequently used in this conventional way in the New Testament. For example, in Acts 12:21 Herod put on (*enduo*) his royal apparel. It is also used in the New Testament in a more metaphysical and spiritual sense. In 2 Cor 5:1–4, it is used to describe a person who is "clothed with (*enduo*) our dwelling from heaven;" and in like manner, in Rom 13:12, it is described as one who has "put on (*enduo*) the armor of light." Being clothed with Christ has a stronger meaning than merely putting on a covering, such as putting on a coat to go out into the cold. In the sense that Paul uses it, it is a covering that declares the nature of the heart and character of the wearer. To be clothed with a particular uniform usually has an identifying quality that distinguishes the wearer as belonging to a

39. Fowler, *More than a Symbol*, 185–86.

40. See "Excursus 2: on the Meaning of *Eis* in the New Testament" at the end of chapter 5.

particular community. Soldiers are seen as distinct from sailors by their uniforms; servers in a restaurant are recognized among the customers by their uniforms. Those who are clothed with Christ are recognized as unique in that they are identified as belonging to Christ.

> Now as they observed the confidence of Peter and John and understood that they were uneducated and untrained men, they were amazed, and began to recognize them as having been with Jesus.[41]

Christians are recognized as distinct from the world because, having been clothed with Christ, they are the image of Christ. When the world observes the purity (*hagiasmos*) of Christ in those who have been "washed," they see a contrast to the corruption and filth that are prevalent around them. The uncleanness of a dirty soul cannot cling to the faithful because they have been baptized into the blood of Christ.

> I have been crucified with Christ; and it is no longer I who live, but Christ lives in me; and the life which I now live in the flesh I live by faith in the Son of God, who loved me and gave himself up for me.[42]

> They [disciples of Jesus] are not of the world, even as I [Jesus] am not of the world. Sanctify [*hagiadzo*] them in the truth; your word is truth.[43]

When the policeman puts on his uniform, he adopts a unique way of life. When he goes off duty, he removes the uniform and steps into civilian life. To put on Christ means to be absorbed into the divine Son, but, unlike most uniforms, being clothed with Christ is not an on-and-off-duty matter; it is a 24/7 commitment for the duration of one's life. This is the commitment that is expected in baptism, a turning from "my will be done" to "your will be done." In baptism the baptizand becomes a different person with a different Lord. It is the beginning of a new existence in which the baptizand is renewed into the image of Christ, who "is all and in all."[44]

---

41. Acts 4:13.
42. Gal 2:20.
43. John 17:16–17.
44. Col 3:11.

Colossians 2:10-14

> and *in him* [*Christ*] *you have been made complete*, and he is the head over all rule and authority; and in him you were also circumcised with a circumcision made without hands, in the removal of the body of the flesh by the circumcision of Christ; having been buried *with* him *in* baptism, by whom also having been raised *with* him by the working in which you were also raised up *with* him through faith in the working of God, who raised him from the dead. When you were dead in your transgressions and the uncircumcision of your flesh, he made you alive together *with* him, having forgiven us all our transgressions, having canceled out the certificate of debt consisting of decrees against us, which was hostile to us; and he has taken it out of the way, having nailed it to the cross.

From Paul's comments in this letter about the church at Colossae, it is obvious that he had very high respect for their faithfulness. One must search this letter in vain for evidence of a corrective tone, or that there was a terrible "heresy" (as most commentators maintain) within the congregation. The popular attempts to identify false teachings within the Colossian congregation—such as an early form of Gnostic heresy, or perhaps a Judaistic legalism such as is found in Galatians, or maybe some pagan religious influence—cannot be found in this letter of Paul's as a problem *within* the church at Colossae.[45] While there are warnings in his letter to the Colossians to beware of such ungodly influences, there is no indication that these problems had yet encroached upon the congregation. There is no scolding language here such as there is in Galatians and 1 Corinthians. Commendations such as Paul lavished upon the Colossian congregation are very absent in the Galatian and Corinthian correspondence.

> We give thanks to God, the Father of our Lord Jesus Christ, praying always for you, since we heard of your *faith* in Christ

---

45. Commentators of significant repute have assumed that the church in Colossae was in the throes of a general abdication of the Gospel with comments such as: "The very existence of spiritual Christianity had been at stake." Robertson, P*aul and the Intellectuals*, 5. See also Guthrie, *New Testament Introduction*, 546; Lightfoot, *Saint Paul's Epistles to the Col. and to Philemon*, 73; Moule, *The Epistles of the Paul the Apostle to the Col. and to Philemon*, 29–34; Martin, *Col.: The Church's Lord and the Christian's Liberty*, 4; and Neill, *Paul to the Col.*, 11.

> Jesus and the *love* which you have for all the saints . . . and he [Epaphras] also informed us of your *love* in the Spirit.[46]
>
> For even though I am absent in body, nevertheless I am with you in spirit, rejoicing to see your *good discipline* and the *stability* of your faith in Christ.[47]

This does not have the sound of an apostle who is upset with his children. His words of warning in the letter strongly suggest that while there were problems facing the congregation from the community around them, none of them had penetrated into the church. We do not know just how menacing the heretic temptations faced by the Colossian Church were, nor do we know how close they were to infiltrating the congregation. Since Paul felt it necessary to strongly warn them, it must have been a significant matter.

"In him [Christ] you have been made complete"

It makes sense that, given the dangers facing the Colossian Church, Paul would strongly remind them that *the fullness of all spiritual blessings is found in Christ* and in him alone. Why should they seek fulfillment elsewhere when they have Jesus as their Lord?

> See to it that no one takes you captive through philosophy and empty deception, according to the tradition of men, according to the elementary principles of the world, rather than according to Christ. For in him all the fullness (*pleiroma*) of Deity dwells in bodily form, and in him [*en ho*: "in whom"] you have been made complete (*pleiroo*), and he is the head over all rule and authority.[48]

In him deity, completeness, rule, and authority are fulfilled. "All the fullness" (*pleiroma*, noun) and "made complete" (*pleiroo*, verb: to fill full, finish, complete) mean that the subject is brought to the point where there is no room for more. A glass is filled (*pleiroo*) with water when it cannot contain so little as one more small drop. For the Christian, the grace available in Christ is their *pleiroma*—"the fullness (*pleiroma*) of him who

---

46. Col 1:3–4, 8.
47. Col 2:5.
48. Col 2:8–10.

fills (*pleiroo*) all in all."⁴⁹ Having been made complete in Christ, they cannot become more complete by bringing into their lives or into the church such heresies as were prevalent in the community around them. When they were buried with him in baptism, they turned their backs on the world's *empty* promises and found perfect *fullness* in Christ.

In the midst of his fatherly concern, Paul exhorted them (as he did the Romans) to look back to their baptism. In their baptism, they were baptized into Christ, buried with him, and raised into the newness of life.⁵⁰ From that moment in the waters of baptism, they received the fullness (completeness) of *every* spiritual blessing in Christ.⁵¹ There was no need, therefore, to seek fulfillment in the heretical practices of their neighbors!

"In him you were also circumcised"

The physical act of circumcision refers to a removal of something by cutting. The Bible first mentions circumcision in Gen 17:10–14, where God instructed Abraham that all males eight days old or older and all male servants purchased from foreigners must be circumcised. God carried this same practice of physical circumcision over into the Law of Moses ("'On the eighth day the flesh of his foreskin shall be circumcised.'"⁵²). However, God meant for circumcision to be more than a physical act. There was a spiritual significance attached to the physical act of circumcision.

> you shall be circumcised in the flesh of your foreskin, and it shall be *the sign of the covenant* between me and you.⁵³

In the Old Testament, without the circumcision of the flesh, there was no covenant between God and the people. It was meant to be both a circumcision of the flesh and of the inner man. Spiritual circumcision was the distinguishing mark that identified God's people as distinct from those who were not his people.

> So circumcise your heart, and stiffen your neck no longer.⁵⁴

49. Eph 1:23.
50. Rom 6:4–5.
51. Eph 1:3.
52. Lev 12:3.
53. Gen 17:11.
54. Deut 10:16.

> Moreover the Lord your God will circumcise your heart and the heart of your descendants, to love the Lord your God with all your heart and with all your soul, so that you may live.[55]

> Circumcise yourselves to the Lord
> And remove the foreskins of your heart,
> Men of Judah and inhabitants of Jerusalem,
> Or else my wrath will go forth like fire
> And burn with none to quench it,
> Because of the evil of your deeds.[56]

> For he is not a Jew who is one outwardly, nor is circumcision that which is outward in the flesh. But he is a Jew who is one inwardly; and circumcision is that which is of the heart, by the Spirit, not by the letter; and his praise is not from men, but from God.[57]

In Colossians 2, Paul did not make baptism out to be the New Testament equivalent of Old Testament circumcision. The new circumcision became "a circumcision made without hands." Nowhere in the New Testament is physical circumcision made a requirement to be in Christ. Paul made it clear that "the true circumcision are those who worship in the Spirit of God and glory in Christ Jesus and put no confidence in the flesh."[58] It is held by some that because circumcision in the Old Testament was practiced on infants and Paul tied baptism into Christ with circumcision in Colossians 2, then the baptism of infants is still binding in our time. However, there is no evidence in the New Testament for the carryover of infant circumcision to the practice of baptism.

In his book, *Baptism in the New Testament*, G. R. Beasley-Murray devoted a whole chapter (eighty pages) to the matter of baptizing infants. He contended that since baptism cannot be divorced from faith, and since infants are incapable of having faith, it is untenable and a violation of Scripture to baptize infants. Even those who defend the practice of infant baptism, he pointed out, recognize that the New Testament does not offer authority for infant baptism. His thorough examination of New Testament passages that bear on this subject demonstrates that infant

---

55. Deut 30:6.
56. Jer 4:4.
57. Rom 2:28–29.
58. Phil 3:3.

baptism cannot be supported by Scripture. For the advocates of infant baptism, the "greater weight must be placed for the defense of the practice upon theological, rather than scriptural grounds."[59]

Another British theologian, Stanley Fowler, in his book *More Than a Symbol*, traces the baptismal history of the British Baptist Churches. He explains how baptism, once viewed as merely a symbolic post-conversion practice in the seventeenth century, evolved down to the twentieth century to a sacramental view that recognized baptism cannot be separated from conversion. Infant baptism had been firmly grounded in earlier Baptist theology, and the controversy played a key role in the evolution of the purpose of baptism. As the trend toward conversion baptism gained acceptance, infant baptism came to be seen as unbiblical and was discarded by many prominent Baptist theologians and churches.

1 Corinthians 1:10–17; 12:12–14

> Now I exhort you, brethren, by the name of our Lord Jesus Christ, that you all agree and that there be no divisions among you, but that you be made complete in the same mind and in the same judgment. For I have been informed concerning you, my brethren, by Chlo's people, that there are quarrels among you. Now I mean this, that each one of you is saying, "I am of Paul," and "I of Apollos," and "I of Cephas," and "I of Christ." Has Christ been divided? Paul was not crucified for you, was he? Or were you baptized in (*eis*) the name of Paul? I thank God that I baptized none of you except Crispus and Gaius, so that no one would say you were baptized in (*eis*) my name. Now I did baptize also the household of Stephanas; beyond that, I do not know whether I baptized any other. For Christ did not send me to baptize, but to preach the gospel, not in cleverness of speech, so that the cross of Christ would not be made void.

> For even as the body is one and yet has many members, and all the members of the body, though they are many, are one body, so also is Christ. For by one Spirit we were all baptized into [*eis*] one body, whether Jews or Greeks, whether slaves or free, and we were all made to drink of one Spirit. For the body is not one member, but many.

---

59. Beasley-Murray, *Baptism*, 309, fn. 2.

In the beginning of Paul's correspondence to the Corinthian Church, he upbraided them for allowing the congregation to be splintered into various cliques. In chapter 12, he counseled them that they were all members of the one Body of Christ and that they were all dependent on one another. He recalled them to their common conversion—the time of their baptism. They all had the same baptism into Christ in common. Regardless of who they were (Jew or Greek, slave or free), regardless of who had taught them the Gospel (Paul, Apollos, Cephas, or even Christ himself), "we" were all baptized by and made to drink of one Spirit. Twice in verse 13 Paul identified himself with them in their baptismal conversion with the use of the pronoun "we" (as he did in Romans 6), thus giving that moment a special significance for them to look back to and rally around.

> For by one Spirit we were all baptized into one body, whether Jews or Greeks, whether slaves or free, and we were all made to drink of one Spirit.[60]

> Has Christ been divided? Paul was not crucified for you, was he? Or were you baptized in the name of Paul?[61]

If they could not answer all three of these questions with a strong negative, the security of their salvation was endangered, and consequently, the church would be splintered, and there would no longer be any light of Christ in the great city of Corinth. In lifting them up to look above their quarrels and divisions, he wanted them to realize that their divisiveness was quite childish, selfish, and worldly. By calling them to remember their baptisms, he focused their attention on the unity inherent in their common baptismal conversion—regardless of who performed their immersion in the water.

So far in this study, we have encountered the preposition *eis* in a number of New Testament passages in which *eis* plays a vital role in understanding the purpose of baptism:

Mark 1:4; Luke 3:3; Matt 3:11	Baptized *into* repentance and forgiveness of sins	John the Baptist
Matt 28:19	Baptized *into* the name of the Father, Son, and Holy Spirit	Jesus—The Great Commission

---

60. 1 Cor 12:13.

61. 1 Cor 1:13.

Acts 2:38	Baptized *into* the forgiveness of sins	Peter at Pentecost
Acts 8:16	Baptized *into* the name of the Lord Jesus	Samaritans
Acts 19:5	Baptized *into* the name of the Lord Jesus	Ephesian disciples of John the Baptist
Rom 6:3	Baptized *into* Christ Jesus	Paul to the Roman Church
Rom 6:3	Baptized *into* Christ's death	Paul to the Roman Church
Rom 6:4	Baptized *into* death	Paul to the Roman Church
Gal 3:27	Baptized *into* Christ	Paul to the Galatian Churches
1 Cor 12:13	Baptized *into* one body	Paul to the Corinthian Church

If it could be legitimately shown that any of these uses of *eis* should be translated as causative ("because of"), would it not stand to reason that they should all be causative? There is a strong parallel in all of them, and to pick and choose some to be causative and some to be purposive would lead to a most unclear message.

In light of the consistent use of *eis* to express the purpose of baptism, it is difficult to escape the realization of how critical, central, and necessary baptism is to initiation into Christ. In 1 Corinthians 1:13, 15, Paul used *eis* to refer to the absurdity that they should want to be followers of him; as if they were "baptized *into* (*eis*) the name of Paul" or "baptized *into* (*eis*) my name" instead of "*into* (*eis*) the name of Christ." These three uses of *eis* lend force to the recognition that Paul and his audience had a common understanding about baptism as an event that identified them with Christ into whom they were being baptized. He did not want them to be identified by his name, nor to be his disciples. If they were baptized into the one body (12:13)—the Body of Christ—it was to Christ that they owed their allegiance, not Paul, Apollos, or Cephas. By calling their attention back to the purpose for which they had been baptized, Paul drove home the awareness that their real identity and loyalty was in Christ.

> This was the basis for unity and showed the fallacy of the divisions in the church at Corinth . . . A depreciation of baptism, therefore, is not to be concluded from this passage, only a depreciation of the administrator of the baptism.[62]

---

62. Ferguson, *Baptism*, 149.

Their common induction into the body could not be accomplished either by the individual who was being baptized, by the one who does the baptism, or by the church (the Body). One could not be brought into the church by human effort or by church consent. *Induction into the Body is solely an act of God, and he has designated baptism as that portal.* God alone is qualified to determine whom he should add to his church.

> And *the Lord was adding* to their number day by day those who were being saved.[63]

> And he put all things in subjection under his [Christ's, see 1:20] feet, and gave him as *head over all things to the church, which is his body*, the fullness of him who fills all in all.[64]

The church was created by God, and by rights of creation, it is his Body (literal: *heitis estin to soma autou* "which is the body of him"). Paul made it clear that the church is the Body of Christ.

> And he gave some as apostles, and some as prophets, and some as evangelists, and some as pastors and teachers, for the equipping of the saints for the work of service, to the building up of *the body of Christ*;[65]

> Jesus answered them, "Destroy this temple, and in three days I will raise it up." The Jews then said, "It took forty-six years to build this temple, and will you raise it up in three days?" But he was speaking of the temple of his body.[66]

In similar language, the church is acknowledged as the dwelling place (temple) of the Holy Spirit.

> Or do you not know that your body [literal: *to soma humon* "the body of you all"] is a temple of the Holy Spirit who is in you, whom you have from God, and that you are not your own?[67]

All Christians are members of the Lord's church, and there are no Christians who are not members of his church. Concerning his Body, Paul said, "we were all baptized into one body." It would seem absurd to Paul

---

63. Acts 2:47.
64. Eph 1:22–23.
65. Eph 4:11–12.
66. John 2:19–21.
67. 1 Cor 6:19.

to suggest that a person can be a Christian or a member of a local congregation without being a member of the church!

1 Corinthians 6:9–11 and Titus 3:3–7

> Or do you not know that the unrighteous will not inherit the kingdom of God? Do not be deceived; neither fornicators, nor idolaters, nor adulterers, nor effeminate, nor homosexuals, nor thieves, nor the covetous, nor drunkards, nor revilers, nor swindlers, will inherit the kingdom of God. Such were some of you; but you were washed, but you were sanctified, but you were justified in the name of the Lord Jesus Christ and in the Spirit of our God.

> For we also once were foolish ourselves, disobedient, deceived, enslaved to various lusts and pleasures, spending our life in malice and envy, hateful, hating one another. But when the kindness of God our Savior and his love for mankind appeared, He saved us, not on the basis of deeds which we have done in righteousness, but according to his mercy, by the washing of regeneration and renewing by the Holy Spirit, whom he poured out upon us richly through Jesus Christ our Savior, so that being justified by his grace we would be made heirs according to the hope of eternal life.

Sin contaminates. Sin produces adverse and dangerous consequences, both in this life and beyond into eternally. Adultery, for example, ruins not only the purity and beauty of a marriage but also damages everyone within that circle of friends and family. Chemical abuse produces adverse harm to the body. That is why these things are called sins. Sin destroys. Sin alienates relationships. Sin upsets societies. Most of all, because sin separates, it results in alienation from God. Satan is the Destroyer who delights in sin, and all of his disciples are also destroyers. Peace and order are displaced by chaos where there is sin. Every sin has adverse consequences, whether "large" or "small."

God alone is pure purity. Consequently, there can be no liaison between God and any who are not equally pure. In Chapter 5 ("Holiness") of this study, we noted that every sin, no matter how small or insignificant, contaminates, leaving the sinner alienated from God.

> . . . for all have sinned and fall short of the glory of God.[68]

---

68. Rom 3:23.

> For whoever keeps the whole law and *yet stumbles in one point*, he has become guilty of all.[69]

From the lists in 1 Corinthians 6 and Titus 3 above, we have very little problem understanding the meaning of "sin" as a violation of God's will. However, we tend to stumble or gloss over the second phrase in Rom 3:23: "fall short of the glory of God" (*hustereo*: "fall short," "come up behind or short," "fail," "to lack"). The glory of God is his holiness—his radiance, his splendor. His beauty is the glory of his perfect purity. To "fall short," then, is *anything* that does not measure up to perfect purity. Paul placed "fall short" on a par with "have sinned"; they both have the same fatal consequences. Anything that "falls short" of that highest of standards dooms the offender for condemnation. No flaw (deliberate or accidental) can be brought into union with him without tarnishing his glory.[70] Hence, the need for a washing, a cleansing that is strong enough to cleanse the most heinous of crimes as well as the little ones tucked away in the remote corners of our life.

To Paul's list of deviant behavior in 1 Cor 6:9–10 and Titus 3:3 can be added his lists in Rom 1:28–32 and Gal 5:19–21.

> And just as they did not see fit to acknowledge God any longer, God gave them over to a depraved mind, to do those things which are not proper, being filled with all unrighteousness, wickedness, greed, evil; full of envy, murder, strife, deceit, malice; they are gossips, slanderers, haters of God, insolent, arrogant, boastful, inventors of evil, disobedient to parents, without understanding, untrustworthy, unloving, unmerciful; and although they know the ordinance of God, that those who practice such things are worthy of death, they not only do the same, but also give hearty approval to those who practice them.[71]

> Now the deeds of the flesh are evident, which are: immorality, impurity, sensuality, idolatry, sorcery, enmities, strife, jealousy, outbursts of anger, disputes, dissensions, factions, envying,

---

69. Jas 2:10.

70. People have a tendency to balk at the idea that "innocent" accidents can alienate people from God. Can a glass of spilled milk be placed alongside of sin to alienate one from God? Who of us has not witnessed in ourselves and others the accidental slip of the tongue, resulting in the wrong (and sometimes embarrassing) use of words? Does not our purity of motive compensate and cover the error? To fall short of divine perfection includes every shortcoming, no matter how small and no matter whether deliberate or accidental.

71. Rom 1:28–32.

drunkenness, carousing, and things like these, of which I forewarn you, just as I have forewarned you, that those who practice such things will not inherit the kingdom of God.[72]

If there is anyone who cannot find themselves somewhere in these lists, their integrity needs to be questioned. The consequences of these violations are devastating. They "will not inherit the kingdom of God," and "those who practice such things are worthy of death." Not only is the practice of such things damning, but the same also applies to those who "give hearty approval to (assent to, find pleasure in) those who practice them;" they share in the guilt and condemnation.

Because such universal guilt among man is so damning, the "washing" in the 1 Corinthian 6 and Titus 3 passages is indeed Good News. There is hope of deliverance from condemnation. There is no doubt that the washing referred to here is the cleansing by the blood of Christ. This washing away of guilt is reminiscent of Paul's words in Rom 6:6–7:

> knowing this, that our old self was crucified with him, in order that our body of sin might be done away with, so that we would no longer be slaves to sin; for he who has died is freed from sin.

The fact that baptism is not specifically mentioned in 1 Cor 6:11 or Titus 3:5 does not negate the fact that it is implied. Beasley-Murray addressed the absence of the word "baptism" in 1 Cor 6:11.

> The question may be raised, 'Is this [1 Cor 6:11] a baptismal saying? Or is the Apostle relating an experience of deliverance independent of any rite of initiation?' There is an understandable reluctance in some quarters to recognize a baptismal context for this statement, especially as it conjoins with the cleansing spoken of justification and sanctification. But the voice of scholarship is unanimous in affirming the association with baptism . . . Accordingly, the majority of exegetes concur in interpreting this statement in the context of baptism.[73]

When 1 Cor 6:11 and Titus 3:5 are taken in conjunction with other passages that do mention baptism, we frequently see the same principles of washing, forgiveness, and renewal associated with baptism. The intimacy between "be baptized" and "wash away your sins" in Acts 22:16 exemplifies this close relation of baptism to washing away of sins. The

---

72. Gal 5:19–21
73. Beasley-Murray. *Baptism*, 162–63.

instruction to "be baptized" and "wash away your sins" in Paul's conversion has the same impact as "washing" in 1 Cor 6:11 and Titus 3:5.

In 1 Cor 6:11 Paul associated "washing" with sanctification and justification. In Titus 3:5 he associated "washing" with God's mercy and renewal by the Holy Spirit. In Romans 6 Paul described baptism as the place where the baptizand is united with the death, burial, and resurrection of Christ "in order that our body of sin might be done away with."[74] In Acts 22:16 Ananias placed baptism and washing away of sin as concurrent. The interweaving of baptism with washing, removal of sin, sanctification, justification, mercy, and renewal in numerous New Testament passages, gives us justification to assume that in 1 Cor 6:11 and Titus 3:5 Paul was describing what happens in baptism even though he did not use the word "baptism."

In Titus 3:5 Paul used the phrase, "washing of regeneration" (*loutrou paliggenesias*) in connection with "He saved us." *Paliggenesias* derives from the joining of *palin* (new) with *genesis* (birth, generated, beginning) and thus means "new genesis."[75] Jesus used *gennao* (verb form of the noun *genesis*) in a similar fashion when speaking with Nicodemus, "Truly, truly, I say to you, unless one is born from above (*genneithei anothen*) he cannot see the kingdom of God."[76] *Genneithei* (verb: aorist, passive, subjunctive of *gennao*), like *genesis* (noun), concerns "birth," "generation." Jesus' two phrases, "born (or generated) from above" and "born of water and Spirit," in John 3:3, 5 are the same as Paul's concept in the phrase, "washing of regeneration" (*loutrou paliggenesias*) in Titus 3:5.

In 1 Corinthians 6:11, there are three phrases in parallel—"you were washed," "you were sanctified," and "you were justified." There has been much discussion concerning the chronological relationship between these three actions. Indisputable is the fact that all three are divine operations of God's grace, and they are all three passive verbs. It is God who washes, sanctifies, and justifies. There are two ways to look at these three actions. One way is to understand all three as separate independent chronological events. The other is to look at them as three concurrent actions in one event. Some have tried to rearrange the chronological order of the three to make them fit their presuppositions,[77] but we must be

---

74. Rom 6:6.

75. Buchsel, "*palingenesia*,"688.

76. See chapter 5 for a fuller account of the conversation between Jesus and Nicodemus.

77. Beasley-Murray, *Baptism*, 163–64.

careful here not to rewrite God's word to suit our own personal theology. When we look at this correspondence through the eyes of the missionary-minded Paul, we need to remember that he is writing to converts, people who had formally been fornicators, idolaters, adulterers, effeminate, homosexuals, thieves, covetous, drunkards, revilers, and swindlers (1 Cor 6:9–10); they were foolish, disobedient, deceived, enslaved to various lusts and pleasures, spending life in malice and envy, hateful, hating one another (Titus 3:3). For them, regardless of what order Paul put their washing, sanctification, and justification, they looked to their baptism as their release from the slavery and destruction brought on by such previous behavior. For the first time in their lives, they experienced a *washing* away of the filth of worldliness, a housecleaning of their souls (*sanctification*), and were at that moment fit to host the Lord himself as a resident in their lives (*justification*). The idea of any chronological separation of these three redeeming events would have sounded like nonsense to Paul and his audience. They would have found the alienation of any of these life-transforming events from their baptism to as the denial of their conversion.

All three of these events serve to point them back (as Paul seems to have a habit of doing) to a time when something of significance was done to them in their past. Paul's use of the passive voice reminded them that their sanctification (*heigiastheite*: aorist, passive, indicative) and justification (*edikaiotheite*: aorist, passive, indicative) were not the result of their own efforts, but were God's work in their lives, just as they are in our lives today. Though *apelousasthe* (aorist, middle, indicative) is in the middle voice, which can be translated "you washed yourselves," the strength of the middle voice is often drawn into, or is even supplanted by, the passive voice. *Apelousasthe* was probably meant to be understood as "you had yourselves washed" or simply, "you were washed."[78] Theirs was a conversion that they had actually experienced as an event, a point in time they could look back to and say, "That was the moment when I became a Christian." We have seen in other similar passages (e.g., Rom 6 and Col 2) instances where their identity with conversion was associated with baptism. There is no other objective event identified in the New Testament to which they could look back upon as the moment of their washing, cleansing, and justification than when they were baptized into Christ. There is no passage in the Bible that identifies the saying of

---

78. Ferguson, *Baptism*, 150. See also Beasley-Murray, *Baptism*, 164.

a "sinner's prayer," going to the "mourner's bench," or any other event except baptism in which conversion is effected. That is why baptism was looked upon by the early Christians as a significant event in their lives. It was their life-changing birth born of heaven.

1 Peter 3:18–21

> For Christ also died for sins once for all, the just for the unjust, so that he might bring us to God, having been put to death in the flesh, but made alive in the spirit; in which also he went and made proclamation to the spirits now in prison, who once were disobedient, when the patience of God kept waiting in the days of Noah, during the construction of the ark, in which a few, that is, eight persons, were brought safely through the water. Corresponding to that, baptism now saves you—not the removal of dirt from the flesh, but an appeal to God for a good conscience—through the resurrection of Jesus Christ, who is at the right hand of God, having gone into heaven, after angels and authorities and powers had been subjected to him.

Though 3:21 is a short reference to baptism, the language of this verse gives the most straightforward and precise statement concerning the purpose and necessity of baptism in the New Testament. It is the only verse that makes reference to baptism in both of Peter's letters; however, historically commentators have suggested that 1 Peter (or at least major portions of it) may have been used by the early church as a baptismal treatise for catechetical use to train those who were to be baptized or had recently been baptized.[79] Dr. Beasley-Murray commenting on this stated,

> Whatever be the truth of its origin, 1 Pt. 1.3–4.11 is unique among New Testament writings in its fullness of baptismal allusions, as a glance through its contents serves to show.[80]

In the verses previous to this passage (3:13–18), Peter gave instructions concerning how Christians should behave in times of suffering. In verse 17 he admonished his readers that if you suffer, it is better to suffer for doing good than for doing wrong. He ended the paragraph by setting

---

79. For a summary of the possibility that 1 Peter was used for catechetical purposes in the early church, see Harrison, *Introduction*, 399–401.

80. Beasley-Murray, *Baptism*, 256.

before them the example of Jesus, who "died for sins once for all, the just for the unjust, so that he might bring us to God, having been put to death in the flesh, but made alive in the spirit" (verse 18). Suffering is not the final end. The suffering of the righteous is overshadowed by hope. The contrast between Jesus "being put to death in the flesh" and his being "made alive in the spirit" reminds his readers that the agony of suffering evaporates in the presence of the glory and joy of deliverance.

As Peter continued in verse 18 and following, his focus was still on Jesus who, according to verse 19, "went and made proclamation to the spirits now in prison." The sudden shift here has caused considerable confusion among commentators. Who are these "spirits?" When and where did this preaching by Jesus take place? The answer to "who" is found in the next verse: those who were disobedient during the days when Noah was building the ark. At the time Peter wrote this treatise, those disobedient souls were "now in prison." Many commentaries on verse 19 believe that Jesus, between his death and resurrection, went into hell and preached to those disobedient souls (or, as some others say, to the fallen angels). However, there is an absence of support for such views, and it misses the main point of these verses. Browsing through numerous articles on the internet concerning this passage, one can find any number of radical and sensational speculations fraught with illogical conclusions. Such speculations distract from the simple meaning of Peter's message. Why would it seem so strange that, in the days when Noah was building the ark, Jesus, with Noah as his messenger (Peter called Noah a "preacher of righteousness" in 2 Peter 2:5), saw fit to preach to that obstinate generation? It would be no stranger than revealing his message to the Asian churches through the apostle John as his spokesman (Rev 1:1–2). The main point of this passage is that *in the days of Noah God was in the business of rescuing people of faith from destruction* ("eight persons were brought safely through the water"). *In like manner, Peter, in verse 21, reassures his readers that God is still rescuing his people.*

"Corresponding to that, baptism now saves you"
(ho kai humas antitupon nun sodsei baptitsma)

The relative pronoun *ho* (which, that) expresses a relationship—either by contrast or similarity—between words, clauses or concepts. It is the bridge that connects that which comes before to that which comes after.

In like manner, the word *antitupos* indicates the comparison of a shape, an idea, or a meaning with that which comes before or after it. Like *ho*, *antitupos* looks both backward and forward for the purpose of comparison. In this case, that which comes before (verse 20) is "eight souls were saved through water." That which comes after (verse 21) is "baptism now saves you." By using *ho* and *antitupos* in this way, Peter called his readers to remember that it is God who delivers the faithful from destruction in baptism, just as it was he who saved in the days of the flood.

In grade school, our English teachers taught us to diagram sentences by the location of the words in the order that they occur in a sentence. In the English language, the subject of a phrase or sentence always comes before the verb with which it is associated; the direct object comes after the verb, as does the indirect object. In the Greek language, such is not the case; the parts of speech can occur anywhere in the phrase or sentence and are identified, not by their location in the sentence, but by the ending of the word. This phrase in 1 Peter 3:21 (*ho kai humas antitupon nun sodzei baptisma* (literally, "which and you corresponding to now it saves baptism") is a good example of this principle. The subject is *baptisma* (baptism: nominative case noun); the verb is *sodzei* (it saves); and the direct object is *humas* ("you"—accusative case pronoun). Thus, *ho kai humas antitupon nun sodzei baptisma* becomes the simple English translation: "And corresponding to that baptism now saves you." With *baptisma* as the subject and *sodzei* as the verbal action, it necessitates the recognition that baptism is the saving event that Peter is emphasizing in this passage. Looking at some of the common translations and paraphrases, it is easy to see the universal emphasis on the intimate connection between the baptismal event and salvation:

Ho kai humas antitupon nun sodzei baptisma	GREEK
Corresponding to that, baptism now saves you	NASU
Baptism, which corresponds to this, *now saves you*	ESV, RSV
and this water symbolizes *baptism that now saves you also*[81]	NIV
which also after a true likeness *doth now save you, (even) baptism*	ASV
The like figure whereunto even *baptism doth also now save us*	KJV
There is also an antitype *which now saves us—baptism*	NKJV

81. The NIV added the word "water," which does not actually occur in verse 21. Likewise, the CEV added the words "flood waters."

Those flood waters were like *baptism that now saves you.*	CEV
which figure also *now saves you, [even] baptism,*	DB
Whereunto *baptism* being of the like form, *now saveth you also*	DRB
which was a symbol pointing to *baptism, which now saves you*	GNT
which was a symbol pointing to *baptism, which now saves you.*	TEV

"Not the removal of dirt from the flesh"
(ou sarkos apotheosis hrupou)

A similarity between the flood and baptism is that they both involve water. Just as it was not the water that saved Noah and his family, so it is not the water that washes away sin in baptism. In both cases, the presence of water is an essential part of the event, but it is not the salvific power. In like manner it was not the Cross itself that effected redemption; it was the Lord on the Cross who, in his death, was the redeeming power. The Cross has become the symbol of what Jesus did. Likewise, it was God, not the water, who saved Noah and his family from the destruction that was experienced by their sinful contemporaries. In like manner, it is God, not the water of baptism itself, who saves the baptizand from eternal destruction. With this negative phrase, "not the removal of dirt from the flesh," Peter sets Christian baptism in contrast to the outward physical ceremonial washings of Judaism and the water ablutions of the pagans.[82]

All through the Bible water has been used symbolically to express spiritual realities. By the water God delivered Noah and his family from death. Peter used the waters of the flood to demonstrate that God also, in the water of baptism, delivers souls from death. In a similar way, by parting of the waters of the Red Sea, God delivered the Israelites safely across on dry land.

> As for you, lift up your staff and stretch out your hand over the sea and divide it, and the sons of Israel shall go through the midst of the sea on dry land.[83]

In the case of the flood and the parting of the Red Sea, the waters marked the difference between the ungodly and the faithful. In like manner, it is

---

82. Beasley-Murray, *Baptism*, 260.
83. Exod 14:16.

the water of baptism that marks/symbolizes the difference between the clean/forgiven and the unclean/guilty.

> Behold, I, even I am bringing the flood of water upon the earth, to destroy all flesh in which is the breath of life, from under heaven; everything that is on the earth shall perish. But I will establish my covenant with you; and you shall enter the ark—you and your sons and your wife, and your son wives with you.[84]

> Then the Lord said to Moses, "Stretch out your hand over the sea so that the waters may come back over the Egyptians, over their chariots and their horsemen."[85]

> He who has believed and has been baptized shall be saved; but he who has disbelieved shall be condemned.[86]

Water also marks a symbolic connection with other spiritual realities throughout the Bible, such as the pouring forth of the Holy Spirit and refreshing of the soul. In Isaiah God set the quenching of thirst by water in parallel to the pouring out of his Holy Spirit and his blessing.

> But now listen, O Jacob, my servant,
> And Israel, whom I have chosen:
> Thus says the Lord who made you
> And formed you from the womb, who will help you,
> "Do not fear, O Jacob my servant;
> And you Jeshurun whom I have chosen.
> For I will pour out water on the thirsty land
> And streams on the dry ground;
> I will pour out my Spirit on your offspring
> And my blessing on your descendants;
> And they will spring up among the grass
> Like poplars by streams of water."[87]

> And the Lord will continually guide you,
> And satisfy your desire in scorched places,
> And give strength to your bones;
> And you will be like a watered garden,
> And like a spring of water whose waters do not fail.[88]

---

84. Gen 6:17–18.
85. Exod 14:26.
86. Mark 16:16.
87. Isa 44:1–4.
88. Isa 58:11.

Jesus used the symbolic meaning of water when talking to the Samaritan woman of Sychar by Jacob's well.

> If you knew the gift of God, and who it is who says to you, "Give me a drink," you would have asked him, and he would have given you living water. She said to him, "Sir, you have nothing to draw with and the well is deep; where then do you get that living water?"[89]

Later, while he was in Jerusalem for the Feast of Booths, Jesus spoke similar words to the multitude:

> Now on the last day, the great day of the feast, Jesus stood and cried out, saying, "If anyone is thirsty, let him come to me and drink. He who believes in me, as the Scripture said, 'From his innermost being will flow rivers of living water.'" But this he spoke of the Spirit, whom those who believed in him were to receive; for the Spirit was not yet given, because Jesus was not yet glorified.[90]

In his vision of the new heaven and new earth John saw this same living water ("the water of life") in the holy heavenly city, the New Jerusalem.

> for the Lamb in the center of the throne will be their shepherd, and will guide them to springs of the water of life; and God will wipe every tear from their eyes.[91]

> Then he said to me, "It is done. I am the Alpha and the Omega, the beginning and the end. I will give to the one who thirsts from the spring of the water of life without cost."[92]

> Then he showed me a river of the water of life, clear as crystal, coming from the throne of God and of the Lamb.[93]

Pilate while sitting as judge during the trial of Jesus recognized the value of water to represent blamelessness.

> When Pilate saw that he was accomplishing nothing, but rather that a riot was starting, he took water and washed his hands in

---

89. John 4:10–11.
90. John 7:37–39.
91. Rev 7:17.
92. Rev 21:6.
93. Rev 22:1.

front of the crowd, saying, "I am innocent of this Man's blood; see to that yourselves."[94]

Obviously, Pilate's hand washing was not for the purpose of removing dirt, but a symbolic declaration of his innocence to the crowd. A similar metaphysical picture of cleansing was used by Paul in the phrase "washing of regeneration" to describe the cleansing of our souls (Titus 3:5). In Eph 5:6 he mentions the same concept as the "washing of water with the word" by which God sanctifies (purifies) his church. Peter explained that baptism also has a symbolic association with water. The water of baptism is not a physical washing, but in that watery burial there is a spiritual cleansing. The physical water is a symbolic portrait of the living heavenly water that is the cleansing agent of the soul.

Water plays a vital role in our daily lives. It brings refreshment to the thirsty; by it we water our plants; with it we wash our bodies; and we find it a very useful cleansing agent for our wounds. We can also see its great power in the rivers and oceans. Why would it seem so unusual for God to choose water to represent his marvelous cleansing work upon the souls of the faithful in redemption?

But an appeal for a good conscience to God
(alla suneideiseos agatheis eperoteima eis theon)

The noun *eperoteima* (appeal) has, from the time of the Greek philosopher Herodotus (484–425 BC), been used to indicate an *inquiry*.[95] The root idea of the verbs *erotao* and *eperotao* indicates "to ask," "to question," "to enquire," "to request," "to petition," "to plead," "to pray."[96] The noun *eperoteima* (a question, an inquiry, a request, a prayer) occurs only in this passage in the New Testament. A question is a request for a response from the one to whom the question is asked. In the New Testament, the verbs are quite numerous (*erotao* fifty-seven times and *eperotao* fifty-eight times) and always indicate an inquiry. *Eperteima* and its verbs, *erotao* and *eperotao*, are never used as an "answer," an "interrogation," a "pledge," or any other *response* to an inquiry. Usually, a question indicates a deficiency in the one asking the question. Sometimes, the questioner already knows

---

94. Matt 27:24.

95. Greeven, "*erotao, eperotao, eperoteima*," 685–88.

96. Greeven, "*erotao, eperotao, eperoteima*," 687. For New Testament examples see Matt. 16:1; Mark 10:2; 1 John 5:16; Acts 10:48.

the correct response and states it in the form of a request/question to elicit some reaction from the one who is questioned. For example, when the chief priests and elders challenged Jesus about his authority, he responded with the request (*eroteiso*: future, active, indicative, "I am going to ask") that they first answer a question about whether the baptism of John the Baptist had its origin with man or with God. Obviously, in this case, Jesus already knew the answer.

> I will also ask you one thing, which if you tell me, I will also tell you by what authority I do these things. The baptism of John was from what source, from heaven or from men?[97]

In light of the evidence from lexicons and the numerous passages in the New Testament, it is obvious that *erotao, eperotao,* and *eperoteima* are to be understood in the sense of requesting a response, not the response itself.

As can be seen in the list below, the NASV, ESV, and RSV translated *eperoteima* as "appeal," which complies with the above idea of a request. In these three translations, the baptizand is making a request to God for a cleansing of the conscience. On the other hand, the NIV, KJV, NKJV, and ASV translated *eperoteima* not as a request but as a response given to God.

"baptism . . . an appeal to God for a good conscience"	NASU, ESV
"baptism . . . an appeal to God for a clear conscience"	RSV
"baptism . . . a pledge of a good conscience toward God"	NIV
"baptism . . . an answer of a good conscience toward God"	KJV, NKJV
"baptism . . . an interrogation of a good conscience toward God"	ASV

If *eperoteima* is made to be a response rather than a request, then the good conscience is made to become the subject who, in baptism, is making a pledge/answer/interrogation to God. *Thus, if it is a response, the baptizand comes to baptism with an already cleansed conscience to make a response to God.* If such were the case, then the conscience is made clean (*agatheis*: good) before baptism, and the cleansed conscience comes to baptism to make a "pledge," "answer," or "interrogation" to God. Rather, if *eperoteima* is taken as a request, Peter's understanding of baptism would

---

97. Matt 21:24–25.

be in conformity with all the other passages about baptism.[98] In their baptism of conversion in which the conscience is cleansed, the convert submits the lordship of their life to God. Consequently, the convert pledges to live a life in obedience. The pledge of obedience is the *result of baptism*. As the passive recipient of God's grace, "baptism is not an offer made by man to God, but an offer made by Christ to man."[99] In contrast "the pledge of a good conscience toward God" makes baptism to be something of value we offer to God as a reward for his salvation.

Grammatically, the genitive phrase *suneideiseos agatheis* (a good conscience) can be translated "for a good conscience" (objective genitive) or "of a good conscience" (subjective genitive). If this is to be taken as an objective genitive, "a good conscience" is the object *requested* by the subject (baptism) of the sentence. If, on the other hand, this is a subjective genitive, the "good conscience" becomes the subject of the sentence that makes a *response* to God in baptism. Technically, *suneideiseos agatheis* can be translated as an objective or a subjective genitive. Two factors within the verse help us to determine which genitive should be used. One factor is the meaning of *eperoteima*, which, as explained above, is a request, not a response. This would require the genitive to be objective.

---

98. Beasley-Murray, *Baptism*, 261. In his commentary on 1 Pet 3:21, Beasley-Murray made the point that,

> The most popularly received interpretation has proceeded on the assumption that *eperoteima* reflects the basic meaning of *eperotao*, to ask or to question, meaning in this context: "the prayer to God for a good conscience." I cannot agree with Reicke that the idea of baptism as a prayer is "quite unthinkable" in a definition of its nature, for the conception of baptism as a vehicle of surrender in faith and obedience to God is inseparable from the thought of prayer in the act of baptism, and the definition so understood would suit the context. Nevertheless, there is evidence for an official use of *eperoteima* in the sense of oracular declaration, and in more popular usage as the equivalent of the Latin *stipulatio*, the clause in an agreement containing a formal question and consent (*homologia*) of two parties making a contract. It seems better to follow this clue and interpret the definition of baptism in our passage as "the pledge to God proceeding from a good conscience." (taking the genitive as objective). On either view the "pledge" is given in response to a demand: the baptismal candidate answers affirmatively to God's request for faith and obedience.

Why Beasley-Murray began this quote recognizing *eperoteima* as a "prayer" (request), but then switching to define *eperoteima* "in the sense of oracular declaration" is confusing. He did not give any biblical evidence to support his switch, and the view he expresses here runs counter to conclusions he made throughout his book.

99. Bonhoeffer, *Cost of Discipleship*, 256.

The other factor is, if *eperoteima* is to be understood as a response (subjective genitive) rather than a request, we are left in the dark as to what that response is supposed to be. What "pledge" (NIV) does the baptizand offer to God in baptism? What is the "answer" (KJV) given to God in baptism? There is a vagueness with the subjective translation, leaving the purpose of baptism allusive and undefined. We are left to guess what the content of that "pledge," "answer," or "interrogation" is, and on such critical matters as salvation, guessing is a dangerous enterprise. As we have previously noted, if baptism is relegated to a post-conversion experience, then we look in vain to find a biblically given purpose for baptism. Many commentators are ready to step up and assign purposes for such a baptism, none of which can be found in the Bible.

Before we leave 1 Peter 3:21, we need to take a look at the word *suneideiseos* (conscience), which occurs thirty-two times in the New Testament. It has to do with the determination of what is right and what is wrong. This working of the conscience is a three-phase process that is common to all humans. The first phase involves a mental effort to examine the available body of facts in an attempt to distinguish between what is true and what is false. The second phase is an internal emotional response in which the acceptance of the facts is processed by the person. The third phase follows with a decision as to how the truth is to be applied to life. This process of intellect, emotion, and will (head, heart, and hand) is Psychology 101. All humans operate on this principle. When a person faces any issue in their life, they must go through this process, and it will consequently determine how they live their life. The resultant quality of life is only as good as the facts available, the interpretation of and emotional reaction to the facts, and the subsequent action taken. Conscience, then, has to do with how we as humans handle truth in life. It is an established fact that no human is capable of applying this process infallibly. Therefore, many mistakes (either intentional or unintentional) are made. That is why Paul wrote, "All have sinned and fall short of the glory of God"[100] and "There is none righteous, not even one."[101] A clean, pure conscience (*suneideiseos*), therefore, is beyond the human ability to attain or maintain; thus, we end up with an impure conscience and we must appeal to God for its cleansing.

---

100. Rom 3:23.
101. Rom 3:10.

> Some, being accustomed to the idol until now, eat food as if it were sacrificed to an idol; and their conscience being weak is defiled.[102]

> Accordingly both gifts and sacrifices [of the first covenant] are offered *which cannot make the worshiper perfect in conscience,* since they relate only to food and drink and various washings, regulations for the body imposed until a time of reformation. But when Christ appeared as a high priest of the good things to come, he entered through the greater and more perfect tabernacle, not made with hands, that is to say, not of this creation; and not through the blood of goats and calves, but through his own blood, he entered the holy place once for all, having obtained eternal redemption. For if the blood of goats and bulls and the ashes of a heifer sprinkling those who have been defiled sanctify for the cleansing of the flesh, *how much more will the blood of Christ, who through the eternal Spirit offered himself without blemish to God, cleanse your conscience from dead works to serve the living God?*[103]

Paul referred to those who had fallen away from the faith and were practicing ungodly behavior as being "seared in their own conscience as with a branding iron" (1 Tim 4:2). In writing to Titus, Paul contrasted a pure conscience against a defiled conscience (Titus 1:15). The Good News is that it is possible for a person's conscience to be cleansed. The only way a conscience can be "good" or "clean" is, as Peter said in verse 21, by coming to God in baptism with an appeal for cleansing by the blood of Jesus Christ.

Conclusion

Over the last three chapters, we have seen an amazing consistency in the way the New Testament writers present to us the significance of the baptismal event. It was that baptismal moment in the lives of the early Christians which Paul told his readers to recall and be reminded of the joy of their conversion. That was the moment they were blessed with all the blessings that are in Christ Jesus. If we were to strip baptism of its salvific importance, we would be left with an event for which the writers of the New Testament gave no reason. Nor would there be any special event

---

102. 1 Cor 8:7.
103. Heb 9:9–14.

to look back to as that moment when the Christians submitted their lives to Christ—i.e., to remember their spiritual birthday.

9

Baptismal Postscripts

TWO THINGS MUST BE kept at the forefront of all discussions about baptism. The first is that holiness (sanctification) is the very heart of the baptismal event which is grounded in the Cross. All other blessings, while significant, are dependent on and secondary to the cleansing power of the blood of Christ. If there is no forgiveness of sin (sanctification), there is no relationship to God (righteousness). If there is no relationship with God, there are no spiritual blessings. The second is that baptism is a thoroughly passive event. Yet, baptism is, in its true sense, a salvation by works; it cost God the death of his Son. It is not a meritorious work done by the baptizand; it is accomplished solely by "the God and Father of our Lord Jesus Christ, who has blessed us with every spiritual blessing in the heavenly places in Christ."[104]

> Baptism, and the Christian faith it embodies, is rooted in the "Christ event," with all that implies, and nothing of man's doing and no theological explanation must ever be allowed to detract from the uniqueness, splendour and power of that event[105]

Baptism is not a doctrine in isolation from other doctrines. It is coupled directly to the death, burial, and resurrection of Christ. It is the event that brings a person into unity with the Father, the Son, and the Holy Spirit. In it, sinners are sanctified (*hagiadzo*), converted into saints (*hagios*). It is a washing in which the guilt of sin is obliterated. It is the initiation into the church, the Body of Christ. It is the resurrection into a new life with its eternal dimensions. A conscientious student of the Bible

---

104. Eph 1:3.
105. Beasley-Murray, *Baptism*, 138.

will approach a study of the meaning of baptism taking the plethora of other associated doctrines into consideration.

Baptism is not an end in itself; it is a portal. Baptism is a transformation (*metamorphoo*), wherein the baptizand is no longer conformed to this world but is transformed into God's Kingdom of Heaven.

> And do not be conformed [*suskeimatidzo*: fashioned according to] to this world, but be transformed [*metamorphoo*: remodeled, re-formed][106] by the renewing of your mind, so that you may prove what the will of God is, that which is good and acceptable and perfect.[107]

> As obedient children, do not be conformed [*suskeimatidzo*] to the former lusts which were yours in your ignorance, but like the Holy One who called you, be holy yourselves also in all your behavior; because it is written, "YOU SHALL BE HOLY, FOR I AM HOLY."[108]

As a transformation, baptism is a conversion (*metanoia*) from sinner to saint; from lost to redeemed; from darkness into his brilliant glory; from despair to hope; from condemned to redeemed. Baptism is a person's induction into a new outlook on life with its new Lord. As we have seen in the previous chapters, John the Baptist and the apostles were emphatic that this conversion into the new life must also result in a transformation of moral behavior.

Baptism and Sanctification/Holiness

Baptism is a washing, the forgiveness of sins. In it, that which is profane[109] is sanctified by the blood of Christ.

---

106. Behm, "*Metamorphoo*," 756–57.
    In Jewish apocalyptic a miraculous change of form is one of the gifts of eschatological salvation which the blessed receive after the resurrection, S. Bar. [*Syrian Apocalypse of Baruch*] 51:3: The appearance of their faces will be transformed into radiant beauty . . . They will be changed into the splendour of angels . . . They will resemble angels, and be like the stars, and will be changed into the form they desire, from beauty to splendour, and from light to the radiance of glory . . . Then will the glory of the righteous be greater than that of the angels.
107. Rom 12:2.
108. 1 Pet 1:14–16.
109. Nasty, obscene, vulgar, dirty, foul, wicked.

> By this [his] will we have been sanctified [*hagiadzo*] through the offering of the body of Jesus Christ once for all.[110]

So long as a person remains unclean, they can have no fellowship with the spotless God. Otherwise, their uncleanness would be an affront to the holy God, and consequently, the gates of heaven would be closed to them. Throughout the Bible and all subsequent history, all people and all things must be made holy (*hagiadzo*) before being admitted into the presence of God. No one and no thing can be allowed to be associated with Deity without first being sanctified (*hagiadzo*). Cleanliness (holiness) is not, as the old saying goes, *next* to godliness. Holiness *is* godliness.

To have a biblical understanding of baptism, it is critical to maintain an accurate awareness of what the Old and New Testaments teach concerning the meaning of holiness (sanctification). This was covered in chapter 5. If the concept of absolute purity and cleanness is not the center and heart of holiness, and if holiness is in any way divorced from the purpose of baptism, then baptism becomes an empty, meaningless ritual. Many wonderful blessings are bestowed in the baptismal event. However, without holiness, all other blessings are futile wishing of a heart searching for what it can never have, leaving it unclean and alienated from the holy God.

Forgiveness and Holiness

The proper starting point in understanding holiness is the recognition that in the Old and New Testaments forgiveness of sin is the essence of holiness. It is sin that separates man from God, and because of that, there cannot be any association between man and God. There must be a cleansing before such a relationship can be established. God's holiness cannot be tainted by even the least of sins. God will have fellowship only with those who are sanctified of all guilt. It is not in man himself to justify the guilt that separates him from God. Therefore, a solution alien to human ability must be found. In sanctification the profane nature is made holy by the washing in the blood of the Cross; guilt is purged of its condemning power. In that cleansing, the baptizand is made holy and fit for the intimacy of divine communion.

---

110. Heb 10:10.

Baptism and Justification / Righteousness

Justification (noun: *dikaiosunei*) is a relationship word. When there is alienation between two parties because of some violation of the relationship, the wrong must be justified (made right—verb: *dikaioo*). It must be brought before the bar of justice, the corruption identified, and the satisfaction for the wrong must be paid to make it righteous. Only then can the relationship be restored. The violation (sin) that separates people from God must be sanctified by the Cross, thus restoring the estranged to a relationship with God who *is* himself justice. Baptism is the place where the foul is cleansed (sanctification), restoring the relationship (righteousness) that was broken.

Baptism and Faith

There are many faiths; everyone has a faith. Faith is that in which a person places their highest loyalty, their primary (ultimate) concern in life.

> Faith is the state of being ultimately concerned . . . If it claims ultimacy it demands the total surrender of him who accepts this claim, and it promises total fulfillment, even if all other claims have to be subjected to it or rejected in its name . . . Faith as ultimate concern is an act of the total personality.[111]

There will arise in everyone's life one concern that becomes of prime importance, around which all other concerns in their life revolve. It may be something noble, such as family, career, patriotism, education, or benevolence. It may be a political ideology, such as democracy, monarchy, or socialism. It might be a more selfish endeavor, such as greed, strife, sensuality, violence, or various addictions. There is only one biblical faith; it is the only truly ultimate faith, which, by its very nature, subjects all other concerns to it. All other faiths will eventually collapse and fail to deliver ultimate security. Being ultimate, biblical faith demands the total devotion of the entire life of the converted.

> *Faith, in the biblical view, is an act of the whole personality.* Will, knowledge, and emotion participate in it. It is an act of self-surrender, of obedience, of assent. Each of these elements must be present. Emotional surrender without assent and obedience would bypass the personal center. It would be a compulsion and

111. Tillich, *Dynamics of Faith*, 1–4.

> not a decision. Intellectual assent without emotional participation distorts religious existence into a nonpersonal, cognitive act. Obedience of the will without assent and emotion leads into a depersonalizing slavery.[112]

This is what Paul meant when he shared with Timothy an intimate look into his faith.

> *I know* [intellect] whom I have believed and *I am convinced* [emotion] that he is able to guard what *I have entrusted* [will] to him until that day.[113]

The Christian faith is the surrender of one's mind, heart, and will to the lordship of Jesus. It is this faith that God accepts as pleasing to him. There is no other way to come to God and the glorious destiny he has for us.

> And without faith [noun: *pistis*] it is impossible to please him, for he who comes to God must believe [verb: *pisteuo*] that he is and that he is a rewarder of those who seek him.[114]

A person's answer to life's most important questions rests on their understanding of faith: Where did I come from? Why am I here? Where am I going? Christian's answer: "I came from God," "I am here to honor God," "I am going to live for eternity with God." God, therefore, becomes life's ultimate concern, rendering all other concerns as pseudo-ultimate, false realities.

When secondary concerns are thought to be and treated as ultimate, they are pseudo-ultimate; their hope of final fulfillment will fail to provide the ultimate benefits and security that a person needs to face this life, survive death, and provide eternal security. Only in God exists absolute trustworthiness to fulfill all human needs. All other concerns, whether honorable or not, to which a person may surrender themselves as if they were ultimate, are illusionary, elusive, and unreliable. Therefore, biblical faith is the plenary surrender of one's whole self—the intellect, the emotion, and the will—to the lordship of God.

> Whatever you do in word or deed, *do all* in the name of the Lord Jesus, giving thanks through him to God the Father.[115]

---

112. Tillich, *Biblical Religion*, 53.
113. 2 Tim 1:12.
114. Heb 11:6.
115. Col 3:17.

Only biblical faith has the substance to provide a hope that ensures eternal life. The classic passage that most people turn to as a definition of faith is Heb 11:1.

> Now faith is the assurance of things hoped for, the conviction of things not seen.[116]

The word "hope" (*elpis*) in this verse means "expectation." For example, when Paul and Silas were preaching in Philippi, they encountered a slave girl who had a spirit of divination, and she was bringing her masters much profit by fortune-telling. When Paul cast the spirit from her, her masters got upset, and when they "saw that their hope (*elpis*) of profit was gone, they seized Paul and Silas and dragged them into the marketplace before the authorities."[117] Her masters were making a profit from this fortune-telling girl, and upon her liberation from the spirit of divination, they lost their expectation (*elpis*) of profit. For her masters, *elpis* meant not wishful thinking but an "expectation" of profit. The "hope" of faith is more than an uncertain dream; it is more than wishful thinking; it is confidence and assurance.

According to Heb 11:1, faith is what gives "substance" to the Christian's expectation of eternal life. The word "substance" (*hupostasis*) means that which stands under (a combination of *statsis*: "stand," "state," "stability," and *hupo*: "under"). Faith, then, is the foundation (or grounding) of the Christian's expectation of things not seen.

The latter part of Heb 11:1, states that faith is what gives "conviction [*elegchos*: proof, test] to things not seen." We are familiar with realities we cannot see, such as wind, electronic signal waves and sound waves that travel through the air, electrical currents moving through conductors, etc. We do not doubt that these exist. We also recognize intangible realities, such as love, hatred, fear, hell, etc. In like manner, there are spiritual realities that we cannot see, such as God, heaven, angels, devils, etc. In all of these, the "conviction" of their reality lies not in their invisible physical appearance but in the effect they have on tangible realities that we can observe. This is what gives the conviction needed for faith.

In both the Old Testament Hebrew and the New Testament Greek, there is only one word for the two English words "faith" and "belief." In *modern* English, the word "faith" is often used to express confidence and trust in someone or something, while "belief" is usually used to express

---

116. Heb 11:1.
117. Acts 16:19.

recognition that something is correct; belief, in this manner, simply indicates a mental acknowledgment of a fact. The Old Testament Hebrew word for both "faith" and "belief" is *emunah* (noun) and its verb, *aman*. In the same way, the New Testament Greek words *pistis* (noun) and *pisteuo* (verb) are used to demonstrate that "faith" and "belief" have the same definition.

Biblical faith is closely allied with baptism. Surrender to the lordship of Christ takes place in baptism. *There can be no biblical faith prior to or without baptism.* If faith is understood as the surrender of one's whole self into the lordship of Christ, and that commitment takes place in baptism, then faith and baptism are so intimately tied together that to separate them into two separate chronological events would destroy the meaning and beauty of both.

> Perhaps we should rather gather that Paul's theological terms are more flexible than we sometimes allow and that faith and baptism are more closely interrelated than the Church has permitted them to be.[118]

A person's faith itself does not accomplish or establish union with God, but it is the indispensable condition God demands in order for him to bring the convert into a relationship with himself.[119] We are not justified by faith, but rather, we are justified on the basis of faith.

> Therefore, having been justified by faith (*ek pisteos*), we have peace with God through our Lord Jesus Christ.[120]

In this verse the noun, *pisteos*, is in the genitive case which, with the preposition *ek*, expresses the reason for justification. Most English translations render *ek* as "by" in this verse which would normally require a dative case noun (*pistei*) to indicate the agent or instrument that accomplishes the action of the verb ("justified"). Thus, Paul's statement, "Therefore, having been justified *on the basis of* faith" gives a more accurate understanding of the relationship between justification and faith. "Justified *by* faith," where faith is understood as the agent which produces justification leads directly into a doctrine of salvation that requires a person's faith to be strong or mature enough to accomplish salvation.

---

118. Beasley-Murray, *Baptism*, 164.
119. Heb 11:6.
120. Rom 5:1.

Faith originates in baptism and is a continually growing process throughout the life of a faithful Christian. Faith can never reach a point where there is no longer any room to grow. Only God has complete and perfect faith. That is why it was necessary for Deity to go to the Cross rather than even the most virtuous human. A Christian's salvation is dependent on the perfect faithfulness of Christ, not on human faith.[121] *It is faith as submission to the lordship of God in baptism that God joins (justifies) the baptizand to himself.*

Baptism and Confession

There is no biblical command for a statement of confession at baptism. However, there is considerable evidence that such was the practice by the apostolic church and is a good practice that we would be wise to follow. In the story of his baptism the Ethiopian eunuch made a confession of faith ("I believe").

> As they went along the road they came to some water; and the eunuch said, "Look! Water! What prevents me from being baptized?" [And Philip said, "If you believe with all your heart, you may." And he answered and said, "I believe that Jesus Christ is the Son of God."] And he ordered the chariot to stop; and they both went down into the water, Philip as well as the eunuch, and he baptized him.[122]

---

121. Rom 3:22.
Even the righteousness of God which is *by faith of Jesus Christ* unto all and upon all them that believe: for there is no difference (KJV).
We here give preference to the King James Version which more accurately expresses the subjective genitive, "of Jesus Christ."

122. Acts 8:36–37. Many have argued that Philip's statement in verse 37 indicates that the Ethiopian had faith (*pistis*) prior to his baptism. A note of caution needs to be observed about this verse. Brackets around verse 37 indicate that this verse is not found in the earliest manuscripts. There has been considerable doubt attached to it, including whether it should be included in Luke's original account and, if so, which of the variant texts that have been inserted throughout Church history should be used in this verse. Verse 37 is included in the KJV and the NKJV. It is also included in the NASU, Youngs, and the AV with brackets around it to indicate its questionable inclusion. The NIV, ESV, and RSV do not include verse 37. None of the major Greek texts, except the Textus Receptus, include verse 37. It was known by some of the early church fathers. In his New Testament commentary on "The Acts of the Apostles" in *The Expositor's Greek Testament* (II:226), R. J. Knowles included verse 37 in the text but made no comment on the verse in the body of his commentary section. He did, however, discuss the genuineness of the verse in a critical footnote in which he noted

There are several other New Testament passages that suggest the probability that a baptismal confession was practiced in the first century church.

> that if you *confess with your mouth* Jesus as Lord, and believe in your heart that God raised him from the dead, you will be saved; for with the heart a person believes, resulting in righteousness, and *with the mouth he confesses*, resulting in salvation.[123]
>
> Fight the good fight of faith; take hold of the eternal life to which you were called, and you made the good *confession in the presence of many witnesses.*[124]
>
> Because of the proof given by this ministry, they will glorify God for *your obedience to your confession* of the gospel of Christ and for the liberality of your contribution to them and to all,[125]
>
> Therefore, since we have a great high priest who has passed through the heavens, Jesus the Son of God, *let us hold fast our confession.*
>
> *Let us hold fast the confession* of our hope without wavering, for he who promised is faithful.[126]

Not only did the baptizand speak their confession at baptism, but confession was also an ongoing practice in their lives.

> Therefore everyone who confesses [*homologomen*: continuous present tense action verb[127]] me before men, I will also confess (continuous present tense) him before my Father who is in heaven."[128]

---

that the *Textus Receptus* included verse 37, and in numerous Patristic quotations there were "various variations" to the wording of the text. He suggested that this verse may have been an early marginal note and was subsequently moved into the text. In *The New International Commentary on the New Testament*, "The Book of Acts," 185, F. F. Bruce did not include verse 37 in the biblical text but added a footnote about it. He wrote, "The grammatical construction of the Ethiopian's confession . . . is un-Lukan." As can be seen by the evidence above, it would be risky to rest a theological viewpoint based on this verse.

123. Rom 10:9–10.
124. 1 Tim 6:12.
125. 2 Cor 9:13.
126. Heb 4:14; 10:23.
127. Present tense, indicating ongoing action in the present time.
128. Matt 10:32.

> Through him then, let us *continually* offer up a sacrifice of praise to God, that is, the fruit of lips that give thanks to [*homologounton*: present tense participle verb, "confessing"] his name.[129]

> If we confess [*homologomen*: present continuous action] our sins, he is faithful and righteous to forgive us our sins and to cleanse us from all unrighteousness.[130]

> ² By this you know the Spirit of God: every spirit that confesses (*ho homologei*: present tense, "who confesses") that Jesus Christ has come in the flesh is from God; ³ and every spirit that does not confess (*ho mei homologei*: present tense) Jesus is not from God; this is the spirit of the antichrist . . . even now many antichrists have come[131]

> Whoever confesses [*homologeisei*: aorist subjunctive, "might confess"] that Jesus is the Son of God, God abides in him, and he in God.[132]

The verb *homologeo* occurs twenty-two times in the New Testament; the noun *homologia* occurs six times. A survey of these passages shows that there are two basic professions included in Christian confession: 1). a declaration that Jesus is the Son of God who came in the flesh, died on the Cross, and was raised from the dead by God, in whom is our hope; and 2). an acknowledgment of sin. The word *homologia* is a compound word: *homoios* (or *homos*) and *logos* (or *logia*). The Greek word *homoios*, which signifies sameness, refers to that which is of like nature. In *homoios*, things that are distinct and separate are brought together into oneness. An example of *homoios* can be seen when milk naturally separates into cream and whey. It is then blended together into the one inseparable homogenized liquid we find in our grocery stores. The second half of *homologeo* comes from *logos*, or *logia* ("a word"). It means a statement that expresses a discourse on a theme. When *homos* and *logia* are brought together to form *homologia*, we might say that "confession" is to speak words that blend lives together. At baptism and subsequently throughout the Christian life, confession is speaking words that blend deity and

---

129. Heb 13:15.
130. 1 John 1:9.
131. 1 John 4:2–3.
132. 1 John 4:15.

humanity into one, and, likewise, when Christians "confess your sins to one another"[133] it builds unity within the Body of Christ.

Confession can also be seen in other interpersonal actions. At weddings, for example, in the vows a confession is made, through which two separate lives are brought together into one life. Not only the vows but the marriage ceremony itself is the public and visible declaration of that confession. In like manner, the baptismal event is both a verbal and physical confession of the baptizand's faith that blends the human will into the divine will—a homogenization.

Is Baptism a Sacrament?

Some have objected to the use of the word "sacrament" (from the Latin *sacramentum*) on the basis that it, like the word "trinity," is not found in the Scriptures. However, the English word "sacrament," like "trinity," is a word that, *when properly used*, does describe a principle that is taught in the Bible. Some of the uneasiness about the term "sacrament" stems from its connection with the mystical powers of the priesthood (sacerdotalism) that suggests the conveyance of spiritual graces by the sacrament regardless of the recipient's faith. The word "sacrament" loses its biblical grounding when the physical elements acquire the power of grace in themselves rather than in God. That God's gracious blessings are made available within the context of a physical event, does not diminish the potency of the blessings so long as they are accompanied by faith. The misuse of the word "sacrament" was a significant reason for the movement in many churches to reject it and move toward the use of the word "ordinance"[134] instead.

While the word "sacrament" as a noun does not occur in the New Testament, it does occur in the New Testament twice as the adjective *hieros* (sacred, holy), thirty-two times as the noun *hiereus* (sacred or holy one, priest), and seventy-one times as the noun *hieron* (sacred or holy place, temple). The root *sacr* can be seen in each of these definitions as in the noun, *sacr*ament.

> Do you not know that those who perform sacred [*hieros*: holy, sacramental] services eat the food of the temple [*hieron*: sacred

---

133. Jas 5:16.
134. Fowler, *More Than a Symbol*, 105–7.

place], and those who attend regularly to the altar have their share from the altar?[135]

The adjective (*hieros*) is also used by Paul to refer to the Scriptures. In his correspondence with Timothy, he wrote,

> and that from childhood you have known the sacred (*hiera*) writings which are able to give you the wisdom that leads to salvation through faith which is in Christ Jesus.[136]

The word "sacred" (*hieros*) is synonymous with the word "holy" (*hagios*). In Chapter 4, we saw that "holy" (*hagios*) was defined as "pure, clean, washed." This synonymous relationship between *hieros* and *hagios* can be seen by comparing Paul's words to Timothy in the above verse concerning the "sacred Writings" and Paul's statement in Rom 7:12.

> So then, the Law is holy (*hagios*), and the commandment is holy (*hagios*) and righteous and good.[137]

As the "Writings" and the "Law" are synonymous, so "sacred" (*hiera*) and "holy" (*hagios*) mean the same thing.

To apply the word "sacrament" to baptism in no way attributes any cleansing power to the water in baptism. If by sacrament it is meant that the water itself in baptism is so blessed that it mystically cleanses the soul of the baptizand of their sins, and if there is no regard for their faith, then the power of the baptismal event is no different than the pagan's reverence for the waters of their streams, rivers, and lakes that we looked at in chapter 2. Salvation in baptism is not some mystical power injected into the water itself. Only God can forgive sin, so how can any water ("blessed" by a church official or not) cleanse the soul? It is quite possible for a person to be immersed in water without becoming holy.

Those who are displeased with the association of the word "sacrament" with the spiritual cleansing in baptism prefer to call baptism an "ordinance." In this move away from "sacrament," the emphasis on mere obedience is an action that is done simply because it is commanded in the New Testament without regard for its spiritual aspects. Baptism is,

---

135. 1 Cor 9:13.

136. 2 Tim 3:15. *Hiera grammata* [*hiera*—accusative, neuter of *hieros* (adjective): "holy," sacred." *Grammata*—"writings," "scriptures"] is translated as "Holy Scriptures" in the NIV, KJV, and NKJV, as "Holy Writings" in the New English Translation and Young's Literal Translation, and as "Sacred Writings" in NASU, ESV, RSV, and ASV.

137. Rom 7:12.

indeed, an ordinance in that it is a biblical command (e.g., Matt 28:19; Acts 2:38). However, to make baptism merely an act of obedience to law without recognizing its sacramental potency strips it of its grace. The sacramental efficacy of baptism is not something accomplished merely as a work of obedience by the baptizand. As mere obedience, baptism would become a salvation by works of Law. Rather, baptism is the work of divine grace that is bestowed *upon* the baptizand *in* baptism. In many cases, the words "ordinance" and "obedience" have been misconstrued as to make baptism a human accomplishment rather than a divine accomplishment. Perhaps the reason many people shun the word "sacrament" is because it has been misused by some among both the Catholic and Protestant traditions. This happens when too much emphasis is attributed to the water of baptism as the cleansing agent or when the act of baptism is regarded as a meritorious work by the baptizand rather than a spiritual transformation wrought by God.

Baptism as a sacrament is a work of God, not of the church or any ecclesiastical pronouncement. This is not meant to say that the church does not have an important role in the baptismal event. It is within the *context* of the church that the teaching of the Gospel takes place, leading to baptism. Membership in the church, the Family of God, is one of the many blessings bestowed upon the baptizand; it is not a privilege given by the church. All Christians are saints and there is no higher office in the church than sainthood! Sainthood is not a blessing or privilege bestowed upon a few; nor is it conferred by the church. Rather, in the waters of conversion, God himself bestows upon the baptizand sainthood and membership in his Kingdom.

Rejecting the sacramental nature of baptism because it involves a physical submersion in water, or because some have abused it, has led many to view baptism as merely a "symbolic" or "spiritual" act with no salvific quality. As a mere symbol, it becomes simply obedience to an ordinance, a confirmation or declaration of a presumed conversion that was already accomplished previous to baptism. As we have already noted above, when the purpose of baptism is stripped of its sacramental nature, it becomes a meaningless ritual, a mere act of obedience with no Scriptural support. With the British Baptist professor, Stanley Fowler, we conclude that:

> For the purpose of this thesis, to say that baptism is "sacramental" is to say that it mediates the experience of salvific union with Christ, i.e., that one submits to baptism as a penitent sinner

in order to experience the forgiveness of sins and the gift of the Holy Spirit, rather than as a confirmed disciple in order to bear witness to a past experience of union with Christ.[138]

Baptism as Both a Physical and a Spiritual Event

Baptism is both a physical and a spiritual event. In the conversion stories of Acts, the converts were baptized *in water*. Somewhere in his teaching, Philip must have convinced the Ethiopian eunuch of the importance of being baptized in water, for when they came to a body of water, the Ethiopian said, "Look! water! What prevents me from being baptized."[139]

> And he ordered the chariot to stop; and they both went down *into the water*, Philip as well as the eunuch, and he baptized him. When they came up *out of the water*, the Spirit of the Lord snatched Philip away; and the eunuch no longer saw him, but went on his way rejoicing.[140]

Water is also specifically mentioned in connection with baptism by Peter at the conversion of Cornelius and his household.

> "Surely no one can refuse the *water* for these to be baptized who have received the Holy Spirit just as we did, can he?" And he ordered them to be baptized in the name of Jesus Christ. Then they asked him to stay on for a few days.[141]

Baptism is not merely getting wet in water; it is also pregnant with spiritual significance. In baptism, all the blessings in Christ Jesus are bestowed upon the baptizand. In passages such as Rom 6:1–11, union with Christ and forgiveness of sins are undeniably wrapped up in the meaning of baptism. The many spiritual symbolisms associated with the physical act of water baptism are strong evidence that they are a picture of what really happens in baptism. While the water itself has no power for the cleansing from sin, water is the symbolic environment in which God chooses to bestow his holiness.

It is no accident that various spiritual symbolisms in the New Testament are brought into play in connection with physical events such as

138. Fowler, *More Than a Symbol*, 6.
139. Acts 8:36.
140. Acts 8:38–39.
141. Acts 10:47–48.

baptism. Water has always been a cleansing agent in a physical sense and is an ideal representative element to reflect spiritual cleansing. Immersion into the water and coming up out of the water carries strong symbolisms of death, burial, and resurrection, which Paul said brings a person into an intimate relationship with the death, burial, and resurrection of Jesus.[142] As an event in which a baptizand does not immerse himself into the water, the symbolism of being lowered into the water by another person emphasizes the passiveness of submission.

There are numerous examples in the Bible where spiritual things are associated with physical things. In Genesis 1 the Creation itself is both a physical and a spiritual event. The sublime example is the life, burial, and resurrection of Jesus. John expressed this in his concise words, "the Word became flesh" (John 1:14). In this phrase the very spiritual "Word" (*Logos*) became united with the very physical "flesh" (*sarx*). Another example of a physical event with strong spiritual meaning is the eucharist whose elements bring the partakers into close union with the death, burial, and resurrection of Jesus. If these, and other events in the Bible, can be recognized as the conjoining of the physical with spiritual meaning, why should the practice of baptism be alienated from the forgiveness of sins?

Necessity of Baptism in John 3:3, 5; Mark 16:16; and 1 Peter 3:21

We dealt with John 3:3, 5 in Chapter 6, at which time the question was raised whether this was a legitimate passage to consider in our quest to determine the purpose of baptism. Jesus made it clear to Nicodemus that without the "birth from above" (baptism) there is no entrance into the Kingdom of Heaven. Also in Chapter 6, we examined Mark 16:16, raising the question whether these last few verses of Mark's Gospel belonged as part of the canon of Scripture. Whether penned by Mark himself or added in subsequent years, it was accepted in the earliest years of the church; and, in his preservation of the text of his word, God did not see fit to give any indication that these verses should be considered illegitimate. In verse 16 Jesus clearly pointed out that the "saved" are those who believed and have been baptized." In Chapter 8 concerning 1 Peter 3:21, we noted that it is clear that these are the genuine words of Peter and the canonicity of the text is on solid ground. This statement by Peter is the

---

142. Rom 6:3–11; Col 2:12–14.

clearest passage affirming baptism as necessary for salvation. The phrase "baptism now saves you" (*nun sodzei baptisma*) leaves no doubt that baptism cannot be separated from salvation. As "an appeal to God for a good conscience" the intimacy between the baptismal event and sanctification cannot be violated.

Are we, therefore, to conclude from these words that *only* those who have been baptized through faith for the forgiveness of sins have the assurance of eternal life? Such questions put the responders in a difficult situation. If they answer in the negative, then the responders stand in danger of contradicting the words of Jesus and his apostles. If the answer is affirmative, then the responder stands in danger of being accused of judging people's eternal destiny.

Because distortions concerning the purpose of baptism are so prevalent among many churches, the necessity of baptism is not an easy topic for loving Christians to deal with. It is hard to draw a line with doctrines such as baptism and make them determining factors of fellowship. Can we be lenient in this matter? Can we make baptism optional? Can a person who has not been baptized but lived an otherwise "spiritual" and "biblical" life be blessed with a heavenly destination? The ramifications of such questions are so numerous and monumental that it becomes an impossible task for any mortal man to give a definitive and responsible response that takes into consideration all circumstances.

We are blessed by God in that we do not have to adjudicate whether anyone is acceptable to God and whether they have eternal life. *There is only one thing God has said that we are responsible to do: preach the word!* God will judge whether we have been his faithful message bearers. If his word falls on receptive ears, it is the hearer's response to God, not to us. If the word falls on unreceptive ears, they must answer to God, not to us. If, because of our slothfulness, they never hear the Gospel message—including the biblical teachings about baptism—the harshness of judgment against us is something that should cause us to tremble. God's words to Ezekiel give us cause to tremble at the responsibility of the Great Commission.

> Son of man, I have appointed you a watchman to the house of Israel; whenever you hear a word from my mouth, warn them from me. When I say to the wicked, "You will surely die," and you do not warn him or speak out to warn the wicked from his wicked way that he may live, that wicked man shall die in his iniquity, but his blood I will require at your hand. Yet if you have

warned the wicked and he does not turn from his wickedness or from his wicked way, he shall die in his iniquity; but you have delivered yourself.[143]

In light of our study in the foregoing chapters, we know that the biblical teaching about conversion into Christ is through faith in baptism. *There is no alternative to baptism as a conversion event mentioned in the Bible.* We also know that "to one who knows the right thing to do and does not do it, to him it is sin."[144] John the Baptist commanded his disciples to be baptized into forgiveness and into repentance. Baptism was practiced in Jesus' ministry, and he commanded his disciples to baptize *the nations* into the Father, the Son, and the Holy Spirit. On the day of Pentecost, Peter commanded his contrite audience to be baptized in the name of Christ into the forgiveness of their sins. In the churches, led by the Holy Spirit through the apostles, all who believed were baptized into Christ. To refuse baptism or to relegate baptism to some meaningless event after conversion is to neglect and distort the abundance of evidence in the New Testament concerning the meaning and purpose of baptism. *Real things of eternal value happen in baptism!*

Because we live as humans in a community wherein there are many different views concerning the purpose, practice, and proper subjects of baptism, we are faced with the question of what our attitude should be toward those who believe that baptism is not a necessary practice, or who believe that the practice of baptism is a post-conversion event that is separate from and subsequent to becoming a Christian. A primary thing we need to keep in mind is that every person is God's creation. God loves every one of them, even the most reprobate. As Christians, we ought to love every one of them also and give them the respect that is due to those created by God. We are responsible to teach them; God will be their judge. This is why Paul said,

> If possible, so far as it depends on you, be at peace with all men.[145]

Paul did not simply say, "Be at peace with all men," he prefaced it with, "*If possible, so far as it depends on you*, be at peace with all men." For our part, we ought not to let our speech, attitude, or behavior be a cause for

---

143. Ezek 3:17–19.
144. Jas 4:17.
145. Rom 12:18.

alienating others from God. There will be cases of alienation that we cannot prevent. If it is due to the other person, then we are innocent of the broken relationship between them and God. If they turn their back on God and refuse to listen to his word, it is God they are rejecting.

In his commentary on Rom 6:3, James Denny's words from 1900 serve us today as a good summary of the importance and necessity of baptism.

> When, it may be asked, did this all-important death [of the old self] take place? The answer is: It is involved in baptism.[146]

Two years later, in his classic volume, *The Death of Christ*, he wrote,

> The New Testament, it may be pointed out, nowhere gives us the idea of an unbaptized Christian, for by one Spirit we were all baptized into one body (1 Cor. xii. 13). Similarly, Paul, in regulating the observance of the Supper at Corinth, regulates it as part of the Christian tradition which goes back for its authority through the primitive church to Christ himself. "I received of the Lord that which also I delivered to you" (1 Cor xi. 23). In other words, *there was no such thing known to Paul as a Christian society without baptism as its rite of initiation, and the Supper as its rite of communion*. And if there was no such thing known to Paul, there was no such thing in the world. (italics added)[147]

Mode of Baptism

It is beyond the purpose of this study to delve into the various modern modes of baptism being practiced by the plethora of churches, except to note how the mode of baptism has an impact on its purpose. In the New Testament, the normal practice for baptizing was by the immersion of adults in water who have been taught and accepted the basics of the Gospel message. There is no reference to any baptism by sprinkling or pouring of water on the baptizand in the New Testament. Nor is there any instruction about any baptism (with or without water) being merely a symbolic, figurative, or optional event. Once a person has been baptized

---

146. Denney, "St. Paul's Epistle to the Romans," 632. James Denny, D.D. (1856–1917) was a Scottish theologian, professor, and preacher.

147. Denney, *The Death of Christ*, 51–52. First published in 1902, this classic has gone through numerous printings.

for the forgiveness of sins, there is no New Testament witness to support the need to be baptized again.

The earliest known alternative to immersion in water is found in the *The Didache*[148] (its longer title: *The Teaching of the Lord Through the Twelve Apostles to the Nations*). It is a document written, probably around 100 AD, by an unknown author.[149] It contains some of the earliest known references to baptism outside the New Testament and gives some insight into both the mode and purpose of baptism as practiced in the early post-apostolic church. The longest quote is found in chapter 7.

> And concerning baptism, baptize this way: Having first said all these things, baptize into the name of the Father, and of the Son, and of the Holy Spirit in living water. But if you have not living water, baptize into other water; and if you cannot in cold, in warm. But if you have not either, pour out water thrice upon the head into the name of Father and Son and Holy Spirit. But before the baptism let the baptizer fast, and the baptized, and whatever others can; but you shall order the baptized to fast one or two days before.[150]

While the *Didache* is an extra-canonical document, it does recognize that, at the turn of the first century, baptism was understood as incorporation into (*eis*) the name of the Trinity (*baptisate eis to onoma eis to onoma tou patros kai tou huios kai tou hagiou pneumatos*). We can see here a reflection of the words of Jesus in Matt 28:19.

The *Didache* deviates from the New Testament by advocating pouring water over the baptizand *only in cases where there is not sufficient water for submersion*. It also goes beyond the New Testament by distinguishing between baptism in living (running) and non-living water and between cold and warm water. Everett Ferguson suggests that there was a common practice of triple pouring, which " . . . was probably an effort to simulate running water . . . the whole body was to come into contact with the water."[151]

---

148. From the Greek, *didakei*: teaching, instruction, doctrine.

149. Some textual authorities place its origin earlier than the turn of the century while others date it later.

150. *Didache*, "Concerning Baptism," 7:1–4.

151. Ferguson, *Baptism*, 205.

Another reference to baptism in the Didache is found in chapter 9, which is concerned with instructions about the eucharist (*eucharistia*: "thanksgiving").[152]

> Now concerning the Thanksgiving . . . But let no one eat or drink of your Thanksgiving, but they who have been baptized into [*eis*] the name of the Lord; for concerning this also the Lord hath said, "Give not that which is holy to the dogs."[153]

In this passage, baptism is considered a necessary prerequisite in order to partake of the Eucharist.

Baptism by immersion in water was the common practice in the early church, and although alternative practices were cropping up as early as the second century, immersion was still the preferred method of baptism. With any other mode of baptism, other than by immersion, the symbolic significance of death, burial, and resurrection is lost.

Baptistries in the Early Years of Church history

In his monumental book, *Baptism in the Early Church*, Everett Ferguson devoted thirty-three pages to a thorough description of early baptistries. They were built in a variety of shapes and sizes, whose symbolism was described by Dr. Ferguson.

> The literary sources give two principal symbolisms for the baptismal font—the tomb of death and resurrection, and the womb of new birth. The former symbolism was reinforced by variations on a cross shape, which became fairly common in the fifth and sixth centuries[154]

Most baptistries were built inside the church's assembly hall. Others were located elsewhere, including some in a room or building specifically designed for baptismal activity. It is interesting to note the variety of shapes of these baptistries.

> About thirty percent of the baptismal *piscinae*[155] are round, sixteen percent are cross-shaped, fourteen percent are rectangular,

---

152. Also commonly called "Lord's Supper," "Communion," "Eucharist," etc.
153. *Didache*, "The Thanksgiving (Eucharist)," 9.1, 5.
154. Ferguson, *Baptism*, 819.
155. *Piscine*: 1. Pertaining to fish. 2. It is also a French noun meaning "swimming pool." 3. The Latin word *piscina* (or *sacrarium*) denotes a shallow basin placed near the

eleven percent are octagonal, nine percent are square and five percent hexagonal.[156]

Besides a variety of shapes, the baptistries were also of various sizes.

> The predominant number of baptismal fonts permitted immersion, and many were so large as to defy any reason for their existence other than for immersion.[157]

In early descriptions of the various designs of baptistries, their constructions "uniformly describe an immersion or imply it as the norm."[158] The earlier baptistries tended to be larger and later ones demonstrated a decrease in size, probably due to the increasing tendency in later years to practice pouring and sprinkling as a substitute for immersion. With the onset of infant baptism, even smaller baptismal fonts were used.

After the first century, numerous other customs, symbols, and traditions came to be associated with baptism. Lengthy catechetical training before baptism, triple immersions, nudeness, limiting the baptismal officiant to church officers, etc., were all post-apostolic practices that were introduced after the first century and became common traditions in many of the churches.

The Timing of Salvation

The purpose and the timing of salvation are very much dependent on their relationship to other doctrines. As has been noted in the previous chapters, repentance, faith, sanctification, justification, etc., are demonstrated by the writers of the New Testament to be chronologically synonymous with salvation-baptism. As we have said before, any attempt to chronologically separate baptism as a post-conversion practice from these vital doctrines leaves baptism a hollow and empty shell of a ritual.

Because faith is a conscious commitment based on biblical teaching, and since faith is a necessary part of the baptismal event, it follows that a person must be old enough to understand these basic doctrines before they are baptized. The "age of accountability" has been a subject of much

---

altar of a church.

156. Ferguson, *Baptism*, 820–21.
157. Ferguson, *Baptism*, 849.
158. Ferguson, *Baptism*, 850.

discussion all down through church history. Nowhere in the New Testament is there an age of accountability assigned to baptism.

Since baptism is a person's initiation into a relationship with God and his salvation, there should be as little time as possible between the recognition for the need to be baptized and the baptismal event. While basic Gospel instruction must precede baptism, lengthy catechetical training beyond the necessary teachings concerning conversion risks endangering a person's eternal salvation. Once a convert has come to the awareness of the need to submit to God in baptism, it behooves them not to linger in being baptized. Examples of conversions such as the three thousand on the day of Pentecost (Acts 2:41), the Ethiopian eunuch (Acts 8:26–38), Paul (Acts 9:18; 22:16), Cornelius and his household (Acts 10:1–48), the jailer at Philippi and his household (Acts 16:22–34), and the men Paul baptized at Ephesus (Acts 19:1–7) were all baptized immediately upon being taught the Gospel.

Post-Baptismal Growth

Christian faith is a growing process. In the New Testament, baptism is depicted as the initiatory rite in which the baptizand is inducted into fellowship with Deity and the Church. Having been "born from above"[159] in baptism, "we are to grow up in all aspects into him who is the head, even Christ."[160] A Christian who ceases to grow becomes stagnant, and their faith perishes. Just as we know a tree is alive because it goes through its annual cycle of blooming, growth, and dormancy, so we know a Christian's faith is alive and growing if it demonstrates spiritual life cycles. If a tree is not going through its growth cycles, we can see and declare it dead. In like manner, a Christian life that is not growing in the fruits of the Spirit is dead. The difference is that once a tree dies there is no hope for revival, but a Christian life always has the potential for revitalization by the power of the Holy Spirit and the teaching/preaching of the word.

Final Thoughts

George Raymond Beasley-Murray (1916–2000) was a British theologian, professor, and preacher whose ministry of the word, both written and

159. John 3:3, 7.
160. Eph 4:15.

oral, marked a major shift in the understanding of the purpose of baptism in England. In 1955 he was part of a consortium of church leaders who came together to study anew the meaning and purpose of baptism. The result of their endeavor was published in 1959 and they chose him to be one of their contributing authors of *Christian Baptism: A Fresh attempt to Understand the Rite in terms of Scripture, History, and Theology* (edited by Alec Gilmore).[161] The book proved to be a landmark turning point for many British Baptist Churches in the restoration of baptism as the sanctifying event in a person's life. From 1954 to 1999, his pen produced numerous volumes, including insightful commentaries and doctrinal discourses. Perhaps his most influential book was his thorough examination of the purpose of baptism as a sacramental event in *Baptism in the New Testament*. His final paragraph in that book makes a fitting conclusion to this project.

> All of us in all the Churches need to consider afresh our ways before God, with the Bible open before us and a prayer for the guidance of the Holy Spirit and a preparedness to listen to what the Spirit is saying to all the Churches.[162]

---

161. Fowler, *More Than a Symbol*, 113.
162. Beasley-Murray, *Baptism*, 395.

Appendix

Baptismal Quotes in Church History

When quoting someone there is always the danger of taking the author's quotes out of context. In spite of the risk, we try to keep the author's whole thesis in mind as we present the following comments. The following quotations about baptism do not necessarily reflect everything the author of the quote had to say about baptism. The inclusion of an author in this list does not imply that we, the authors of this book, concur with all their views, or even those expressed in their quotation. This is not a comprehensive list of quotes about baptism, but it is provided to give the reader an idea of prevailing views expressed concerning the purpose of baptism at various times in church history.

Some of the dates, especially during the early years of church history, are approximate. In many cases, scholars have debated over when they were written. This list gives a generally agreed-upon date so that the reader may have an approximate idea of the time of their origin. It is difficult to properly document some of the earlier writer's bibliographical information, but enough should be given to lead the reader to the source.

All dates for these writings are AD ("Anno Domini"). The Latin expression "Anno Domini" translates to "Year of Our Lord," and is equivalent to CE ("Common Era"). To make it easier to find specific writings, the chart below lists all the authors or titles in the order of their date.

WRITING	DATE
Epistle of Barnabas	100
Epistles of Ignatius	100
Justin Martyr	147

Shepherd of Hermas	140s
Irenaeus	180
Clement of Alexandria	198
Tertullian	200
Origen of Alexandria	238
Cyprian of Carthage	246
Cyril of Jerusalem	350
Athanasius of Alexandria	356
Basil the Great	375
Apostolic Constitutions	375
Gregory of Nazianzus	381
John Chrysostom	389
Ambrose of Milan	387
Augustine of Hippo	397
Thomas Aquinas	1485
Desiderius Erasmus	1503
Martin Luther	1520
John Calvin	1536
Menno Simmons	1540
Benjamin Keach	1689
John Wesley	1756
Alexander Campbell	1839
Henry Alford	1862
Moses E. Lard	1863
William Sandy and Arthur Headlum	1895
James Denny	1900
A. T. Robertson	1927
Otto Procksch	1933
Karl Barth	1933
Kenneth S. Weust	1935
Dietrich Bonhoeffer	1937
Henry C. Thiessen	1949
T. F. Torrance	1953
William Barclay	1958
Gleason L. Archer	1959
Emil Brunner	1959

George R. Beasley-Murray	1962
F. F. Bruce	1963, 1969
D. Martyn Lloyd-Jones	1972
Robert H Stein	2006
Thomas R. Schreiner	2006
Everett Ferguson	2009
David Platt	2009
Wally Morris	2017

Didache

100

This brief treatise was written by an unknown pseudonymous author. It is also known as The Teaching Through the Twelve Apostles to the Nations. *Some have placed its date before the turn of the century.*

"Concerning Baptism"

And concerning baptism, thus baptize ye: Having first said all these things, baptize into the name of the Father, and of the Son, and of the Holy Spirit, in living water. 2. But if thou have not living water, baptize into other water; and if thou canst not in cold, in warm. 3. But if thou have not either, pour out water thrice upon the head into the name of Father and Son and Holy Spirit. 4. But before the baptism let the baptizer fast, and the baptized, and whatever others can; but thou shalt order the baptized to fast one or two days before.[1]

"The Thanksgiving (Eucharist)"

But let no one eat or drink of your Thanksgiving (Eucharist), but they who have been baptized into the name of the Lord; for concerning this also the Lord hath said, "Give not that which is holy to the dogs."[2]

---

1. *Didache*, 7.1–4.
2. *Didache*, 9.5.

Epistle of Barnabas

The exact date this epistle was written is unknown—between 70 and 132. Some early Church Fathers attributed this epistle to Paul's companion, Barnabas; however, it is now well established it was an unknown author of perhaps the same name or one who used the name of Barnabas, the companion of Paul in Acts, to lend authority to the work.

"Baptism and the Cross Prefigured in the Old Testament"

100

> Perceive how he defines the water and the cross together. For he says this: "Blessed" (Ps.1.1) are those who with hope in the cross went down into the water. 11. He means this: that we go down into the water full of sins and uncleanness, and we come up bearing as fruit in our heart reverence and having hope in Jesus in our spirit. And "whoever eats from these (trees by the water) will live forever" (Ezek. 3.19; Gen 3.22) means this: Whoever, he says, hears these when they speak and believes will live forever.[3]

Ignatius, Bishop of Antioch

Ignatius Theophorus was a bishop at Antioch at the turn of the 1st century. During a period of persecution in Antioch, Ignatius was arrested. He was being transported by Roman soldiers to Rome when he wrote ahead to congregations along the route (Ephesus, Magnesia, Tralles, Rome, Philadelphia, and Smyrna) appealing to them not to interfere with his road to martyrdom. He considered his martyrdom to be a witness to the victory of Christ. We know nothing for sure about him except what is revealed in his letters.

---

3. Ferguson, *Baptism*, 211.

Epistles of Ignatius

100

"The Epistle of Ignatius to the Trallians"

Be ye subject to the bishop as to the Lord, for he watches for your souls, as one that shall give account to God. Wherefore also, ye appear to me to live not after the manner of men, but according to Jesus Christ, who died for us, in order that, by believing in His death, ye may by baptism be made partakers of His resurrection. It is therefore necessary, whatsoever things ye do, to do nothing without the bishop.[4]

"The Epistle of Ignatius to the Smyrnaeans"

It is not lawful without the bishop either to baptize or to celebrate a love-feast; but whatsoever he shall approve of, that is also pleasing to God, so that everything that is done may be secure and valid.[5]

Justin Martyr

Justin Martyr was born in 100 and died as a Christian martyr. Before becoming a Christian, he studied the philosophies of numerous schools of thought of his day. His search for truth was a quest for the understanding of divine things. One day while walking in a remote place he encountered an old man with whom he began discussing philosophy. The old man introduced him to the Old Testament prophets and the apostles of Jesus. As a result of his investigation into their writings, he found what he was looking for and wrote down his encounter with the old man in Dialogue of Justin with Trypho, a Jew. *He was arrested on the charge of refusing to sacrifice to the pagan gods. He, along with six of his students during the term of the Prefect Junius Rusticus (162–68), were condemned to death in the year 165. Along with the Apostle John, he stands tall as one of the earliest Christian philosophers.*

---

4. Ignatius, *Epistles*, 2.8-9.
5. Ignatius, *Epistles*, 8.1.

Dialogue of Justin with Trypho, a Jew

Circa 147–61

By reason, therefore, of this laver of repentance and knowledge of God, which has been ordained on account of the transgression of God's people, as Isaiah cries, we have believed, and testify that that very baptism which he announced is alone able to purify those who repent; and this is the water of life. But the cisterns which you have dug for yourselves are broken and profitless to you. For what is the use of that baptism which cleanses the flesh and body alone? ... And we, who have approached God through Him, have received not carnal, but spiritual circumcision, which Enoch and those like him observed. And we have received it through baptism, since we were sinners, by God's mercy; and all men may equally obtain it.[6]

First Apology

150

I will also relate the manner in which we dedicated ourselves to God when we had been made new through Christ; lest, if we omit this, we seem to be unfair in the explanation we are making. As many as are persuaded and believe that what we teach and say is true, and undertake to be able to live accordingly, are instructed to pray and to entreat God with fasting, for the remission of their sins that are past, we praying and fasting with them. Then they are brought by us where there is water, and are regenerated in the same manner in which we were ourselves regenerated. For, in the name of God, the Father and Lord of the universe, and of our Saviour Jesus Christ, and of the Holy Spirit, they then receive the washing with water. For Christ also said, "Except ye be born again, ye shall not enter into the kingdom of heaven."

And for this [baptismal rite] we have learned from the apostles this reason. Since at our birth we were born without our own knowledge or choice, by our parents coming together, and were brought up in bad habits and wicked training; in order that we may not remain the children of necessity and of ignorance, but may become the children of choice and knowledge, and may

---

6. Justin Martyr, *Dialogue*, chap. 1.

obtain in the water the remission of sins formerly committed, there is pronounced over him who chooses to be born again, and has repented of his sins, the name of God the Father and Lord of the universe; he who leads to the laver the person that is to be washed calling him by this name alone.[7]

Shepherd of Hermas

The treatise, Shepherd of Hermas, *was written by Hermas whose brother was Pius, bishop of Rome (139–54). It was probably written in the 140s, though an earlier date has been claimed by some. It is an allegory that calls the faithful to repent of their sins.*

Mandates

140s

"I have heard, Sir, from some teachers that there is no other repentance except that one when we descended into the water and received the forgiveness of our former sins." He said to me, "You heard correctly, for it is so. He who has received forgiveness of sins ought to sin no more but to live in purity."[8]

Visions

140s

"Do you wish to know who are the other stones which fall near the waters and are not able to be rolled into the water? These are those who heard the word and wanted to be baptized into the name of the Lord [*baptistheinai eis to onoma tou kuriou*], but when they remember the purity of the truth they change their minds and return again to their evil desires."[9]

---

7. Justin Martyr, *First Apology*, chap. 61.
8. Ferguson, *Early Christians Speak*, 33.
9. Ferguson, *Baptism*, 215.

Irenaeus

Irenaeus (Greek: "peaceful"), of Greek heritage, was born in 130 (approximate) and died in Lyons around the turn of the second and third centuries. He grew up in Smyrna in Asia Minor and had the privilege of the close acquaintance with the Smyrna bishop, Polycarp, who was likely a disciple of the Apostle John. He left Smyrna for Gaul (France) and settled in the remote town of Lugdumum (Lyons). When the local bishop died, the Church turned to Irenaeus to be their bishop. He is noted for his polemic against the Gnostic heresies.

Against Heresies

180

But it is evident from Peter's words that he did indeed still retain the God who was already known to them; but he also bare witness to them that Jesus Christ was the Son of God, the Judge of quick and dead, into whom he did also command them to be baptized for the remission of sins; and not this alone, but he witnessed that Jesus was Himself the Son of God, who also, having been anointed with the Holy Spirit, is called Jesus Christ.[10]

Clement of Alexandria

Titus Flavius Clemens was born in 150 and died in 215. A Christian theologian and philosopher, he taught at the Catechetical School of Alexandria. His pupils included Origen and Alexander of Jerusalem. A convert to Christianity, he was an educated man who was familiar with classical Greek philosophy and literature.

---

10. Irenaus, *Against Heresies*, 3.12.7.

Instructor [Paedagogus, or Tutor]

198

"The Name Children Does Not Imply Instruction in Elementary Principles"

> Being baptized, we are illuminated; illuminated, we become sons; being made sons, we are made perfect; being made perfect, we are made immortal. "I," says He, "have said that ye are gods, and all sons of the Highest." This work is variously called grace, and illumination, and perfection, and washing: washing, by which we cleanse away our sins; grace, by which the penalties accruing to transgressions are remitted; and illumination, by which that holy light of salvation is beheld, that is, by which we see God clearly. Now we call that perfect which wants nothing. For what is yet wanting to him who knows God? . . . Accordingly, they confess that the spirit in repentance retraces its steps. In the same way, therefore, we also, repenting of our sins, renouncing our iniquities, purified by baptism, speed back to the eternal light, children to the Father.[11]

Tertullian

Quintus Septimius Florens Tertullianus was born at Carthage around 160 to heathen parents and died around 220–25. Not much is known of his personal life except a few references in his writings. Eusebius and Jerome claimed that he was a trained lawyer and an ordained priest. He was the first Latin-writing Christian author and the first post-apostolic author to offer a major apologetic for Christianity.

---

11. Bettenson, *Early Christian Fathers,* 49–51, 65.

On Baptism [De Baptismo]
200
"Introduction. Origin of the Treatise"

Happy is our sacrament of water, in that, by washing away the sins of our early blindness, we are set free and admitted into eternal life![12]

"The Primeval Hovering of the Spirit of God Over the Waters Typical of Baptism"

And accordingly, it makes no difference whether a man be washed in a sea or a pool, a stream or a fount, a lake or a trough . . . All waters, therefore, in virtue of the pristine privilege of their origin, do, after invocation of God, attain the sacramental power of sanctification; for the Spirit immediately supervenes from the heavens, and rests over the waters, sanctifying them from Himself; and being thus sanctified, they imbibe at the same time the power of sanctifying. Albeit the similitude may be admitted to be suitable to the simple act; that, since we are defiled by sins, as it were by dirt, we should be washed from those stains in waters.[13]

"Of the Unction"

After this, when we have issued from the font, we are thoroughly anointed with a blessed unction . . . Thus, too, in our case, the unction runs carnally, (i.e., on the body) but profits spiritually; in the same way as the act of baptism itself too is carnal, in that we are plunged in water, but the effect spiritual, in that we are freed from sins.[14]

Origen of Alexandria

Origen Adamantius of Alexandria and later of Caesarea was born in 184 and died in 253 from injuries he suffered in prison. He is credited with writing about 2,000 books. There is no single major discussion of baptism

---

12. Tertullian, *On Baptism*, chap. 1.
13. Tertullian, *On Baptism*, chap. 3.
14. Tertullian, *On Baptism*, chap. 7.

in Origen's works, but his voluminous writings contain abundant references to the subject. Origen could be quite flexible in his biblical interpretations, at one time giving one explanation and another time a different one. He may have been considering in his mind at various times different possible meanings, or given his advocacy of multiple meanings of Scripture, he may have considered all the possibilities as correct (provided, of course, that they contributed to edification and spiritual progress). Be cautious, therefore, about committing too rigidly to any analysis of his comments on baptism.

Homilies on Numbers

238-44

Let every one of the faithful recall the words he used in renouncing the devil when first he came to the waters of Baptism, when he took upon himself the first seals of faith and came to the saving fountain; he proclaimed that he would not deal in the pomps of the devil, nor his works, nor would he submit to his servitude and his pleasures.[15]

Commentary on Romans

No Date

The one who has died to sin and is truly baptized into the death of Christ, and is buried with him through baptism into death (Rom 6:3-4), he is the one who is truly baptized in the Holy Spirit and with the water from above (John 3:5).[16]

Cyprian of Carthage

Thascius Caecilius Cyprianus was born into a rich, pagan, Roman African family in 200 and suffered death by martyrdom on September 14, 258. He was a member of a legal fraternity in Carthage, an orator, a "pleader in the courts," and a teacher of rhetoric. He was Converted from paganism in 245 or 246. He served as the bishop of Carthage during 248-58. He was honored by the poor of Carthage due to the benevolent distribution of his wealth.

---

15. Bettenson, *Early Christian Fathers*, 246. A sermon delivered between 238-244.
16. Ferguson, *Baptism*, 408

APPENDIX

The Epistles of Cyprian

"To Donatus"

246

These were my frequent thoughts. For as I myself was held in bonds by the innumerable errors of my previous life, from which I did not believe that I could possibly be delivered, so I was disposed to acquiesce in my clinging vices; and because I despaired of better things, I used to indulge my sins as if they were actually parts of me, and indigenous to me. But after that, by the help of the water of new birth, the stain of former years had been washed away, and a light from above, serene and pure, had been infused into my reconciled heart, after that, by the agency of the Spirit breathed from heaven, a second birth had restored me to a new man.[17]

"To Fidus On the Baptism of Infants"

No date

But in respect of the case of the infants, which you say ought not to be baptized within the second or third day after their birth, and that the law of ancient circumcision should be regarded, so that you think that one who is just born should not be baptized and sanctified within the eighth day, we all thought very differently in our council. For in this course which you thought was to be taken, no one agreed; but we all rather judge that the mercy and grace of God is not to be refused to any one born of man.[18]

"To Magnus, on Baptizing the Novatians, and Those Who Obtain Grace on a Sick-Bed"

255

You have asked also, dearest son, what I thought of those who obtain God's grace in sickness and weakness, whether they are to be accounted legitimate Christians, for that they are not to be washed, but sprinkled, with the saving water . . . "And thus shalt thou do unto them, to cleanse them: thou shall sprinkle them with the water of purification." And again: "The water of

---

17. Cyprian, *The Epistles of Cyprian*, 1.4.
18. Cyprian, *Epistles of Cyprian*, 58.2.

sprinkling is a purification." Whence it appears that the sprinkling also of water prevails equally with the washing of salvation; and that when this is done in the Church, where the faith both of receiver and giver is sound, all things hold and may be consummated and perfected by the majesty of the Lord and by the truth of faith.[19]

"To Januarius and Other Numidian Bishops, on Baptizing Heretics"

256

When we were together in council, dearest brethren, we read your letter which you wrote to us concerning those who seem to be baptized by heretics and schismatics, (asking) whether, when they come to the Catholic Church, which is one, they ought to be baptized ... we put forward our opinion, not as a new one, but we join with you in equal agreement, in an opinion long since decreed by our predecessors, and observed by us, judging, namely, and holding it for certain that no one can be baptized abroad outside the Church, since there is one baptism appointed in the holy Church.[20]

The Treatises of Cyprian

"On the Dress of Virgins"

248

All indeed who attain to the divine gift and inheritance by the sanctification of baptism, therein put off the old man by the grace of the saving laver, and, renewed by the Holy Spirit from the filth of the old contagion, are purged by a second nativity.[21]

Cyril of Jerusalem

Cyril of Jerusalem was born in 313 and died in 386. In 350, he became Bishop of Jerusalem but was exiled and reinstated several times due to the influence of the Arian bishop Acacius of Caesarea.

19. Cyprian, *Epistles of Cyprian*, 75.12.
20. Cyprian, *The Epistles of Cyprian*, 69.1.
21. Cyprian, *The Treatises of Cyprian*, 2.23

APPENDIX

Catechetical Lectures

350

Great is the Baptism that lies before you: a ransom to captives; a remission of offences; a death of sin; a new-birth of the soul; a garment of light; a holy indissoluble seal; a chariot to heaven; the delight of Paradise; a welcome into the kingdom; the gift of adoption![22]

This is in truth a serious matter, brethren, and you must approach it with good heed. Each one of you is about to be presented to God before tens of thousands of the Angelic Hosts: the Holy Ghost is about to seal your souls: ye are to be enrolled in the army of the Great King. Therefore make you ready, and equip yourselves, by putting on I mean, not bright apparel, but piety of soul with a good conscience. Regard not the Laver as simple water, but rather regard the spiritual grace that is given with the water.[23]

When going down, therefore, into the water, think not of the bare element, but look for salvation by the power of the Holy Ghost: for without both thou canst not possibly be made perfect . . . Neither doth he that is baptized with water, but not found worthy of the Spirit, receive the grace in perfection; nor if a man be virtuous in his deeds, but receive not the seal by water, shall he enter into the kingdom of heaven.[24]

If any man receive not Baptism, he hath not salvation; except only Martyrs, who even without the water receive the kingdom. For when the Saviour, in redeeming the world by His Cross, was pierced in the side, He shed forth blood and water; that men, living in times of peace, might be baptized in water, and, in times of persecution, in their own blood.[25]

Having gone down dead in sins, thou comest up quickened in righteousness. For if thou hast been united with the likeness of the Saviour's death, thou shalt also be deemed worthy of His Resurrection.[26]

---

22. Cyril of Jerusalem, *Catechetical Lectures*, Procatechesis, par. 16.
23. Cyril of Jerusalem, *Catechetical Lectures*, lect. 3, par. 3.
24. Cyril of Jerusalem, *Catechetical Lectures*, lect. 3.
25. Cyril of Jerusalem, *Catechetical Lectures*, lect. 3.
26. Cyril of Jerusalem, *Catechetical Lectures*, lect. 3.

But He came down to clothe the Apostles with power and to baptize them; for the Lord says, ye shall be baptized with the Holy Ghost not many days hence. This grace was not in part, but His power was in full perfection; for as he who plunges into the waters and is baptized is encompassed on all sides by the waters, so were they also baptized completely by the Holy Ghost. The water however flows round the outside only, but the Spirit baptizes also the soul within, and that completely.[27]

Athanasius of Alexandria

Athanasius of Alexandria was born between 296 and 298 and died in 373. His parents were of high rank and wealth. He received an extensive liberal education. He was influential in the defense of the Trinity against the teaching of Arius. Most of his writings are concerned with trinitarian doctrines. Although he had no discourses on baptism, he had high regard for baptism and makes references to it.

Discourses Against the Arians

356–60

For where the Father is, there is the Son, and where the light, there the radiance; and as what the Father worketh, He worketh through the Son, and the Lord Himself says, "What I see the Father do, that do I also;" so also when baptism is given, whom the Father baptizes, him the Son baptizes; and whom the Son baptizes, he is consecrated in the Holy Ghost. And again as when the sun shines, one might say that the radiance illuminates, for the light is one and indivisible, nor can be detached, so where the Father is or is named, there plainly is the Son also; and is the Father named in Baptism? Then must the Son be named with Him.[28]

Basil the Great

Basil was born in 330 and died in 379. He was the bishop of Caesarea in Cappadocia, Asia Minor. Together with his friend, Gregory (329–89) of

---

27. Cyril of Jerusalem, *Catechetical Lectures*, lect. 17.
28. Athanasius, *Four Discourses*, disc. 2, chap. 18.

Nazianzus, also in Cappadocia, and Basil's brother, Gregory (335–95) of Nyssa, also in Cappadocia, they have come to be known as the Cappadocian Fathers. They were the fourth-century theologians who are best known for developing and perfecting the trinitarian theology of St. Athanasius the Great (295–373). Through their theological endeavors, the Orthodox Christian trinitarian theology of the Trinity was established. He was a theologian and intellectual of the first order, but was also a consummate ecclesiastical statesman, organizer, and liturgist.

On the Holy Spirit

375

Whence is it that we are Christians? Through our faith, would be the universal answer. And in what way are we saved? Plainly because we were regenerate through the grace given in our baptism. How else could we be? And after recognizing that this salvation is established through the Father and the Son and the Holy Ghost, shall we fling away "that form of doctrine" which we received?[29]

Let no one be misled by the fact of the apostle's [Paul] frequently omitting the name of the Father and of the Holy Spirit when making mention of baptism, or on this account imagine that the invocation of the names is not observed . . . For the naming of Christ is the confession of the whole, shewing forth as it does the God who gave, the Son who received, and the Spirit who is the anointing . . . Faith and baptism are two kindred and inseparable ways of salvation: faith is perfected through baptism, baptism is established through faith, and both are completed by the same names. For as we believe in the Father and the Son and the Holy Ghost, so are we also baptized in the name of the Father and of the Son and of the Holy Ghost.[30]

---

29. Basil the Great, *On the Holy Spirit*, 10.26.
30. Basil the Great, *On the Holy Spirit*, 12.28.

APPENDIX

Apostolic Constitutions

375–80

Also known as "Constitutions of the Holy Apostles." The author is unknown, but it was probably written by a Syrian. It is made up of eight treatises on discipline, worship, and doctrine. It was intended to guide teachers and supposedly was the work of the twelve Apostles.

Book 7: "Concerning the Christian Life, and the Eucharist, and the Initiation into Christ."

Section 3: "On the Instruction of Catechumens, and Their Initiation into Baptism"

Paragraph 43: "Thanksgiving Concerning the Mystical Water"

> He has sent His Son to become man for man's sake, and to undergo all human passions without sin. Him, therefore, let the priest even now call upon in baptism, and let him say: Look down from heaven, and sanctify this water, and give it grace and power, that so he that is to be baptized, according to the command of Thy Christ, may be crucified with Him, and may die with Him, and may be buried with Him, and may rise with Him to the adoption which is in Him, that he may be dead to sin and live to righteousness. And after this, when he has baptized him in the name of the Father, and of the Son, and of the Holy Ghost, he shall anoint him with ointment.[31]

Gregory of Nazianzus

Gregory was born in 329 and died in 390. He was a fourth-century Archbishop of Constantinople, a theologian, and along with Basil the Great and Gregory of Nyssa, he was known as one of the Cappadocian Fathers.

---

31. *Apostolic Constitutions*, bk. 7, sect. 3, par. 43.

Orations

381

"On Holy Baptism"

And as Christ the Giver of it [baptism] is called by many various names, so too is this Gift, whether it is from the exceeding gladness of its nature (as those who are very fond of a thing take pleasure in using its name), or that the great variety of its benefits has reacted for us upon its names. We call it, the Gift, the Grace, Baptism, Unction, Illumination, the Clothing of Immortality, the Laver of Regeneration, the Seal, and everything that is honourable. We call it the Gift, because it is given to us in return for nothing on our part; Grace, because it is conferred even on debtors; Baptism, because sin is buried with it in the water; Unction, as Priestly and Royal, for such were they who were anointed; Illumination, because of its splendour; Clothing, because it hides our shame; the Laver, because it washes us; the Seal because it preserves us, and is moreover the indication of Dominion. In it the heavens rejoice; it is glorified by Angels, because of its kindred splendour. It is the image of the heavenly bliss. We long indeed to sing out its praises, but we cannot worthily do so.[32]

How shall this be? Remember always the parable, and so will you best and most perfectly help yourself. The unclean and malignant spirit is gone out of you, being chased by baptism. He will not submit to the expulsion, he will not resign himself to be houseless and homeless: He goes through waterless places, dry of the Divine Stream, and there he desires to abide. He wanders, seeking rest; he finds none. He lights on baptized souls, whose sins the font has washed away. He fears the water; he is choked with the cleansing, as the Legion were in the sea.[33]

John Chrysostom

John Chrysostom (Greek: "Golden Mouth") was born in Antioch in 347 and died in exile in 407. His father was an officer of high rank in the Roman military. He was baptized sometime between 368 and 373. Because of his

---

32. Gregory of Nazianzus, *Orations*, par. 4.
33. Gregory of Nazianzus, *Orations*, par. 35.

father's rank, who died soon after John was born, he lived a privileged life. His mother made sure he had the best of learning. He was headed for a lucrative career in Rhetoric but as a young man turned his studies to theology under Diodore of Tarsus. Longing for a higher spiritual maturity, he retreated into a monastic life for six years in the mountains outside Antioch. Because of his rigid ascetic lifestyle during those years, he suffered damage to his stomach and kidneys that bothered him the rest of his life. John had a great devotion and love for the Scriptures. He set much of the Old and New Testaments to memory. He had an honest and forthright approach to the Bible, setting him in contrast to the allegorical style of biblical interpretation practiced in the Alexandrian Churches. His eloquent preaching and exposition of the Bible focused on practical Christian living and moral behavior. When the bishop of Constantinople (the city was then being hailed as the "New Rome") died, the bishop of Alexandria, Theophilus, tried to get that high-ranking position in the Church for his protégé, but it went to Chrysostom instead. When Theophilus found out that John Chrysostom was given the bishopric of Constantinople instead of his protege, he became a major thorn in John's side. John was loved by the people for his plain and forthright teaching of moral Christian living, but not so much by the rich and powerful who, with the backing of Theophilus, succeeded in getting him banished to exile in a remote mountain village where he lived out the rest of his days in isolation. Though his presence in the pulpit was torn from him, while in exile he continued to write profusely and sent it to friends back in Constantinople. Next to Origen of Alexandria and Augustine of Hippo, he was the most prolific authors in the early Church.

Instructions to Catechumens

389

"First Instruction"

But, if you will, let us discourse about the name which this mystic cleansing bears: for its name is not one, but very many and various. For this purification is called the laver of regeneration. "He saved us," he saith, "through the laver of regeneration, and renewing of the Holy Ghost." It is called also illumination, and this St. Paul again has called it, "For call to remembrance the former days in which after ye were illuminated ye endured a great conflict of sufferings;" and again, "For it is impossible for those who were once illuminated, and have tasted of the heavenly gift, and then fell away, to renew them again unto repentance." It is called also, baptism: "For as many of you as were baptized into Christ did put on Christ." It is called also burial: "For we were buried" saith he, "with him, through baptism, into death." It is called circumcision: "In whom ye were also circumcised, with a circumcision not made with hands, in the putting off of the body of the sins of the flesh." It is called a cross: "Our old man was crucified with him that the body of sin might be done away."[34]

Ambrose of Milan

Aurelius Ambrosius was born in 340 and died in 397. He was the Archbishop of Milan (Northwest Italy). He served as the Roman governor of Liguria and Emilia, headquartered in Milan before popular acclamation propelled him into becoming Bishop of Milan in 374. He was a staunch critic of Arianism.

Concerning the Mysteries

387

Then he [Naaman] began to think within himself that he had the better waters of his own country, in which he had often dipped without being cleansed from leprosy, and drawn away by this thought, he was minded to disobey the prophet's commands; but he yielded to the advice and solicitations of his servants, and dipped; and he was straightway cleansed, and understood that it was due not to water, but to grace, that each one was cleansed.[35]

Thou receivedst after this white raiment for a sign that thou hast put off the covering of sins, thou hast put on the chaste garments of innocence . . . For he who is baptized is plainly cleansed both according to the Law and according to the Gospel.[36]

But Christ seeing his Church in white garments—the Church for whom he had put on filthy garments, as thou readest in the

---

34. John Chrysostom, *Instructions to Catechumens*, par. 2.
35. Ambrose, *Concerning the Mysteries*, chap. 3.17, p. 51.
36. Ambrose, *Concerning the Mysteries*, chap. 7.37, p. 59.

book of the prophet Zechariah [3:3]—or seeing, it may be, the soul clean and washed by the laver regeneration...."[37]

De Sacramentis (Concerning the Sacraments)

390

Thou didst enter, thou sawest the water, thou sawest the priest, thou sawest a levite. Let not some one haply say, "Is this all?" Yes, it is all. It is truly all, where all is innocency, all is godliness, all is grace, all is sanctification.[38]

There are many kinds of baptisms: but the Apostle cries, *one baptism*. Why? There are baptisms of the Gentiles, but they are no baptisms. They are baths, baptisms they cannot be. The flesh is washed, but guilt is not washed away; nay, it is contracted in that bath.[39]

Therefore the Apostle cries, as you have heard in the lesson just read, that whosoever is baptized, is baptized in the death of Jesus. What is in the death? It is that, as Christ died, so thou also shouldst taste of death; that, as Christ died unto sin, and liveth unto God, so thou also shouldst be dead unto the former allurements of sins through the sacrament of baptism, and shouldst rise again through the grace of Christ. It is a death, therefore; but not a death in the reality of bodily death, but in the likeness. For when thou dippest thou takest on the likeness of death and burial, thou receivest the sacrament of that cross, because Christ hung on the cross, and his body was pierced with nails.[40]

Therefore thou didst dip, thou camest to the priest. What did he say to thee? "God the Father Almighty," he saith, "who hath regenerated thee by water and the Holy Ghost, and hath forgiven thee thy sins, himself anoint thee unto eternal life."[41]

Yesterday we discoursed on the font, whose appearance is somewhat like that of a tomb in shape; into which, believing in the

---

37. Ambrose, *Concerning the Mysteries*, chap. 7.37, p. 60–61.
38. Ambrose, *Concernding the Sacrtamentis*, chap. 3.10, p. 79.
39. Ambrose, *De Sacrtamentis*, 85.
40. Ambrose, *De Sacrtamentis*, 94.
41. Ambrose, *De Sacrtamentis*, 94.

Father and the Son and the Holy Ghost, we are received, and plunged, and emerge, that is, we are raised up.[42]

Therefore, what is resurrection, but when we rise from death to life? So, therefore, in baptism also, since there is a likeness of death, without doubt when thou dost dip and rise again, there is a likeness of the resurrection. Rightly, therefore, according to the interpretation of the Apostle Peter, as that resurrection was a regeneration, so also is this resurrection a regeneration.[43]

Augustine of Hippo

Aurelius Augustinus was born in Thagaste, Algeria in 354 and died in 430. Before he found Christ, and eventually became the bishop of Hippo in Algeria, he had a restless mind, always wondering and questioniing. He was keenly aware that, because of his lust and sin, he stood alienated from God; this alienation put him on his quest to find answers for his restless heart. For several years in his youth, he sought those answers in the wrong places, especially in material success and sexual activities. In 386, under the example of dedicated Christians and the influence of Ambrose, the bishop in Milan, his spiritual quest led him to find peace and rest in Jesus. At the turn of the fourth and fifth centuries, he published The Confessions *which, in the first paragraph he made his famous statement, "Thou awakes us to delight in Thy praise; for Thou madest us for Thyself, and our heart is restless until it repose in Thee."*[44]

On Christian Doctrine

397

For a sign is a thing which, over and above the impression it makes on the senses, causes something else to come into the mind as a consequence of itself; as when we see a footprint, we conclude that an animal whose footprint this is has passed by . . . Nor is there any reason for giving a sign except the desire of

---

42. Ambrose, *De Sacrtamentis*, 96.
43. Ambrose, *De Sacrtamentis*, 97.
44. Augustine, *The Confessions*, 1.

drawing forth and conveying into another's mind what the giver of the sign has in his own mind.[45]

City of God

413–26

And the fact that the ancient church [Israel] offered animal sacrifices, which the people of God nowadays read of without imitating, proves nothing else than this, that those sacrifices signified the things which we do for the of drawing near to God, and inducing our neighbor to do the same. A sacrifice, therefore, is the visible sacrament or sacred sign of an invisible sacrifice... In the words of this prophet [Micah 6:6–8], these two things are distinguished and set forth with sufficient explicitness, that God does not require these sacrifices for their own sakes and that He does require the sacrifices which they symbolize.[46]

Enchiridion

420

And after this discussion of punishment through one man [Adam] and grace through the Other [Jesus], as he deemed sufficient for that part of the epistle, the apostle passes on to speak of the great mystery of holy baptism in the cross of Christ, and to do this so that we may understand nothing other in the baptism of Christ than the likeness of the death of Christ. The death of Christ crucified is nothing other than the likeness of the forgiveness of sins—so that in the very same sense, in which the death is real, so also is the forgiveness of our sin real, and in the same sense in which his resurrection is real, so also in us is there authentic justification... If therefore, the fact that we are baptized into the death of Christ shows that we are dead to sin, then certainly infants who are baptized in Christ die to sin, since they are baptized into his own death... Thus, to those baptized into the death of Christ—into which not only adults but infants

---

45. Augustine, *On Christian Doctrine*, 636–37.
46. Augustine, *City of God*, 301.

as well are baptized—he says, "So also you should reckon yourselves to be dead to sin, but alive to God in Christ Jesus."[47]

The angels are in concord with us even now, when our sins are forgiven. Therefore, in the order of the Creed, after the reference to "holy Church" is placed the reference to "forgiveness of sins." For it is by this that the part of the Church on earth stands; it is by this that "what was lost and is found again" is not lost again. Of course, the gift of baptism is an exception. It is an antidote given us against original sin, so that what is contracted by birth is removed by the new birth—though it also takes away actual sins as well, whether of heart, word, or deed. But except for this great remission—the beginning point of man's renewal, in which all guilt, inherited and acquired is washed away—the rest of life, from the age of accountability (and no matter how vigorously we progress in righteousness), is not without the need for the forgiveness of sins.[48]

Thomas Aquinas

Thomas Aquinas was born in 1225 and died in 1274. He was a Catholic humanist, philosopher, and theologian. Aquinas was a strong advocate that all seven sacraments of the Catholic church (baptism, confirmation, holy eucharist, penance, extreme unction, holy orders, and matrimony) convey grace upon those who practice them. His famous Summa Theologica, *though unfinished at his death, has had a powerful influence on subsequent generations of theologians and philosophers.*

Summa Theologica

Published in 1485 (written 1265–74)

"Treatise on the Sacraments"

In like manner the corporeal sacraments by their proper operation, which they exercise on the body that they touch, accomplish through the Divine institution as instrumental operation on the soul; for example, the water of baptism, in respect of its proper power, cleanses the body, and thereby, since it is the

---

47. Augustine, *Enchiridion*, 42–43.
48. Augustine, *Enchiridion*, 50.

instrument of the Divine power, cleanses the soul, since from soul and body one thing is made.[49]

Now the sacraments are ordered to certain special effects which are necessary in the Christian life; thus Baptism is ordered to a certain spiritual regeneration, by which man dies to vice and becomes a member of Christ, which effect is something special in addition to the actions of the soul's powers; and the same holds true of the other sacraments.[50]

Desiderius Erasmus

Desiderius Erasmus of Rotterdam, Netherland was born in 1466 (or thereabouts) and died in 1536. He was a Dutch theologian, a philosopher, and a Catholic priest. He has become known as a "Christian humanist" because he endeavored to make Christ and His message more relevant to the Christian's daily life. As a "primitive theologian" he was an avid student of the Scriptures and the early Church Fathers. His love of the Greek language made him one of the great Bible translators of Medieval Europe. In contrast to the Reformation leaders of his day, Erasmus remained within the Roman Church as he strove to bring about its much-needed reforms.

"The Handbook of the Militant Christian"

1503

Perhaps you are not aware, O Christian soldier that when you were initiated into the mysteries of life-giving Baptism, you gave yourself by name to Christ as your leader.[51]

An Inquiry Concerning Faith

1524

But in this society even one's own good works do not further his salvation, unless he is reconciled to the holy congregation; and

---

49. Aquinas, *Summa Theologica*, 859.
50. Aquinas, *Summa Theologica*, 860.
51. Erasmus, *Handbook*, 30.

therefore follows, "the forgiveness of sin," because outside of the Church there is no remission of sins, though a man should pine himself away with repentance and perform works of charity. In the Church, I say, not of heretics, but the Holy Church, there is forgiveness of sins by baptism, and after baptism by repentance and the keys given to the Church.[52]

Paraphrase on the Gospel According to Matthew

1522

When you have taught them these things, if they believe what you have taught, if they repent of their former lives, if they are ready to embrace the gospel teaching, then bathe them with water in the name of the Father and of the Son and of the Holy Spirit, so that by this sacred symbol they may trust that they have been freed from the filth of all their sins by the free benefit of my death, and have now been admitted into the company of the sons of God. Let no one be circumcised, let no one be baptized in the name of Moses or of any man. Let them all acknowledge to whom they owe their salvation, upon whom, accordingly, they ought to depend completely.[53]

Martin Luther

Martin Luther was born in 1483 and died in 1546. He was a German professor of theology, composer, priest, and a former Augustinian monk. In spite of great risk to his life by the Catholic Church, he opened the way for a return to Scripture as the only basis for faith. On May 25, 1521, following the edict of the Diet of Worms, the Holy Roman emperor declared Luther an outlaw, banned his literature, and ordered his arrest. Due to the protection of Prince Frederick III, Elector of Saxony, he was assured of safe conduct to and from the meeting. On his return from Worms, Frederick III had him abducted and escorted to the Wartburg Castle at Eisenach where he stayed in retreat for the next several months before returning to Wittenburg.

---

52. Erasmus, *An Inquiry Concerning Faith*, 219.
53. Erasmus, *Paraphrase on the Gospel According to Matthew*, 377–78.

Large Catechism

1520

You should first of all note that these words stand as God's command and ordinance. Basing yourself on these words, you are not to doubt that Baptism is a divine act, not something devised or invented by man. For as truly as I can affirm that the Ten Commandments, the Creed, and the Lord's Prayer were not spun out of any human being's head, but revealed and given by God Himself, so joyously can I affirm that Baptism is no human trifle, but that it was established by God Himself. Moreover, He earnestly and solemnly commanded that we must be baptized or we shall not be saved. No one is to think that it is an optional matter like putting on a red coat. It is of the greatest importance that we hold Baptism in high esteem as something splendid and glorious. The reason why we are striving and battling so strenuously for this view of Baptism is that the world nowadays is full of sects that loudly proclaim that Baptism is merely an external form and that external forms are useless. Well, be it external as it may, nevertheless here stands God's Word and command that institutes, establishes, and confirms Baptism. And what God institutes and commands cannot be useless; it is altogether priceless and precious even though it were as insignificant in appearance as a spear of straw.[54]

To be baptized in God's name is to be baptized not by man but by God Himself. Although Baptism is indeed performed by human hands, yet it is truly God's own action . . .

Learn from this to come to a correct understanding and to find the answer to the question, What is Baptism? It is not simple ordinary water, but water comprehended in God's Word and thus made holy. It is nothing else than a divine water, not because the water in itself is something more special than other water, but because God's Word and commandment are added to it . . . It is from the Word that Baptism derives its nature as a sacrament, as St. Augustine has taught: "Accedat verbum ad elementum et fit sacramentum," which means, "When the Word is joined to the element or natural substance, the outcome is a sacrament," that is, a holy, divine thing and sign.[55]

---

54. Luther, *Luther's Large Catechism*, 98.
55. Luther, *Luther's Large Catechism*, 99–100.

Stated most simply, the power, effect, benefit, fruit, and purpose of Baptism is to save. No one is baptized for the purpose making him a prince, but as the words say, that he may "be saved."[56]

John Calvin

John Calvin was born in 1509 and died in 1564. His Institutes of the Christian Religion *was first published in 1536. Calvin published later editions, each with more sections until his magnum opus reached its final form in 1559.*

Institutes of the Christian Religion

1536

Baptism is the initiatory sign by which we are admitted to the fellowship of the Church, that being ingrafted into Christ we may be accounted children of God.[57]

We ought to consider that at whatever time we are baptised, we are washed and purified once for the whole of life. Wherefore, as often as we fall, we must recall the remembrance of our baptism, and thus fortify our minds, so as to feel certain and secure of the remission of sins.[58]

And of what nature is this preaching? That we are washed from our sins by the blood of Christ. And what is the sign and evidence of that washing if it be not baptism? We see, then, that that forgiveness has reference to baptism.[59]

Wherefore, there can be no doubt that all the godly may, during the whole course of their lives, whenever they are vexed by a consciousness of their sins, recall the remembrance of their baptism, that they may thereby assure themselves of that sole and perpetual ablution which we have in the blood of Christ.[60]

---

56. Luther, *Luther's Large Catechism*, 101.
57. Calvin, *Institutes*, 2513.
58. Calvin, *Institutes*, 2514.
59. 57 Calvin, *Institutes*, 2515.
60. 58 Calvin, *Institutes*, 2515.

(Rom. 6:3–4). By these words, he not only exhorts us to the imitation of Christ, as if he said, that we are admonished by baptism, in like manner as Christ died, to die to our lusts, and as he rose, to rise to righteousness; but he traces the matter much higher, that Christ by baptism has made us partakers of his death, ingrafting us into it.[61]

These things, I say, we ought to feel as truly and certainly in our mind as we see our body washed, immersed, and surrounded with water. For this analogy or similitude furnishes the surest rule in the sacraments—viz. that in corporeal things we are to see spiritual.[62]

God in baptism promises the remission of sins, and will undoubtedly perform what he has promised to all believers.[63]

Whether the person baptised is to be wholly immersed, and that whether once or thrice, or whether he is only to be sprinkled with water, is not of the least consequence: churches should be at liberty to adopt either, according to the diversity of climates, although it is evident that the term baptise means to immerse, and that this was the form used by the primitive Church.[64]

Menno Simmons

Menno Simmons was born in 1496 and died in 1561. He was consecrated as a Roman Catholic priest at Utrecht, The Netherlands in 1516. He rejected the Catholic Church and the priesthood on January 12th, 1536, casting his lot with the Anabaptists. His followers became known as Mennonites.

His writing on baptism is a substantial reading. Simmons stepped into the Anabaptist movement when it was in a weakened state and built it to become a significant part of the Reformation alongside men like Luther, Zwingli, Calvin, and others. In these quotes can be seen a good example of the evolution of the purpose of baptism as it is moved from being an initiation into one's relationship with God as an act of conversion to an event chronologically removed from and subsequent to salvation. Sometimes, it seems that Simmons is advocating an immediate connection between remission of sin and baptism, and at other times, he seems to remove remission

61. 59 Calvin, *Institutes*, 2520.
62. 60 Calvin, *Institutes*, 2522.
63. 61 Calvin, *Institutes*, 2524.

of sins and baptism from each other. He appears to divide baptism into two baptisms, one an inner spiritual baptism with which he associates faith and remission of sins, and another physical outer baptism for which he gives no purpose other than it is the water baptism that is taught in the New Testament.

Simmons made it quite clear that his view places faith prior to baptism. It also appears that he considered faith as God's gift that He imputes into a person, rather than man's response to God's grace.

Concerning Baptism

1540

Even as Christ commanded, so the holy apostles also taught and practiced, as may be plainly perceived in many parts of the New Testament. Thus Peter said, "Repent, and be baptized every one of you in the name of Jesus Christ for the remission of sins, and ye shall receive the gift of the Holy Ghost," Acts 2:38. Again, Philip said to the eunuch, "If thou believest with all thine heart, thou mayest," Acts 8:37. Here, faith did not follow baptism, but baptism followed faith, Mark 16:16 . . . In the beginning the gospel was to be preached and faith followed hearing, and baptism followed faith; this is incontrovertible, for so the Scriptures teach, Rom. 10:17.[65]

Beloved Reader, take heed to the word of the Lord, for this also Paul teaches, who received not his gospel of men, but of the Lord himself; even as Christ died and was buried, so also ought we to die unto our sin, and be buried with Christ in baptism; we are not to do this after we have been baptized, but we must commence and do all this before hand . . . Therefore beware, for the intent of baptism is to bury sin, and to rise with Christ into a new life, which can by no means, be the case with infants; therefore, consider well what the word of the Lord teaches you on this subject.[66]

Beloved sirs, friends, and brethren, awake and delay not, render the Most High his due praise and honor, and give ear to his holy word, for those who maintain that the baptism of children that are incapable of understanding, is a washing of regeneration, do

---

65. Simmons, "Concerning Baptism," 24.
66. Simmons. "Concerning Baptism," 25.

violence to the word of God; resist the Holy Ghost; make Christ a liar, and his holy apostles false witnesses; for Christ and his apostles teach that regeneration comes through faith from God and his word, which word is not to be taught to those who are unable to hear or understand, but to those who have the ability, both to hear and understand; this is incontrovertible.[67]

Here [1 Peter 3:21] Peter teaches us how the inward baptism saves us, by which the inner man is washed, and not the outward baptism by which the flesh is washed; for only this inward baptism, as already stated, is of value in the sight of God, while outward baptism follows only as an evidence of obedience which is of faith . . . [discussion on 1 Pet. 3:21] Not, my beloved, that we believe in the remission of sins through baptism; by no means; because by baptism we cannot obtain faith and repentance, neither do we receive the forgiveness of sins, nor peace, nor liberty of conscience.[68]

It is true, Peter says, "Repent and be baptized every one of you in the name of Jesus Christ, for the remission of sins." But this is not to be understood, that we receive the remission of our sins through baptism. O no! for if it be so, then Christ and his merits must fall. (31) [69]

Benjamin Keach

Born in 1640 and died in 1704, Benjamin Keach was a Particular Baptist preacher and author who advocated for hymn singing in the Baptist church in London. He wrote 43 books, one of which, The Child's Instructor *(a children's catechism), brought on such controversy that he was locked in the public stocks on the pillory.*

Gold Refin'd; or Baptism in its Primitive Purity

1689

Consider the great Promises made to those who are obedient to it, amongst other things, Lo, I am with you always, even to the end of the world. And again, He that believeth, and is baptized,

---

67. Simmons, "Concerning Baptism," 26–27.
68. Simmons, "Concerning Baptism," 27.
69. Simmons, "Concerning Baptism," 31.

shall be saved. If a Prince shall offer a Rebel his Life in doing two things, would he neglect one of them, and say this I will do, but the other is a trivial thing, I'll not do that? Surely no, he would not run the hazard of his Life so foolishly . . . And then in Acts 2:38. Repent, and be baptized every one of you for Remission of Sin, and ye shall receive the Gift of the Holy Spirit. See what great Promises are made to Believers in Baptism.[70]

John Wesley

John Wesley was born in 1703 and died in 1791. He was an English preacher, theologian, and ordained as a priest in the Church of England in 1728. He subsequently became identified with a group known as the Moravian Christians. In May of 1738, he had a conversion experience. After several years of seeking to attain a pure heart before God, He discovered that he did not have a real conviction of salvation. He described his awakening:

"In the evening I went very unwillingly to a society in Aldersgate Street, where one was reading Luther's 'Preface to the Epistle to the Romans.' About a quarter before nine, while he was describing the change that God works in the heart through faith in Christ, I felt my heart strangely warmed. I felt I did trust in Christ, Christ alone for salvation, and an assurance was given me that he had taken away my sins, even mine, and saved me from the law of sin and death."[71]

Even after the Aldersgate experience, he continued to search for a sense of inward holiness. After leaving the Moravians, he wandered throughout Great Britain and Ireland as an itinerant preacher establishing small groups of Christians that came to be known as Methodism.

A Treatise on Baptism

1756

Concerning baptism I shall inquire, what it is; what benefits we receive by it; whether our Saviour designed it to remain always in his Church; and who are the proper subjects of it.

1.1 What it is. It is the initiatory sacrament, which enters us into covenant with God. It was instituted by Christ, who

---

70. Fowler, *More Than a Symbol*, 29.
71. Ward and Heitzenrater, *Works of John Wesley*, 249–50.

alone has the power to institute a proper sacrament, a sign, seal, pledge, and means of grace, perpetually obligatory on all Christians[72]

The matter of this sacrament is water; which, as it has a natural power of cleansing, is the more fit for this symbolical use. Baptism is performed by washing, dipping, or sprinkling the person, in the name of the Father, Son, and Holy Ghost, who is hereby devoted to the ever-blessed Trinity.[73]

What are the benefits we receive by baptism is the next point to be considered. And the first of these is, the washing away the guilt of original sin, by the application of the merits of Christ's death.[74]

By baptism we enter into covenant with God; into that everlasting covenant.[75]

By baptism we are admitted into the Church, and consequently made members of Christ, its Head. The Jews were admitted into the Church by circumcision, so are the Christians by baptism.[76]

In all ages, the outward baptism is a means of the inward; as outward circumcision was of the circumcision of the heart. Nor would it have availed a Jew to say, "I have the inward circumcision, and therefore do not need the outward too:" That soul was to be cut off from his people.[77]

If infants are guilty of original sin, then they are proper subjects of baptism; seeing, in the ordinary way, they cannot be saved, unless this be washed away by baptism. It has been already proved, that this original stain cleaves to every child of man; and that hereby they are children of wrath, and liable to eternal damnation.[78]

---

72. Wesley, *A Treatise on Baptism*, 1. https://nebula.wsimg.com/3bbcf98fce4854b613be820513e26dba?AccessKeyId=4A680661BDCD9E70158F&disposition=0&alloworigin=1.
73. Wesley, *A Treatise on Baptism*, 1.
74. Wesley, *A Treatise on Baptism*, 2.
75. Wesley, *A Treatise on Baptism*, 3.
76. Wesley, *A Treatise on Baptism*, 3.
77. Wesley, *A Treatise on Baptism*, 4.
78. Wesley, *A Treatise on Baptism*, 4.

But to baptize infants has been the general practice of the Christian Church, in all places and in all ages. Of this we have unexceptionable witnesses.[79]

Alexander Campbell

Alexander Campbell was born in 1788 and died in 1866. Along with Barton W. Stone and others, Campbell was a moving force behind the movement in America that came to be known as the Restoration Movement. He was a prolific writer, educator, and popular preacher. Campbell's views on the purpose of baptism evolved over the years, which makes it difficult to choose his words on the subject. The following quotes serve as an example of his main attitude toward the purpose of baptism.

"Essay on the Religion of Christianity"

1827

Now this internal religion, externally manifested by certain acts and exercises of divine appointment, is what is commonly called worship, and rightly too. See the whole Bible upon this word. The first instituted act of Christian worship is baptism into the name of the Father, and of the Son, and of the Holy Ghost. Why is it translated "in the name," &c. contrary to the literal and almost universal translation of the particle *eis*? In the name of any dignified character, universally imports, by the authority of such a person. Whereas, this is not the proper and obvious meaning of the baptismal institution. For although it is done by virtue of the divine authority enjoining it, that is, by the authority of Christ; yet its proper and primary import is not a mere exhibition of authority on the part of the institutor, and of submission on the part of the baptized, though this is certainly implied in every act of worship; but it is of a much more consolatory, and blissful import, being an expression of faith and obedience on the part of the baptized; nay, the very first instituted act of obedience of faith, in and by which the believing worshipper is openly declared to be of the household of faith and of the family of God, being baptized into "the name of the Father," of whom the whole redeemed family in heaven and earth is named; and into the name of the Redeemer, the Son, and heir of all things

---

79. Wesley, *A Treatise on Baptism*, 7.

who makes his people free; and into the name of the Holy Spirit, the sanctifier, the comforter, and perfecter of the saints; that by virtue of his indwelling and sanctifying presence . . . by the Spirit. He is declared free—justified from the guilt, and washed from the pollution of sin, by this washing of regeneration and renewing of the Holy Ghost.[80]

The Christian System

1839

Baptism is, then, designed to introduce the subjects of it into the participation of the blessings of the death and resurrection of Christ; who "died for our sins," and "rose again for our justification." But it has no abstract efficacy. Without previous faith in the blood of Christ, and deep and unfeigned repentance before God, neither immersion in water, nor any other action, can secure to us the blessings of peace and pardon. It can merit nothing. Still to the believing penitent it is the means of receiving a formal, distinct, and specific absolution, or release from guilt. Therefore, none but those who have first believed the testimony of God and have repented of their sins, and that have been intelligently immersed into his death, have the full and explicit testimony of God, assuring them of their pardon.[81]

Sermons and tracts of all dimensions are continually issuing from the press, containing only reiterations of the opinion of one or two men who happened to live some three hundred years ago—affirming that baptism is not for the remission of sins, but for no reason at all—a dispensable, unmeaning, ceremonial for making a Christian profession. The opposition has assumed singular forms of reason and argument. Now we have learned dissertations on certain Greek particles—such as *eis, kai,* and *en*—by preachers who have a little knowledge of the Greek *alphabet*—affirming that *eis* means "*because of,*" and *kai,* "*even,*" when baptism is alluded to. These *ex post facto* laws, manufactured at some of the machine shops in Pittsburgh or Birmingham, in Wales or New Holland, for the express purpose of proving that Peter meant "*be baptized because of the remission of your sins,*" and that Jesus meant "born of water, *even* of the

---

80. Campbell, "Essay," 62.
81. Campbell, *The Christian System,* 42.

Spirit," are most fatally formed by persons who were born both deaf and blind. They are the most suicidal things in the world.[82]

Henry Alford

Henry Alford was born in 1810 and died in 1871. As an English churchman, he was a theologian, textual critic, scholar, poet, hymnodist, preacher, and author. He is primarily remembered for his commentary on the Greek text, *The Greek Testament*. His commentary was conceived in 1845, and the first volume was published in 1849, the last in 1861.

"The Gospel According to Matthew"

1849

[Commenting on Matthew 28:19: *eis to onoma tou patros kai tou uiou kai tou agiou pneumatos*—"into the name of the Father and the Son and the Holy Spirit"]. Reference is apparently made to the Baptism of the Lord himself, where the whole Three Persons of the Godhead were in manifestation ... It is unfortunate again here that our English Bibles do not give us the force of the *eis*. It should have been 'into' (as in Gal. iii.27 al.) both here and in 1 Cor. x.2, and wherever the expression is used ... Baptism is the *contract of espousal* (Eph. v. 26) between Christ and His Church.[83]

"The Epistle to the Ephesians"

1862

Commentary on Eph 5:26:

> **He might sanctify her, having purified her** (*hagiasei* and *katharisas* might be contemporaneous, and indeed this is the more common usage of past participles with past finite verbs in the N. T. But here, inasmuch as the sanctifying is clearly a gradual process, carried on till the spotless presentation [ver. 27]. And the washing cannot be separated from the introductory rite of

---

82. Campbell, *The Millennial Harbinger*, 417.
83. Alford, "Gospel According to Matthew," 291.

baptism, it is best to take the ***katharisas*** as antecedent to the ***hagiasei*)[84] [Greek words are transliterated by author]

Moses E. Lard

Moses E. Lard was born in 1818 and died in 1880. He was a self-educated preacher and author in Missouri and Kentucky.

"Do the Unimmersed Commune?"

1863

That belief in Christ, a fixed purpose to forsake sin, and the immersion of the body in water, are necessary to constitute a man a Christian—always and everywhere necessary. In other words, and generally, it is here assumed that it takes two things to constitute a man a Christian; namely: 1. The right spirit or mental frame; 2. The right act or acts; and that no more can a right spirit, without the right acts constitute him a Christian, than can the right acts, without the right Spirit.[85]

I cannot repress in my heart the deep, honest convictions thereof; at least I will not. It is high time that the world understood the present point; and that we understood ourselves. If we mean to teach without mincing the matter, that immersion, for this is the only difficulty in the way, is necessary, always and everywhere, since the founding of the kingdom, to constitute a Christian, let it be unqualifiedly said; and then let it stand forever as the unalterable expression of our faith. Or if we do not mean to teach thus, let us avow what we do mean to teach. Candidly, I am tired of publishing to the world a tenet, as something taught in Holy Writ, and in the same breath proclaiming a set of inferences which falsify it. If a man can be a Christian without immersion, let the fact be shown; or if a man can or may commune without being a Christian, let the fact be shown. I deny both. Immovably I stand here. But I shall be told that this is Phariseeism, that it is exclusivism. Be it so; if it be true and this is the only question with me respecting it, then I am so far the

---

84. Alford, "The Epistle Ephesians," 137.
85. Lard, "Do the Unimmersed Commune?" 41.

defendant of Phariseeism and exclusivism. I stagger at nothing if true, at everything if false.[86]

Let the unimmersed be told of their error with a spirit as sweet and kind as that in which you would address the wife of your bosom, but at the same time with a purpose as firm and uncompromising as that in which you would snatch the hand of your child from theft.[87]

William Sanday and Arthur C. Headlum

William Sanday was born in 1843 and died in 1920. He was an English theologian and priest. As a professor of theology at Oxford, he authored numerous theological works. He was one of the editors of the 1880 Variorum Bible *and contributed articles to the* Encyclopaedia Biblica *and* The American Journal of Theology.

Arthur Headlum was born in 1862 and died in 1947. He was also an English theologian, Professor of Dogmatic Theology at King's College London and, later, Regius Professor of Divinity at Oxford. He also served as Bishop of Gloucester from 1923 to 1945.

A Critical and Exegetical Commentary on the Epistle to the Romans

1895

"The Mystical Union of the Christian with Christ" (*Comments on Romans 6:1–14*)

When we descended into the baptismal water, that meant that we died with Christ—to sin. When the water closed over our heads, that meant that we lay buried with Him, in proof that our death to sin, like His death, was real . . . For it is a matter of experience that our Old Self—what we were before we became Christians—was nailed to the Cross with Christ in our baptism: it was killed by a process so like the Death of Christ and so

---

86. Lard, "Do the Unimmersed Commune?" 43.
87. Lard, "Do the Unimmersed Commune?" 47.

wrought in conjunction with Him that it too may share in the name and association of His Crucifixion.[88]

baptistheimen eis Christon Ieisoun: "were baptized unto union with" (not merely "obedience to") "Christ." The act of baptism was an act of *incorporation* into Christ . . . This conception lies at the root of the whole passage. All the consequences which St. Paul draws follow from this union, incorporation, identification of the Christian with Christ.[89] [Greek words are transliterated by author]

James Denney

James Denney was born in 1856 and died in 1917. As a Scottish theologian, he was an accomplished author, professor, and preacher. In 1897 he became Professor of Systematic Theology at his old alma mater, Free Church College Glasgow, and spent the rest of his life teaching there.

St. Paul's Epistle to the Romans

1900

[Comments on Rom 6:3] When, it may be asked, did the all-important death take place? The answer is: It is involved in baptism . . . In the same way *baptistheinai eis ton thanaton autou* ["were baptized into His death"] might certainly mean to be baptized with Christ's death in view as the object of faith. This is the interpretation of Lipsius. But it falls short of the argumentative requirements of the passage, which demand the idea of an actual union to, or incorporation in, Christ. This is more than Lipsius means, but it does not exclude what he means. The baptism in which we are united to Christ and to His death is one in which we confess our faith, looking to Him and His death. To say that faith justifies but baptism regenerates, breaking the Christian life into two unrelated pieces, as Weiss does—one spiritual and the other magical—is to throw away the Apostle's case. His whole point is that no such division can be made . . . Therefore we were buried with Him (in the act of immersion) through that baptism into His death—burial being regarded as the natural

---

88. Sandy and Headlam, "The Mystical Union," 154.
89. Sandy and Headlam, "The Mystical Union," 156.

sequence of death, and a kind of seal set to its reality.[90] [Greek phrase changed from Greek to English letters]

The Death of Christ

1902

The answer is apparent if we consider the context in which the ideas found in this commission are elsewhere found in the New Testament. In all its forms the commission has to do either with baptism (as in Matthew and Mark) or with the remission of sins (as in Luke and John). These are but two forms of the same thing, for in the world of New Testament ideas baptism and the remission of sins are inseparably associated.[91]

It does not seem to me in the least illegitimate, but on the contrary both natural and necessary, to take all these references to the forgiveness of sins and to baptism as references at the same time to the saving significance 'in relation to sin' of the death of Jesus.[92]

The New Testament, it may be pointed out, nowhere gives us the idea of an unbaptized Christian for by one Spirit we were all baptized into one body (1 Cor. xii. 13) . . . In other words, there was no such thing known to Paul as a Christian society without baptism as its rite of initiation, and the Supper as its rite of communion.[93]

[Concerning Romans 6] But the new life is involved in the faith evoked by the sin-bearing death of Christ, and in nothing else; it is involved in in this, and this pictorially presented in baptism. Hence the use which Paul makes of this sacrament in the same chapter. He is able to use it in his argument in the way he does because baptism and faith are but the outside and the inside of the same thing. If baptism, then, is symbolically inconsistent with the continuance in sin, as is apparent to everyone, faith is really inconsistent with it.[94]

---

90. Denny, "St. Paul's Epistle to the Romans," 2:632.
91. Denny, *The Death of Christ*, 46.
92. Denny, *The Death of Christ*, 51.
93. Denny, *The Death of Christ*, 51–52.
94. Denny, *The Death of Christ*, 107.

A. T. Robertson

Archibald Thomas Robertson was born in 1863 and died in 1934. He was a Southern Baptist preacher and a biblical scholar, and he wrote a monumental classic Greek grammar that is still in use today.

Robertson's Word Pictures of the New Testament

1927

"Acts 2:38"

The first thing to do is make a radical and complete change of heart and life. Then let each one be baptized after this change has taken place, and the act of baptism be performed "in the name of Jesus Christ" (*en to onomat Ieisou Christou*) . . . One will decide the use here [Acts 2:38] according as he believes that baptism is essential to the remission of sins or not. My view is decidedly against the idea that Peter, Paul, or anyone in the New Testament taught baptism as essential to the remission of sins or the means of securing such remission. So I understand Peter to be urging baptism on each of them who had already turned (repented) and for it to be done in the name of Jesus Christ on the basis of the forgiveness of sins which they had already received. [95]

A New Short Grammar of the Greek Testament

1931

Hence a case like Acts 2:38 (*eis aphesin ton hamartion*) can mean either on the basis of forgiveness of sins (cf. Mk. 1:4f, "confessing their sins") or with a view to forgiveness of sins. There is nothing in *eis* to compel either result. One will interpret according to his theology.[96]

---

95. Robertson, "Acts 2:38."
96. Robertson, *A New Short Grammar*, 256.

Otto Procksch

Otto Procksch was born in 1874 and died in 1947. He was a German Evangelical Lutheran theologian and Old Testament scholar. In 1925 he assumed the Old Testament chair in Erlangen.

"hagios"

1933

There is here [Hebrews 13:12] a clear connection between the concept of atonement and that of sanctification . . . Sanctification is not moral action on the part of man, but a divinely affected state . . . the baptismal washing showing that in the baptismal fellowship of Christ (R. 6:4; Col. 2:12) lies the basis of sanctification and justification (cf. 1 Cor. 1:30) . . . the concept of holiness approximates to that of purity in wholly Jewish style . . . The presupposition here is that they are *hagioi* (1 Pet 1:16), so that Christ dwells in them as His temple, and will not suffer any impurity.[97]

Karl Barth

Karl Barth was born in 1886 and died in 1968. Barth was a Swiss Reformed theologian, professor of theology, preacher, and world-renowned author. His unfinished five-volume masterpiece, Church Dogmatics *was published 1932–67. He began his career as a liberal theologian, but with the publication* The Epistle to the Romans *he abandoned liberal theology and became a leader of Neo-orthodox theology.*

The Epistle to the Romans

1933

Baptism mediates the new creation: it is not itself grace, but from first to last a means of grace.[98] . . . To those who are not ignorant the sign of baptism speaks of death. To be baptized means to be immersed, to be sunk in a foreign element, to be

---

97. Procksch, "*hagios*," 1:112.
98. Barth, *Epistle to the Romans*, 192.

covered by a tide of purification. The man who emerges from the water is not the same man who entered it. One man dies and another is born. The baptized person is no longer to be identified with the man who died. Baptism bears witness to the death of Christ, where the radical and inexorable claim of God upon men triumphed.[99]

With this [grace] the act of baptism is concerned: "Your baptism is nothing less than grace clutching you by the throat: a gracefull throttling, by which your sin is submerged in order that ye may remain under grace. Come thus to thy baptism. Give thyself up to be drowned in baptism and killed by the mercy of thy dear God, saying: 'Drown me and throttle me, dear Lord, for henceforth I will gladly die to sin with Thy Son.'" (Luther). This death is grace.[100]

Kenneth S. Wuest

Kenneth S. Wuest was born in 1893 and died in 1961. He was a professor of Greek grammar and New Testament studies. He wrote several books on the New Testament and was one of the translators for the New American Standard Bible.

Romans in the Greek New Testament for the English Reader

1935

It [*baptidzo*] refers to the act of God introducing a believing sinner into vital union with Jesus Christ, in order that the believer might have the power of his sinful nature broken and the divine nature implanted through his identification with Christ in His death, burial, and resurrection, thus altering the condition and relationship of that sinner with regard to his previous state and environment, bringing him into a new environment, the kingdom of God.[101]

---

99. Barth, *Epistle to the Romans*, 193.
100. Barth, *Epistle to the Romans*, 194.
101. Wuest, *Romans in the Greek*, 97.

Dietrich Bonhoeffer

Dietrich Bonhoeffer was born in 1906 and was executed by the Germans for his association with a plot to kill Hitler on April 9, 1945, just days before the collapse of the Nazi regime. He was a professor of Systematic Theology at the University of Berlin for a short while before Hitler took over Germany. He drafted the Barmen Declaration, which was adopted by the newly founded Confessing Church in opposition to the state-supported church. He wrote several books on theology and ethics.

The Cost of Discipleship

1937

Baptism is not an offer made by man to God, but an offer made by Christ to man. It is grounded solely on the will of Jesus Christ, as expressed in his gracious call. Baptism is essentially passive—being baptized, suffering the call of Christ. In baptism man becomes Christ's own possession. When the name of Christ is spoken over the candidate, he becomes a partaker in this Name, and is baptized "into Jesus Christ (*eis*, Rom. 6.3; Gal. 3.27; Matt. 28:19). From that moment he belongs to Jesus Christ. He is wrested from the dominion of the world, and passes into the ownership of Christ.

Baptism therefore betokens a breach. Christ invades the realm of Satan, lays hands on his own, and creates for himself his Church. By this act past and present are rent asunder. The old order is passed away, and all things have become new. This breach is not effected by man's tearing off his own chains through some unquenchable longing for a new life of freedom. The breach has been effected by Christ long since, and in baptism it is effected in our own lives. We are now deprived of our direct relationship with all God-given realities of life. Christ the Mediator has stepped in between us and them. The baptized Christian has ceased to belong to the world and is no longer its slave. He belongs to Christ alone, and his relationship with the world is mediated through him.

The breach with the world is complete. It demands and produces the death of the old man. In baptism a man dies together with his old world. This death, no less than baptism itself, is a passive event.[102]

---

102. Bonhoeffer, *The Cost of Discipleship*, 256–57.

When he called men to follow him, Jesus was summoning them to a visible act of obedience. To follow Jesus was a public act. Baptism is similarly a public event, for it is the means whereby a member is grafted onto the visible body of Christ (Gal. 3.27f; 1 Cor. 12.13).[103]

Henry C. Thiessen

Henry C. Thiessen was born in 1883 and died in 1947. He served as Professor of New Testament Literature and Exegesis at Dallas Theological Seminary and as Chairman of the Bible and Theology Department at Wheaton College.

Lectures in Systematic Theology

1949

Some see baptism as a necessary prerequisite to regeneration, but this makes salvation dependent upon works. Clearly, Cornelius was born again before he received baptism (Acts 10:47). Acts 2:38 must be understood in the sense of being baptized because of the forgiveness of sins, rather than in order that they would be forgiven; just as John baptized because of repentance, rather than in order that those who were being baptized would repent (Matt. 3:11).[104]

T. F. Torrance

Thomas Forsyth Torrance was born in 1913 and died in 2007. He was a Scottish Protestant theologian and minister. Torrance served for 27 years as professor of Christian dogmatics at New College in the University of Edinburgh. In 1953, a Special Commission on Baptism, under the leadership of Dr. Torrance, was appointed by the General Assembly of the Church of Scotland, "to carry out a fresh examination of the Doctrine of Baptism" in order to lead the church to "theological agreement and uniform practice." The project was to be "founded on the teaching of Holy Scripture."

---

103. Bonhoeffer, *The Cost of Discipleship*, 259.
104. Thiessen, *Lectures in Systematic Theology*, 280.

The Commission was established after years of disagreement related to the meaning of baptism and its administration, especially in light of infant baptism.[105]

The Biblical Doctrine of Baptism, A Study Document issued by The Special Commission on Baptism of the Church of Scotland

1958

The New Testament doctrine of Baptism is wholly Christocentric: it is grounded on the Person and Work of Christ—what He was, and did, and is for evermore.

The New Testament writers found the meaning of Baptism primarily in what God has done in Christ for our salvation, and what He still does, and has promised to do, through His Word and Spirit. It is because God is faithful to His Word and Promise, active to realize in His Church what has been accomplished for all men in Christ, that Baptism is significant.[106]

In the New Testament Baptism is referred to as a washing or cleansing, and especially as a washing away of sins . . . The New Testament links Baptism as the washing away of sins with cleansing in the blood and through the death of Christ.

An example of the way the New Testament speaks of Baptism as washing is seen in Acts xxii.16, where S. Paul recalls that Ananias said to him, "Arise and be baptized and wash away thy sins, calling on the name of the Lord." The connexion between this washing and the death of Christ is seen in passages like I Corinthians vi.11, "but ye are washed, but ye were sanctified, but ye were justified in the name of the Lord Jesus, and by the Spirit of our God"; and Ephesians v.25f, "Christ also loved the Church and gave Himself for it, that He might sanctify and cleanse it by the washing of water by the Word, that He Might present it to Himself a glorious Church, not having spot or wrinkle . . . but that it should be holy and without blemish." In these passages Christ's work is described as a cleansing of the Church and of believers, in language reminiscent of the Old Testament ideas of covenant and sacrifice. Since believers are first incorporated in Christ's work by means of Baptism in water and Spirit, it is

---

105. Torrance, "Introductory Note," 5.
106. Torrance, *Biblical Doctrine of Baptism*, 26.

inevitable that this language of cleansing should be applied to Baptism—whether the two passages cited refer directly to Baptism or not.[107]

Comments on Rom 6:4:

> The action of Baptism, with its symbolism of death and resurrection, is not merely symbolic. It is the act of transfer into the new age; it is God's act bestowing participation in Christ which is no less real than our former participation in the sinful humanity represented by Adam . . . S. Paul's assertion is that what happened for us in the death and resurrection of Christ has happened to us in Baptism, committing us to a personal death to sin and a personal resurrection to newness of life. This is a change which controls our whole life ever afterward. Our personal dying and rising with Christ are not our own work, but Christ's life-giving death and resurrection life now active in us (cf. among many passages Galatians ii. 19f.), for He who died and rose again is Himself really, and not merely symbolically, present to the baptized, uniting them to Himself in their faith and life.[108]

> If the condition of entrance into the Kingdom of God is at the same time being born of water and of the Spirit, and becoming like a little child, it is incredible that our Lord would have us refuse Baptism to those children whom even adult candidates for Baptism need to resemble in order to enter the Kingdom of God. It is "as little children" that all must be baptized, whatever the actual age . . . Our Lord, who bids His disciples receive little children in His name, cannot refuse to receive them Himself in the sacrament of Baptism.[109]

Theology in Reconciliation, Essays towards Evangelical and Catholic Unity in East and West

1975

Certainly ritual and ethical acts have their proper place in the administration of baptism, but baptism itself is focused beyond those acts upon the one saving act of God embodied in Jesus

---

107. Torrance, *Biblical Doctrine of Baptism*, 22–23.
108. Torrance, *Biblical Doctrine of Baptism*, 26.
109. Torrance, *Biblical Doctrine of Baptism*, 50–51.

Christ in such a way that, when the Church baptizes in his name, it is actually Christ himself who is savingly at work, pouring out his Spirit upon us and drawing us within the power of his vicarious life, death and resurrection.[110]

For us baptism means that we become one with him, sharing in his righteousness, and that we are sanctified in him as members of the messianic people of God, compacted together in one Body in Christ ... That is the one baptism common to Christ and his Church which every act of baptism in the Church presupposes, and from which it derives its significance and efficacy. Thus whenever the Church in obedience to the command of Christ baptizes specific individual with water in the Name of the Father and the Son and the Holy Spirit, it believes that Christ himself is present baptizing with his Spirit, acknowledging and blessing the action of the Church as his own, fulfilling in the baptized what he has already done for them and making them share in the fruit of his finished work. While in this sense baptism is both the act of Christ and the act of the Church, they may well be distinguished but may not be separated, for their content, reality and power are the same. Hence the baptism of individual people is to be understood as their initiation into and sharing in the one vicarious *baptisma* of Christ. Through his birth they have a new birth and are made members of the new humanity. Through his obedient life and death as the incarnate Son their sins are forgiven and they are clothed with a new righteousness ... As an ordinance, then, baptism sets forth not what we do, nor primarily what the Church does to us, but what God has already done in Christ, and through His Spirit continues to do in and to us. Appropriately, therefore, we *are baptized*. Baptism is administered to us in the name of the Triune God, and our part is only to receive it, for we cannot add anything to Christ's finished work.[111]

William Barclay

William Barclay was born in 1907 in Wick, Scotland, and died in 1978. He was a Scottish author, radio and television speaker, Church of Scotland minister, and Professor of Divinity and Biblical Criticism at the University

---

110. Torrance, *Theology in Reconciliation*, 83.
111. Torrance, *Theology in Reconciliation*, 87–88.

of Glasgow. He was a prolific writer and wrote a popular set of Bible commentaries on the New Testament that sold 1.5 million copies.

The Letters to the Galatians and Ephesians

1958

The early Christians looked on baptism as something which really and truly produced a real union with Christ ... Baptism was no mere outward form or ceremony; it was a real union with Christ, Paul goes on to say that they had put on Christ.[112]

Gleason L. Archer

Gleason Leonard Archer Jr. was born in 1916 and died in 2004. He was a member of the Massachusetts Bar and a biblical professor, theologian, and author. He was also one of the fifty original translators of the New American Standard Version of the Bible and worked on the team that translated the New International Version of the Bible. He was noted as an able defender of the doctrine of biblical inerrancy.

The Epistle to the Romans, A Study Manual

1959

The transaction signified by baptism is both a cleansing from sin and a union with Christ in His death, so that we in effect died on the cross with Him.[113]

Emil Brunner

Heinrich Emil Brunner was born in 1889 and died in 1966. He was a Swiss Reformed theologian. Along with Karl Barth, he is commonly associated with neo-orthodoxy.

---

112. Barclay, *Letters*, 35.
113. Archer, *Epistle to the Romans*, 33.

The Letter to the Romans, A Commentary

1959

Thus we too who are baptized, in having not only been submerged but also having emerged again, have been immersed not only into the death of Christ, but above all into his life, his resurrected life, his divine life ... Baptism makes us partakers of the future resurrection.[114]

G. R. Beasley-Murray

George Raymond Beasley-Murray was born in 1916 and died in 2000. He was a prominent British Baptist scholar who made significant contributions toward a return to the biblical approach to baptism. His book, Baptism in the New Testament, *is a highly acclaimed and influential examination of the purpose of baptism in the New Testament. He was Principal of Spurgeon's College, London, and later, Professor of New Testament Interpretation at Southern Baptist Theological Seminary. He wrote several books on theological topics and commentaries on John's Gospel and Revelation.*

Baptism in the New Testament

1962

If then baptism was practiced in the earliest church, what significance was assigned to it? In the judgement of [Rudolph] Bultman, the rite at this period must have been essentially similar in import to the baptism of John; it was "a bath of purification for the coming Reign of God."[115]

Baptism is an overt, public act that expresses inward decision and intent; since it is performed in the open, and not in secret, it becomes by its nature a confession of a faith and allegiance embraced. If baptism "in the name of Jesus" is a baptism "with respect to Jesus", and so distinguished from all other kinds of baptism by its relation to Him, then to submit to it becomes a confession of trust in Him. It is but natural that what is involved

---

114. Brunner, *Letter to the Romans*, 50.
115. Beasley-Murray, *Baptism in the New Testament*, 99.

in the event itself should be brought to explicit mention and that the confession, "Jesus is Lord", be uttered by the one baptized.[116]

On the basis of the exposition offered above [first four chapters], and without any attempt to give exhaustive references, the "grace" available to man in baptism is said by the New Testament writers to include the following elements: forgiveness of sin, Acts 2.38 and cleansing from sin Acts 22.16, 1 Cor. 6.11; union with Christ, Gal. 3.27, and particularly union with Him in his death and resurrection, Rom. 6.3 ff, Col. 2.11 f, with all that implies of release from sin's power, as well as guilt, and the sharing of the risen life of the Redeemer, Rom. 6.1-11; Participation in Christ's sonship, Gal. 2.26 f; consecration to God, 1 Cor. 6.11, hence membership in the Church, the Body of Christ, 1 Cor. 12.13, Gal. 3.27-29; possession of the Spirit, Acts 2.38, 1 Cor. 6.11, 12.13, and therefore the new life in the Spirit, i.e. regeneration, Tit. 3.5, Jn 3.5; grace to live according to the will of God, Rom. 6.1 ff, Col. 3.1 ff; deliverance from the evil powers that rule this world, Col. 1.13; the inheritance of the Kingdom of God, Jn 3.5, and the pledge of the resurrection of the body, Eph. 1.13 f, 4.30.[117]

In baptism the Gospel proclamation and the hearing of faith become united in one indissoluble act, at one and the same time an act of grace and faith, and act of God and man . . . for *in the New Testament precisely the same gifts of grace are associated with faith as with baptism*. Forgiveness, cleansing and justification are the effect of baptism in Acts 2.38, 22.16, 1 Cor. 6.11.[118]

F. F. Bruce

Frederick Fyvie Bruce was born in 1910 and died in 1990. As a British biblical scholar, he was instrumental in preserving the historical reliability of the New Testament. Professor Bruce, besides being a popular teacher and lecturer, wrote numerous articles and books and commentaries that have become classics in New Testament studies.

---

116. Beasley-Murray, *Baptism*, 101.
117. Beasley-Murray, *Baptism*, 263-64.
118. Beasley-Murray, *Baptism*, 72.

The Epistle of Paul to the Romans, An Introduction and Commentary

1963

Faith in Christ and baptism were, indeed, not so much two distinct experiences as parts of one whole; faith in Christ was an essential element in baptism, for without it the application of water, even accompanied by the appropriate words, would not have been baptism.

But when believers were baptized, what happened? This says Paul. Their former life came to an end; a new began. They were, in fact, 'buried' with Christ when they were plunged in the baptismal water, in token that they had died so far as their old life of sin was concerned; they were raised again with Christ when they emerged from the water, in token that they received a new life, which was nothing less than participation in Christ's own resurrection life . . . Baptism thus seals the believer's exodus, his deliverance from the bondage of sin.[119]

Paul: Apostle of the Heart Set Free

1977

That Paul himself at his conversion was baptized and so had his sins washed away is the testimony of Acts 22:16 (cf. 9:18). When in his letters he reminds his Christian readers of the meaning of their baptism he associates his own baptism with theirs: "all of us who were baptized into Christ Jesus were baptized into his death" (Romans 6:3); "in one Spirit we were all baptized into one body" (1 Corinthians 12:13). At the same time he gives baptism—theirs and his—a new depth of meaning. Baptism, in Paul's teaching, initiates believers into their state of being "in Christ", so that his historical death and resurrection become part of their spiritual experience; the baptism in the Spirit which the risen Lord then effects incorporates them into one body with him—or, as Paul puts it to the Galatians, "as many of you as were baptized into Christ have put on Christ . . . you are all one in Christ Jesus" (Galatians 3:27f) . . . It is unlikely that they [the Corinthian converts] dissociated the washing from their baptism in water, but it was the divine action in their lives that gave

---

119. Bruce, *Paul to the Romans*, 136–37.

their baptism effective meaning and caused Paul to use what has been called the language of sacramental realism.[120]

Paul gives his readers no ground for supposing that baptism makes no practical difference or that it is an optional extra in Christian life. He takes it for granted that all believers have been baptized, just as he takes it for granted that they have all received the Spirit.[121]

D. Martyn Lloyd-Jones

David Martyn Lloyd-Jones was born in 1899 and died in 1981. He was a Welsh Protestant minister and medical doctor. For almost 30 years, he was the minister of Westminster Chapel in London. In his commentary on Romans 6, he argued strongly that baptism is what brings us into unity with Christ, but that in Romans 6, this baptism is not a baptism in water, the water baptism comes later after conversion.

Romans: The New Man, Exposition of Chapter 6

1972

The teaching of the New Testament is that the people who are to be baptized are those who have already given evidence that they are regenerated; it is believers who are baptized in the New Testament. So it is not the act of baptism that makes them believers, it is because they are believers, or are presumed to be believers, that they are baptized ... The cases given in the New Testament itself clearly show that, far from giving life and union, baptism is rather meant to be something that seals a preceding happening, or is given as an attestation or a seal of an accomplished fact.[122]

The conclusion therefore at which I arrive is that baptism by water is not in the mind of the Apostle at all in these two verses [Romans 6:3–4]; instead it is the baptism that is wrought by the Spirit.[123]

---

120. Bruce, *Paul*, 280–81.
121. Bruce, *Paul*, 282.
122. Lloyd-Jones, *Romans*, 31.
123. Lloyd-Jones, *Romans*, 36.

Baptism is important, baptism is a command which must be carried out; but do not go to the sixth chapter of Romans for it. You can discuss it and argue about it from some other texts, but do not bring it here.[124]

Robert H. Stein

Robert H. Stein (1935–present) is a retired senior professor of New Testament interpretation at The Southern Baptist Theological Seminary in Louisville, Kentucky. He previously taught for 28 years at Bethel Theological Seminary in Arden Hills, Minnesota. He is a well-known scholar of the Synoptic Gospels.

Baptism in Luke–Acts

2006

The intercourse of repentance, faith, and baptism is witnessed too by the fact that they all lead to the forgiveness of sins. It would certainly be wrong to think that Luke believed these were three separate ways of receiving forgiveness: the "repentance" way, the "faith" way, and the "baptism" way. On the contrary, he understood them as all part of the experience of becoming a Christian. This is even more evident on the occasions where these components are paired together in Acts as bringing about the forgiveness of sins.[125]

Within the Book of Acts water-baptism "in/into the name of Jesus/Lord Jesus/Jesus Christ" is understood as an essential part of becoming a Christian.[126]

Thomas R. Schreiner

Thomas R. Schreiner, born in 1954, is the James Buchanan Harrison Professor of New Testament Interpretation and the Associate Dean for the Scripture and Interpretation Division at The Southern Baptist Theological Seminary in Louisville, Kentucky. He previously taught at Bethel

---

124. Lloyd-Jones, *Romans*, 37.
125. Stein, "Baptism in Luke-Acts," 51.
126. Stein, "Baptism in Luke-Acts," 63.

Theological Seminary and Azusa Pacific University. He is also the New Testament editor of the English Standard Version Study Bible.

"Baptism in the Epistles: An Initiation Rite for Believers"

2006

[Comments on 1 Peter 1:21] Baptism is only saving if there is an appeal to God for a good conscience through the resurrection of Jesus Christ. In other words, baptism saves only because it is anchored to the death and resurrection of Jesus Christ. The waters themselves do not cleanse as is the case when a bath removes dirt from the body. Indeed, the objective work of Jesus Christ in his death and resurrection does not save unless there is a subjective element as well. The one receiving baptism also appeals to God for a good conscience, which means that he asks God to cleanse him of his sins on the basis of Christ's death and resurrection . . . It seems to me that the notion of appeal is slightly preferable since it: (1) fits the verbal form of the word (*eperotao*); (2) does not focus on the promise to live a godly life but on God's saving work based on Christ's cross and resurrection; and (3) fits with what occurs at the inception of the Christian life—the forgiveness and cleansing of sin.[127]

Everett Ferguson

Everett Ferguson was born in 1933. He is a Distinguished Scholar in Residence at Abilene Christian University in Abilene, Texas. He is the author of numerous books on early Christian studies.

Baptism in the Early Church

2009

Christian sources consistently saw the antecedent to Christian baptism in the practice of John the Baptizer. They applied the same distinctive terminology, *baptisma* (other dippings were

---

127. Schreiner, "Baptism in the Epistles," 70.

designated by the word *baptismos*), and the same purpose, "forgiveness of sins," to John's baptism as they did to their own.[128]

The apostle Paul is a central figure for the study of Christian baptism. His own experience and the evidence of his letters show baptism to have been practiced from the earliest days of the church. He included himself with his readers as baptized (1 Cor. 12:13), and his conversion must be placed within a very few years of the crucifixion. He takes baptism for granted as common ground with his readers and refers to it in order to make an argument about something else. The frequent references to baptism in his writings offer a profound understanding of its significance.[129]

The predominant number of baptismal fonts permitted immersion, and many were so large as to defy any reason for their existence other than for immersion.[130]

The New Testament and early Christian literature are virtually unanimous in ascribing a saving significance to baptism . . . Only a few (fringe) heretics of the ancient church tried to dehydrate the new birth.[131]

David Platt

David Platt was born in 1978. He is a Southern Baptist preacher, an author, and a teacher at McLean Bible Church, a mega-church in the Washington D.C. area.

"Baptism: Identification with the New Covenant"

March 22, 2009

The primary reason to be baptized is not to become a member of a church, the primary reason to be baptized is to obey Christ, period. Baptism is not primarily a church membership issue. Baptism is primarily an obedience issue. And this is the primary reason every single follower of Christ in this room needs to be

---

128. Ferguson, *Baptism*, 83.
129. Ferguson, *Baptism*, 146.
130. Ferguson, *Baptism*, 849.
131. Ferguson, *Baptism*, 854.

baptized, to follow the example of Christ, and to obey the command of Christ because not to be baptized is to live in disobedience, to live in sin.[132]

"Baptism: More Than Just a Symbol"

October 10, 2011

What is the meaning of baptism? Number one, I believe that baptism is a celebration of the grace of Christ . . . Baptism is a celebration of that grace. The Scriptures teach very clearly that it is trust, faith in the grace of Christ alone that brings us to salvation. What that means is that baptism is not necessary for salvation. Let me say that again, baptism is not necessary for salvation. It's not something we do to earn salvation . . . Baptism is not necessary for salvation. That doesn't mean it's not important, but it does mean it is not necessary. It's a celebration of grace . . . When you see someone being baptized, that's not their salvation. It's the illustration, it's the representation of what Christ has done in their life . . . Baptism is a declaration to the world that we belong to Jesus.[133]

Wally Morris

Wally Morris is a minister in the Charity Baptist Church in Huntington, IN, and he is a contributing author on the website Proclaim & Defend, *a blog of the online voice of the Foundations Baptist Fellowship International.*

"Acts 2:38 and Baptismal Regeneration"

2017

Acts 2:38 uses the same preposition as Matthew 3:11. Prepositions have a wide variety of meaning and to base a major doctrinal belief only on prepositions is risky. However, prepositions have their place in exegesis. If we take the reasoning of supporters of baptismal regeneration in Acts 2:38 and apply that same reasoning to Matthew 3:11, then John the Baptist baptized

---

132. Platt, "Baptism."
133. Platt, "Baptism."

people so that they would receive repentance or that they would repent. Actually, John refused to baptize people until they demonstrated some evidence of repentance (Matthew 3:8). In other words, John baptized people because they had already repented or when they demonstrated evidence of repentance. Their repentance became the basis of John's baptism.[134]

---

134. Morris, "Acts 2:38."

Bibliography

Alford, Henry. "The Gospel According to Matthew." in *The Greek Testament*. 4th ed., 1:1-292. London: Gilbert and Rivington, 1859.

———. "The Epistle to the Ephesians." in *The Greek Testament*. 3rd ed., 3:6-25. London: Gilbert and Rivington, 1859.

Allen, Ronald B. "*ahtsab*." in *Theological Wordbook of the Old Testament*, Edited by R. Laird Harris, 1:687-88. Chicago: Moody, 1980.

Ambrose. *St. Ambrose On the Mysteries and the Treatise on the Sacraments*. Edited by J. H. Strawley. Translated by T. Thompson. New York: Alpha Editions, 2020.

"Apostolic Constitutions." in *Ante-Nicene Fathers of the Christian Church*. vol. 7, Edited by Alexander Roberts and James Donaldson. PC Study Bible electronic database. Seattle: Biblesoft, Inc., 2010.

Aquinas, Thomas. *Summa Theologica*. in *Great Books of the Western World*. vol. 20, Edited by Robert Hutchins, Translated by Fathers of the English Dominican Province. Chicago: Encyclopaedia Britannica, Inc., 1952.

Archer, Gleason, Jr. *The Epistle to the Romans: A Study Manual*. Shield Bible Study Series. Grand Rapids: Baker Book House, 1959.

Athanasius of Alexandria. *Discourses Against the Arians*. in *Nicene and Post-Nicene Fathers*. Vol. 4, Edited by Archibald Robertson and Philip Schaff. PC Study Bible electronic database. Seattle: Biblesoft, Inc., 2010.

Augustine. *The Confessions*. in *Great Books of the Western World*, Edited by Robert Hutchins, Translated by Edward Bouverie Pusey, 18:1-125. Chicago: Encyclopaedia Britannica, 1952.

———. *The City of God*. in *Great Books of the Western World*, Edited by Robert Hutchins, Translated by Marcus Dodds, 18:129-618. Chicago: Encyclopaedia Britannica, 1952.

———. *Enchiridion*. Radford, VA: Wilder Publications, 2012.

———. *On Christian Doctrine*. in *Great Books of the Western World*, Edited by Robert Hutchins, Translated by J.F. Shaw, 18:621-98. Chicago: Encyclopaedia Britannica, 1952.

Barclay, William. *The Letters to the Galatians and Ephesians*. The Daily Study Bible Series, 2nd ed. Philadelphia: Westminster, 1958.

Barnes, Albert. "Acts 2:37." In *Barnes Notes on the Old and New Testaments*. PC Study Bible electronic database. Seattle: Biblesoft, Inc., 2010.

Barth, Karl. *The Epistle to the Romans*. Translated by Edwyn C. Hoskyns. 6th ed. London: Oxford University, 1968.

Basil the Great. *On the Holy Spirit.* in *Nicene and Post-Nicene Fathers* Vol. 8, Edited by Archibald Robertson and Philip Schaff. PC Study Bible electronic database. Seattle: Biblesoft, Inc., 2010.

Baur, Walter. *A Greek-English Lexicon of the New Testament and Other Early Christian Literature.* 2nd ed. Revised by F. Wilbur Gingrich and Frederick W. Danker. Chicago: The University of Chicago, 1979.

Beasley-Murray, George R. *Baptism in the New Testament.* Grand Rapids: Eerdmans, 1962.

Behm, Johannes. "*Metamorphoo*." in *Theological Dictionary of the New Testament,* Edited by G. Kittel and G. Friedrich, Translated by G. W. Bromiley, 4:755–59. Grand Rapids: Eerdmans, 1976.

Bonhoeffer, Dietrich. *The Cost of Discipleship.* New York: Macmillan, 1963.

Bettenson, Henry, ed. and trans. *The Early Christian Fathers: A Selection from the Writings of the Fathers from St. Clement of Rome to St. Athanasius.* New York: Oxford University Press, 1956.

Blass, F., and A. Debrunner. *A Greek Grammar of the New Testament and Other Early Christian Literature.* 10th ed. Translated and revised by Robert W. Funk. Chicago: University of Chicago Press, 1961.

Brents, Thomas Wesley. *The Gospel Plan of Salvation.* 14th ed. Nashville: Gospel Advocate, 1957.

Bruce, F. F. *The Book of Acts.*in *The New International Commentary on the New Testament,* Edited by F.F. Bruce. Grand Rapids: Eerdmans, 1981.

———. *The English Bible: A History of Translations from the Earliest English Versions to the New English Bible.* New York: Oxford University Press, 1970.

———. *The Epistle of Paul to the Romans, An Introduction and Commentary.* Tyndale New Testament Commentaries. Edited by R. V. G. Tasker. Grand Rapids: Eerdmans, 1963.

———. *Paul: Apostle of the Heart Set Free.* Grand Rapids: Eerdmans, 1977.

Bruner, Frederick Dale. *A Theology of the Holy Spirit.* Grand Rapids: 1970.

Brunner, Emil. *The Letter to the Romans: A Commentary.* Philadelphia: The Westminster, 1959.

Buchsel, Friedrich. "*palingenesia*." in *Theological Dictionary of the New Testament,* Edited by G. Kittel and G. Friedrich, Translated by G. W. Bromiley, 1:688–89. Grand Rapids: Eerdmans, 1964.

Burton, Ernest De Witt. *Syntax of the Moods and Tenses in New Testament Greek.* 3rd ed. Edinburgh: T. & T. Clark, 1973.

Calvin, John. *Institutes of the Christian Religion.* Translated by Henry Beveridge. Edinburgh: Calvin Translation Society, 1845. https://ccel.org/ccel/calvin/institutes/institutes.i.html.

Campbell, Alexander. *The Christian System.* Nashville: Gospel Advocate, 1974.

Cauley, Kevin. "Were the Sins of Those Under the Old Covenant 'Rolled Forward'?" March 17, 2005. https://gewatkins.net/were-the-sins-of-those-under-the-old-covenant-rolled-forward/. G. E. Watkins

Chrysostom, John. *Instructions to Catechumens.* in *Nicene and Post-Nicene Fathers* Vol. 9, Edited by Philip Schaff. PC Study Bible electronic database. Seattle: Biblesoft, Inc. 2010.

Clement of Alexandria. *Instructor (also known as Tutor or Pedagogue).* in *Ante-Nicene Fathers of the Christian Church* Vol. 2, Edited by Rev. Alexander Roberts and

James Donaldson. Seattle: PC Study Bible electronic database. Seattle: Biblesoft, Inc., 2010.

"Confused Prepositions." ProWritingAid. https://prowritingaid.com/grammar/1000 145/Confused-epositions#:~:text=Prepositions%20are%20words%20that%20 show%20a%20relationship%20between,include%20to,%20on,%20for,%20at,%20 in,%20and%20of. Chris Banks, CEO.

Cowper, William. "God Moves in a Mysterious Way." in *Songs of Faith and Praise*, West Monroe, LA: Howard Publishing, 1994.

Cyprian of Alexandria. *The Epistles of Cyprian.* in *Ante-Nicene Fathers of the Christian Church* Vol. 5, Edited by Rev. Alexander Roberts and James Donaldson. PC Study Bible electronic database. Seattle: Biblesoft, Inc. 2010.

———. *The Treatises of Cyprian.* in *Ante-Nicene Fathers of the Christian Church* Vol. 5, Edited by Alexander Roberts and James Donaldson. PC Study Bible electronic database. Seattle: Biblesoft, Inc. 2010.

Cyril of Jerusalem. *Catechetical Lectures.* in *Nicene and Post-Nicene Fathers of The Christian Church* Vol. 7, Edited by Philip Schaff and Henry Wace. PC Study Bible electronic database. Seattle: Biblesoft, Inc. 2010.

Dana, H. E., and Julius Mantey. *Manual Grammar of the Greek New Testament.* Toronto: Macmillan, 1927.

Debate.org. "Did Jesus Ever Sin?" http://www.debate.org/opinions/did-jesus-ever-sin. Debate.org was a free online community where people from around the world could come to debate online and read the opinions of others. It is no longer online.

Denny, James. *The Death of Christ.* Edited by R. V. G. Tasker. London: Tyndale, 1951.

———. "St. Paul's Epistle to the Romans." in *The Expositor's Greek Testament,* Edited by W. Robertson Nicoll, 2:555–725. Grand Rapids: Eerdmans, 1961.

Didache (The Teaching of the Twelve Apostles). in *Ante-Nicene Fathers of the Christian Church.* Vol. 7. Edited by Alexander Roberts and James Donaldson. PC Study Bible electronic database. Seattle: Biblesoft, Inc. 2010.

Erasmus, Desiderius. *The Handbook of the Militant Christian.* in *The Essential Erasmus,* Translated by John P. Dolan, 24–93. New York City: Meridian, 1964.

———. *An Inquiry Concerning Faith.* In *The Essential Erasmus,* 205–21 Translated by John P. Dolan. New York City: Meridian, 1964.

———. *Paraphrase on the Gospel According to Matthew.* in *The Collected Works of Erasmus,* Edited by Robert D. Sider,Translated by Dean Simpson. Toronto: University of Toronto, 2008.

Ferguson, Everett. *Baptism in the Early Church: History, Theology, and Liturgy in the First Five Centuries.* Grand Rapids: Eerdmans, 2009.

———. *Early Christians Speak.* Abilene, TX: ACU Press, 1981.

Fowler, Stanley K. *More Than a Symbol: The Baptist Recovery of Baptismal Sacramentalism.* Eugene, Oregon: Wipf & Stock, 2006.

Gregory of Nazianzus. *Orations.* in *Nicene and Post-Nicene Fathers* Vol. 7, Edited by Philip Schaff and Henry Wace. PC Study Bible electronic database. Seattle: Biblesoft, Inc. 2010.

Greeven, Heinrich. "*erotao, eperotao, eperoteima.*" in *Theological Dictionary of the New Testament,* Edited by G. Kittel and G. Friedrich, Translated by G. W. Bromiley, 2:685–89. Grand Rapids: Eerdmans, 1964.

Grundmann, Walter. "*dexomai*." in *Theological Dictionary of the New Testament*, Edited by G. Kittel and G. Friedrich, Translated by G. W. Bromiley, 2:50–59. Grand Rapids: Eerdmans, 1964.

———. "On the Use of *soun* and of *metah* with the Genitive." in *Theological Dictionary of the New Testament*, Edited by G. Kittel and G. Friedrich, Translated by G. W. Bromiley, 7:766–67. Grand Rapids: Eerdmans, 1971.

Guthrie, Donald. *New Testament Introduction*. Downers Grove, IL: Inter-Varsity, 1970.

Hagner, Donald A. "Matthew 1–13." in *Word Biblical Commentary* Vol. 33A, Edited by David A. Hubbard and Glen W. Barker. Dallas: Word Books, 1993.

Harrison, Everett F. *Introduction to the New Testament*. Grand Rapids: Eerdmans, 1964.

Hauck, Walter. "*hagnos, hagnidzo, hagneia, hagnoteis, hagnismos*." in *Theological Dictionary of the New Testament*, Edited by G. Kittel and G. Friedrich, Translated by G. W. Bromiley, 1:122–24. Grand Rapids: Eerdmans, 1964.

Hawn, C. Michael. "History of Hymns: 'Nothing but the Blood.'" *Discipleship Ministries*, July 2, 2013. https://www.umcdiscipleship.org/resources/history-of-hymns-nothing-but-the-blood.

Ignatius. *Epistles of Ignatius*. in *The Apostolic Fathers*, edited by Kirsopp Lake. PC Study Bible electronic database. Seattle: Biblesoft, Inc. 2010.

Irenaeus. *Against Heresies*. in *Ante-Nicene Fathers of the Christian Church*. Vol. 1, Edited by Alexander Roberts and James Donaldson. PC Study Bible electronic database. Seattle: Biblesoft, Inc. 2010.

Josephus, Flavius. *Antiquities of the Jews*. in *The Works of Josephus*. Translated by William Whiston. 15th printing, 27-542. Peabody, MA: Hendrickson Publishers, 1987.

Justin Martyr. *Dialogue With Trypho, a Jew*. in *Ante-Nicene Fathers of the Christian Church*. Vol. 1. Edited by Rev. Alexander Roberts and James Donaldson. PC Study Bible electronic database. Seattle: Biblesoft, Inc. 2010.

———. *First Apology*. in *Ante-Nicene Fathers of the Christian Church*. Vol. 1. Edited by Alexander Roberts and James Donaldson. PC Study Bible electronic database. Seattle: Biblesoft, Inc. 2010.

Keach, Benjamin. *Gold Refin'd; or Baptism in its Primitive Purity*. in *More Than a Symbol: The Baptist Recovery of Baptismal Sacramentalism*. Stanley K. Fowler. Eugene, Oregon: Wipf & Stock, 2006.

Keil, C. F. "The First Book of Moses (Genesis)." in *Commentary on the Old Testament*. 1:19–268. By C. F. Keil and F. Delitzch, Translated by James Martin. 3rd printing. Massachuetts: Hendricksen Publishers Marketing. 2011.

———. "Ezekiel." in *Commentary on the Old Testament*. 9:3-480. By C. F. Keil and F. Delitzch, Translated by James Martin. 3rd printing. Massachuetts: Hendricksen Publishers Marketing. 2011.

Knowles, R. J. "The Acts of the Apostles." *The Expositor's Greek Testament*. 2:1–554. Edited by W. Robertson Nicoll. Grand Rapids: Eerdmans, 1961.

Lambdin, Thomas O. *Introduction to Biblical Hebrew*. New York: Charles Scribner's Sons, 1971.

Lard, Moses E. "Baptism in One Spirit Into One Body." *Lard's Quarterly* 1 (1864) 271–82. Kansas City: Old Paths Book Club, 1949.

———. "Do the Unimmersed Commune?" *Lard's Quarterly* 1 (1863) 41–52. Kansas City: Old Paths Book Club, 1949.

Lewis, Jack P. "EIS, 'For the Forgiveness' or 'Because of Forgiveness?'" *Forgiven in Christ.* http://www.forgiveninchrist.org/eis.shtml.

Lightfoot, J. B. *Saint Paul's Epistles to the Colossians and to Philemon.* Grand Rapids: Zondervan, 1961.

Lloyd-Jones, D. Martyn. *Romans: An Exposition of Romans 6, The New Man.* Grand Rapids: Zondervan, 1972.

Locke, John. *An Essay Concerning Human Understanding.* Victoria, Canada: Anodos Books (a subsidiary of ABE Books). 2019

Louw, Johannes P. and Eugene A. Nida. *Greek-English Lexicon of the New Testament.* PC Study Bible electronic database. Seattle: Biblesoft, Inc., 2010.

Luther, Martin. *Luther's Large Catechism: A Contemporary Translation with Study Questions.* Translated by F. Samuel Janzow. St. Louis, MO: Concordia. 1978.

Machen, James Gresham. *New Testament Greek for Beginners.* New York: Macmillan, 1923.

Mantey, Julius R. "The Causal Use of *Eis* in the New Testament." *Journal of Biblical Literature* 70, no. 1 (1951) 45–48.

———. "On Causal *Eis* Again." *Journal of Biblical Literature* 70, no. 4 (1951) 309–11.

Marcus, Ralph. "The Elusive Causal *Eis*." *Journal of Biblical Literature* 71, no. 1 (1952) 43–44.

———. "On Causal *Eis*." *Journal of Biblical Literature* 70, no. 2 (1951) 129–30.

Martin, Ralph. "Approaches to New Testament Exegesis." in *New Testament Interpretation: Essays on Principles and Methods*, Edited by Ian Howard Marshall, 220–51. Exeter: Paternoster. 1977.

———. *Colossians: The Church's Lord and the Christian's Liberty.* Exeter: Paternoster, 1972.

McComiskey, Thomas E. "*qadash*." in *Theological Wordbook of the Old Testament*, Edited by R. Laird Harris, 2:786–87. Chicago: Moody, 1980.

McGee, J. Vernon. *The Tabernacle: God's Portrait of Christ.* Rev. ed. Pasadena: Thru the Bible Radio Network, 2002. https://ttb.org/docs/default-source/booklets/tabernacle.pdf?sfvrsn=2.

McIntyre, Luther B. "Baptism and Forgiveness in Acts 2:38." *Bibliotheca Sacra* 153 (Jan–Mar 1996) 53–62. http://faculty.gordon.edu/hu/bi/ted_hildebrandt/ntesources/ntarticles/bsac-nt/mcintyre-baptforgive-acts2-bs.pdf.

Michel, Otto. "*metamelomai, ametameleitos*." in *Theological Dictionary of the New Testament*, Edited by G. Kittel and G. Friedrich, Translated by G. W. Bromiley, 4:626–29. Grand Rapids: Eerdmans, 1967.

Morris, Wally. "Acts 2:38 and Baptismal Regeneration." *Proclaim & Defend.* November 27, 2017. https://www.proclaimanddefend.org/2017/11/27/acts-238-and-baptismal-regeneration/.

Moule, C. F. D. *The Epistles to the Colossians and to Philemon.* in *The Cambridge Greek Testament Commentary*, Edited by C. F. D. Moule. Cambridge: Cambridge University Press, 1957.

Neill, Stephen. *Paul to the Colossians.* New York: Association, 1964.

Newell, William. "Years I Spent in Vanity." in *Songs of Faith and Praise*, West Monroe, LA: Howard Publishing, 1994.

Oekpe, Albrecht. "*baptw, baptidzw*." in *Theological Dictionary of the New Testament*,Edited by G. Kittel and G. Friedrich, Translated by G. W. Bromiley, 1:529–46. Grand Rapids: Eerdmans. 1964.

———. "louo, apolouo, loutron." in *Theological Dictionary of the New Testament*, Edited by G. Kittel and G. Friedrich,Translated by G. W. Bromiley, 4:295–307. Grand Rapids: Eerdmans, 1967.

Ovid. *Fasti*. Translated by A. S. Kline. Poetry in Translation, 2004. https://www.poetryintranslation.com/PITBR/Latin/OvidFastiBkTwo.php#anchor_Toc69367683

Perrine, Tim. *Institutes of the Christian Religion by John Calvin.* in *Christian Classics Ethereal Library*. Translated by Henry Beveridge. https://www.ccel.org/ccel/calvin/institutes.

Philo, Julius. *On the Cherubim*. in *The Works of Philo*, 5th printing. Translated by C. D. Yonge. 80–93. Peabody, Massachusetts: Hendrickson, 2000.

"Pillory." Wikipedia. Wikimedia Foundation, April 11, 2022. https://en.wikipedia.org/wiki/Pillory .

Plato. *Cratylus*. in *Great Books of the Western World*, Edited by Robert Maynard Hutchins, Translated by Benjamin Jopwett, 7:85–114. Chicago: Encyclopaedia Britannica, 1952.

Platt, David. "Baptism: Identification with the New Covenant." Radical.net. Video, 1:00:21. March 22, 2009. https://radical.net/baptism-more-than-just-a-symbol/.

———. "Baptism - more than just a symbol." You Tube video, 43:22. October 2, 2011. https://youtu.be/pAmGifIjo5w.

Plutarch. *On Isis and Osiris*. in *Moralia* 5, Translated by Loeb Classical Library edition.1936
https://penelope.uchicago.edu/Thayer/E/Roman/Texts/Plutarch/Moralia/Isis_and_Osiris*/A.html.

Polhill, John B. *Acts: An Exegetical and Theological Exposition of Holy Scripture*. New American Commentary Vol. 26. Nashville: Broadman, 1992.

Procksch, Otto. "hagios." in *Theological Dictionary of the New Testament,* Edited by G. Kittel and G. Friedrich,Translated by G. W. Bromiley, 1:88–115. Grand Rapids: Eerdmans, 1964.

Reeve, Simon. "Sacred Rivers: the Nile, the Ganges, and the Yangtze—Cradles of Civilisation." *Globalisation for the Common Good*. October 21, 2014. http://www.gcgi.info/index.php/blog/632-sacred-rivers-the-nile-the-ganges-and-the-yangtze-cradles-of-civilisation.

Robertson, A. T. "Acts 2:38." *Robertson's Word Pictures of the New Testament*. StudyLight.org. https://www.ccel.org/ccel/robertson_at/word/word.viii.ii.html. 1927

———. *A Grammar of the Greek New Testament in the Light of Historical Research*. Nashville: Broadman, 1934.

———. *Paul and the Intellectuals*. Nashville: Broadman, 1956.

Robertson, A.T., and W. Hersey Davis. *A New Short Grammar of the Greek Testament*. 10th ed. Grand Rapids: Baker Book House, 1977.

Sandy, William, and Arthur C. Headlam. "The Mystical Union of the Christian with Christ." in *Critical and Exegetical Commentary on The Epistle to the Romans*, 5th ed., Edited by S.R. Driver, A. Plummer, and C. A. Briggs, 153–66. Edinburgh: T & T Clark, 1902.

Schreiner, Thomas R. "Baptism in the Epistles: An Initiation Rite for Believers." in *Believer's Baptism, Sign of the New Covenant in Christ*, Edited by Thomas R Schreiner and Shawn D. Wright, 67–96. Nashville: B & H Publishing Group, 2006.

BIBLIOGRAPHY

Simmons, Menno. "Concerning Baptism." in *The Complete Works of Menno Simmon, Trans. from the Original Dutch or Holland*. Christian Classics Ethereal Library. https://ccel.org/ccel/simon/works1/works1.iv.vii.html.

Smith, W. T., and W. J. Harrelson. "Holiness." In *Dictionary of the Bible*, Edited by James Hastings, Revised by Frederick C. Grant and H. H. Rowley, 387-88. New York: Charles Scribner's Sons, 1963.

Stein, Robert H. "Baptism in Luke-Acts." in *Believer's Baptism, Sign of the New Covenant in Christ*, Edited by Thomas R. Schreiner and Shawn D. Wright, 35–65. Nashville: B & H Publishing Group, 2006.

Thiessen, Henry C. *Lectures in Systematic Theology*. Revised by Vernon Doerksen. Grand Rapids: Eerdmans, 1979.

Tillich, Paul. *Biblical Religion and the Search for Ultimate Reality*. Chicago: The University of Chicago Press, 1955.

———. *Dynamics of Faith*. New York: Harper & Brothers, 1957.

Tertullian. *On Baptism*. in *Ante-Nicene Fathers of the Christian Churc*. Vol. 3, Edited by Rev. Alexander Roberts and James Donaldson. PC Study Bible electronic database. Seattle: Biblesoft, Inc. 2010.

Torrance, T. F. *The Biblical Doctrine of Baptism: A Study Document Issued by The Special Commission on Baptism of the Church of Scotland*. Edinburgh: Saint Andrew, 1958.

———. *Theology in Reconciliation: Essays towards Evangelical and Catholic Unity in East and West*. Grand Rapids: Eerdmans, 1975.

Trueblood, Elton. *Philosophy of Religion*. New York: Harper & Row, 1957.

Vermes, G., translator. "The Damascus Rule" in *The Dead Sea Scrolls in English*, 2nd ed., 95–117. London: Penguin Books, 1975.

———. "The Hymns." In *The Dead Sea Scrolls in English*, 2nd ed., 149–201. London: Penguin Books, 1975.

———. "The Manual of Discipline" In *The Dead Sea Scrolls in English*, 2nd ed., 72–94. London: Penguin Books, 1975.

Weingreen, J. *A Practical Grammar for Classical Hebrew*. Oxford: Oxford University Press, 1959.

Wesley, John. *A Treatise on Baptism*. in United Methodist Resources. https://danielhixon.blogspot.com/2015/07/john-wesleys-treatise-on-baptism.html.

———. *The Works of John Wesley: Journals and Diaries*, Edited by Ward, W. Reginald and Richard P. Heitzenrater, 18:249–50. Nashville: Abingdon, 1988–2003. https://wesleyscholar.com/wesleys-warmed-heart-at-aldersgate-what-really-happened/#_ftn1.

Wilson, R. "*nacham*," in *Theological Wordbook of the Old Testament*, Edited by R. Laird Harris, 2:570–71. Chicago: Moody, 1980.

Wycliffe, John. *Trialogus*. Edited by Robert Vaughan. London: Blackburn and Pardon, 1845.

Wuest, Kenneth. *Romans in the Greek New Testament for the English Reader*. Grand Rapids: Eerdmans, 1935.

Subject Index

ablutions, 7n2, 48
  characteristics, 11
  pre-Christian, 7
  of Qumran community, 44–46
Abraham, 48, 149
adzomai (pure, clean), 33
age of accountability, 192
ahtsab (Hebrew; displease, hurt), 51
Akkadian language, 28
Alford, Henry, 87, 230–31
alienation from God, 25, 50, 100, 126, 155, 189
allegiance to Christ, 153
aman (Hebrew; faith belief), 178
Amarna heresy, 11n9
Ambrose of Milan, 214–16
Ananias, 116–18, 128, 158
anastas baptisai (Greek), 118
anastas ebaptisthei (Greek), 118
anothen (Greek; again), 96–97
anthropos (Greek; man), 133
Antioch, 198–99
antitupos (Greek), 161
apallotrioo (Greek; estranged), 37
apelousathe (Greek; washed), 159
aphoridzo (Greek; separate, divide), 37
Apollos, 64
apostles, 113, 124, 125, 173. See also disciples of Jesus
  and early church, 126
  and repentance, 78
apostolic church, 179
apostolic constitutions, 211
Aquinas, Thomas, 218–19

Arabia
  Paul in, 128
  war with Herod, 53
Arabic language, 28
Aramaic language, 28
Archer, Gleason L., 243
Ark of the Covenant, 15
Atenism, 11n9
Athanasius of Alexandria, 209
Athanasius the Great (295-373), 210
atonement, 44, 59–60, 129–30, 236
Augustine of Hippo, 216–18

bahdal (Hebrew; separated), 27–28
baptidzo (Greek; baptize), 86, 91
baptidzontes (Greek; baptize), 86
baptism, 133
  beauty of, 142
  being saved, 90
  as birth, 99
  and closeness to God, 32, 87
  and confession, 179–82
  as conversion, 99
  distortions of purpose, 187
  early Christians and, 160
  in early church, 100–126
  of Ephesian disciples of John, 115–16
  and forgiveness, 52, 57–63, 67, 69, 71, 77, 100, 105, 108
  glory of, 141
  and Holy Spirit, 119, 121, 124
  by immersion, 189, 191, 231–32
  of infants, 150–51, 192, 206, 217, 227–28

(baptism continued)
  initiation into Christ, 153
  and Jesus, 79–99, 187
  by John the Baptist, 48
  John the Baptist vs. Jesus' teachings, 63–64
  mode of, 189–91
  modern modes of, 189
  necessity of, 186–87
  new life through, 141
  in New Testament, 49, 100
  in Old Testament, 198
  origins of, 43–48
  by Paul, 64
  as post-conversion experience, 17, 69–70
  power of, 136
  purification and, 22
  purpose of, 68, 71, 86
  redemption and, 25
  and repentance, 49–52, 78, 81, 93, 108
  restoration of, 194
  and salvation, 106, 115, 135
  and sanctification, 100
  as special moment, 135
  as symbolic event, 138
  understanding, 16
  union with Trinity, 120
  in water, 99, 135
  waters of, 137, 166
  as work of God, 106
baptism doctrine, ix
Baptism in the Early Church (Ferguson), 191–92
Baptism in the New Testament (Beasley-Murray), 150, 194
baptisma (Greek; baptism), 162
baptisma matanoias (Greek), 52, 57
baptismal event, 183, 193
baptismal fonts, 192
baptismal formula, Father and Holy Spirit in, 111
baptismal regeneration, 136
baptismal sacramentalism, 87
  recovery of, 87
Baptist radio preachers, 106
baptistheis (Greek), 92

baptistheito (be baptized), 107
baptistries, in early Church years, 191–92
baptizand, as passive recipient, 138–39
Barclay, William, 242–43
Barnabas, epistle of, 198
Barth, Karl, 236–37
Basil the Great, 209–11
Bathseba, 56
Beasley-Murray, George Raymond, 46n11, 87, 112, 121, 142, 144, 150, 157, 160, 168n98, 192–94, 244–45
being set apart, 27–28, 36–37, 39–40
belief, 177–78
  in Christ, 144
Bhramaputra River, 10
Bible
  accuracy of, 62–63
  approaches to, 4–5
  first English, 71
  history, 136
  lack of reasoning for Jesus' baptism, 82
  redefined words, 6
  study of, 66
Bible translations, 71–72, 73, 162–63, 167
  born from above, or born again, 96–97
Bible translators, 71
biblical faith, 175–78
biblical support, 82
biblical teaching, and commitment, 192
Bibliotheca Sacra, 107
Bildad, 15
blashemy, consequences, 21
blessings, 182
blood, importance to life, 130
blood of Christ, 60, 78, 81, 129, 137, 146, 170, 172
  cleansing power of, 100
Body of Christ, 152–53, 172
  induction into, 154
  offering of, 58
body of saint, 132

SUBJECT INDEX

Bonhoeffer, Dietrich, 238–39
Book of the Law, 4
born again, 94, 95n47, 96–98, 200–201, 239
born from above, 95, 95n47, 96, 99, 142, 158, 193
Brents, Thomas, 55
British baptismal doctrine, 144
British Baptist Church, 87, 194
Bruce, Frederick Fyvie, 134, 245–47
Bruner, Frederick, 56, 122
Brunner, Emil, 243–44

Calvin, John, 222–23
Campbell, Alexander, 26, 228–30
Cappadocia, 209
Cappadocian Fathers, 210
Catholic traditions, for sacrament, 184
Cauley, Kevin, 62
chahlal (profaned), 31
charismata, 123–24
children of God, 125
choris (Greek; separate), 37
Christ. See Jesus Christ
Christian Baptism: A Fresh attempt to Understand the Rite in terms of Scripture, History, and Theology, 194
Christian discipleship, 87
Christian doctrines, Paul and, 127–29
Christian life, 181
  growth, 193
The Christian System (Campbell), 26n34
Christianity, as religion of victory or defeat, 129–30
Christians, 130
  distinctiveness of, 146
church, 154–55
  baptism in early, 101
  baptistries in early years, 191–92
  divisions over baptism purpose, 17
  doctrinal statements, 82
  and holiness, 23
  initiation into, 172
  as pure virgin, 35
  role in baptismal event, 184

Church of Christ, 106
circumcision, 47, 149–50
  of Christ, 147
  in New Testament, 150
  physical act of, 136
cleanliness, 174
cleansing, 34, 35, 60, 104, 142, 156, 169, 185
  with blood of Christ, 100
  by forgiveness, 62
  power, 137
cleansing, rituals, 44
cleansing, and sanctification, 39
cleansing agent, 184
Clement of Alexandria, 202–3
comfort, physical display of, 50
commitment to Christ, 90, 146, 178
communication, and relationships, 26
compassion, physical display of, 50
concord, grammar rule, 108
condemnation, deliverance from, 157
confession
  baptism and, 152, 179–82
  New Testament on, 180–81
congregation, 155
conscience, 169–70
consecration, 30
Constantinople, bishopric of, 213
conversion, 50, 51, 52, 76, 90, 133, 173, 188
  and baptism, 57, 68, 141–42, 152, 167
  of Gentile proselytes to Judaism, 97
  and Holy Spirit, 121, 126
  intellectual, 56
  John's call to, 48
  from Judaism to Christianity, 127
  and moral standard, 85
  need for, 95
  from pagan religions, 47
  of Paul, 128
  at Pentecost, 102
  in relationship with God, 52
  repentance and, 110
Corinth, 64
Cornelius, 114–15, 119, 185
  timing of baptism, 193

covenant
  for forgiveness of sins, 78
  with God, 83
Cowper, William, 121
Cross, 63, 84, 125, 129–32, 137, 141, 143–44, 163, 172, 175, 179
  and forgiveness, 60
  in heaven vs. Jerusalem, 132
  Jesus' baptism as precursor, 82
  in Old Testament, 198
  Paul on, 128–29
crucifixion, 131, 138, 140
  responsibility for, 103–4
cultic rituals, 29
Cyprian of Carthage, 205–7
Cyril of Jerusalem, 207–9

Dallas Theological Seminary, 107
Damascus road, Paul on, 117, 127–28
David (king), 14, 56
  on guilt, 61–62
de (Greek), 88
"dead works," 51
The Death of Christ (Denney), 189
death of Jesus, 144, 161, 163. *See also* crucifixion
deity, water and, 8
deliverance, from condemnation, 157
Denney, James, 189, 233–35
dexomai (Greek; receive), 75
dia (Greek; because of), 67, 71
Didache, 190–91, 197
didasko (Greek), 87
didaskontes (Greek; teach), 87
dikaioo (Greek; made right), 175
dikaios (Greek; righteous, just), 34, 75
dikaiosunei (Greek; justification), 83n19, 175
disciples in Qumran community, 45
disciples of Jesus, 75, 94, 187
  baptisms by, 84–85
  commissioning, 43
  making, 86–87, 90, 92, 94, 111
  at Pentecost, 102–4
disciples of John the Baptist, 57, 80, 119, 153
  in Ephesus, 64
disciples of Satan, 155

discipline, of faith, 148
disgrace, images of, 129
distinctness, 19, 26, 32. *See also* being set apart
divine mercy, 45
divine origin of baptism, of John's practices, 47–48
dove, Holy Spirit as, 79

ean (Greek; if), 98
Ean mei tis genneithei (Greek), 98
ebaptistheimen (we have been baptized), 138
edikaiotheite (Greek; justification), 159
Egyptians, purification by, 8
eigapeisen (Greek), 40
eis (Greek; for, into), 51–52, 57, 86, 102, 111, 115–16, 135, 140, 151–53, 190
  in New Testament, 66–78, 109, 145
eis aphesin hamartion (Greek; for forgiveness of sins), 93
eis Christo (into Christ), 145
eis Christon (into Christ), 135
eis metanoia, 93
eis onoma (Greek; into the name), 75
ek (Greek), 178
ek pisteos (justified by faith), 178
ekastos (each one), 109
elambanon (Greek), 124
elegchos (Greek; proof), 177
Elihu, 15
Elijah, 65
Eliphaz, 15, 24
Elizabeth, 79n1
elpis (hope), 177
emotional distress, 51
emotions, 5
emunah (Hebrew; faith, belief), 178
en Christo (in Christ), 145
en onoma (Greek; in the name), 76
enduo (clothed), 145–46
English language, 161
English translations of Bible, 71–72, 113, 178
  questionable verse origins, 88–89
Enoch, 3

SUBJECT INDEX

Epaphras (love), 148
eperotao (Greek; to question), 166–67
eperoteima (Greek; a question), 166–69
eperoteima (Greek; appeal), 166
Ephesus, 64
    John the Baptist's disciples in, 115, 119
epi (resting upon), 110–11
epipeptokos (not yet fallen), 124
Erasmus, Desiderius, 219–20
erotao (Greek; to ask), 166–67
eroteiso (Greek; I am going to ask), 167
Essene sect, 43
eternal life, 177, 187
Ethiopian eunuch, 185
    confession of faith, 179
    timing of baptism, 193
Ethiopic language, 28
eucharist, 186, 191, 197
eucharistia (thanksgiving), 191
Euphrates River, 10
exclusivism, Jewish mindset of, 93

faith, 133, 142, 144, 180–82, 187–88, 193, 224, 246
    and baptism, 90, 144–45, 175–78
    as commitment, 192
    discipline and stability of, 148
    and forgiveness, 114, 115
    meaning of, 114
    in New Testament, 90
"faith toward God," 51
fear, 11
Feast of Booths, 165
fellowship, 187
    with God, 50
Ferguson, Everett, 249–50
    Baptism in the Early Church, 190–91
flood, 163
forgiveness, 23, 26, 49, 71, 106, 108, 115, 125, 172–73, 185–87
    baptism and, 57–58, 68–69, 93, 108
    and holiness, 174
    hope of, 104
    John the Baptist's preaching on, 65
    Old Covenant and, 62
    potential or actual, 62
    timing of, 59
Fowler, Stanley, 120, 144, 184–85
    More Than a Symbol, 151
Fowler, Stanley K., 87

Galilee, 80, 84–85
Ganges River, 10
genesis (birth), 158
gennao (*genesis* verb form), 158
genneithei (Greek; birth), 158
genneithei anothen (Greek; born from above), 96
Gentiles
    Jewish church and, 120
    proselyte conversion to Judaism, 97
Gingrich, Wilbur, 68–69
God. See also Yahweh
    being out of favor with, 51
    as creator, 14
    David's sin against, 56
    glory of, 156
    holiness of, 19–22
    judgment by man, 131
    love and, 38
    message of, 25
    obedience to, 82
    omniscience of, 63
    oneness with, 141
    personal relationship with, 83
    perspective of, 63
    relationship with, 26, 46, 48, 172
    sons of, 144
    union with, 178
    word of, 48, 113
gods, ancient pagan worship, 12
Gospel
    central message of, 125
    power of, 143
grace, 45–46, 133–34, 251
    need for, 143
Great Commission, 85–94, 100, 118, 119, 152, 187
Greek language, 25, 33, 67–68
    New Testament, 177
    Old Testament translation into, 29
    participles, 88
    parts of speech, 161

Greek-English Lexicon, 68
Greeks, purification by, 8
Gregory (329-89) of Nazianzus, 209, 211-12
Gregory (335-95) of Nyssa, 210
guilt
    David on, 61-62
    solution to, 104

hagiadzo (Greek; sanctified), 172, 174
hagiasei (Greek; he sanctified), 39, 40
hagiasmos (purity), 146
hagios (Greek; holiness, sanctification), 26, 29, 33-37, 57, 172, 183
Hagner, Donald, 75
hagnidzo (Greek), 33
hagnos (Greek; cleansing), 33, 35, 36
hand washing, 165-66
Headlum, Arthur C., 232-33
heart, 103
heaven, 19-20, 130, 137, 145, 174
    Jesus' authority in, 111
    kingdom of, 43, 173, 186. See also kingdom of God
    union fit for, 23
Hebrew language, 25, 28
    Old Testament translation from, 29
    tenses, 59-60
Hebrew people. See also Jewish people
    God and, 13-17
    prophets, 120
    religion, 11, 14
Hebrew scriptures, 15. See also Old Testament
heigiastheite (Greek; sanctification), 159
heimon (us), 140
Henotheism, 14n3
Heraclitus of Ephesus, 9
heresies, 149
heretics, baptizing of, 207
Hermas, 201
Herod, 84
Herod Antipas, 53
Herodias, 53
Herodotus, 8, 166
hiera (Greek; sacred), 183

hieron (Greek; sacred), 183
hieros (holy), 182-83
Hindu people, 10
ho (Greek; which, that), 92, 161
ho homologei (Greek; who confesses), 181
ho mei homologei (Greek; not confess), 181
holiness, 18-38, 57, 83-84, 135, 156, 172, 174
    baptism and, x, 100
    cleansing rituals and, 46-47
    etymology of, 26-29
    God's grace and, 18
    in New Testament, 33-37
    in Old Testament, 25, 29-33
    vs. sanctification, 19
Holy Spirit, 67, 111-13, 119-20, 122
    and baptism, 42, 63-64, 121
    church and, 154
    as dove, 79
    gift of, 101
    at Jesus' baptism, 80
    in New Testament, 34
    and Paul's ministry, 127
    and Peter, 107
    power from, 93, 94, 105
    promise of, 103
    receiving, 118-26
homologeisei (might confess), 181
homologeo (Greek), 181
homologia (Greek), 168n98, 181
homologounton (Greek; confessing), 181
hope, suffering and, 161
hospitality, 75
hote (Greek; when), 113-14
human body, transformation to spiritual, 132
humanism, 130
humon (your), 107, 109
hupostasis (Greek, eternal life), 177
hustereo (Greek; fall short), 156

idols, 12
Ignatius (Bishop of Antioch), 198-99
images of disgrace, 129
Immanuel, 32

SUBJECT INDEX

immersion, baptism by, 189, 191
  necessity of, 231–32
impurities, 46, 101
incarnation of Jesus, 83
India, 10
Indus Rier, 10
infant baptism, 150–51, 192, 206, 217, 227–28
initiation into church, 172
initiatory rite, 193
intellectual conversion, 56
interpretation, exegetical method of, 77
intimacy, 32
Irenaeus, 202
Isaiah, 47
Isis, 10
Israel
  losses in batle, 15
  place in world, 43
  restoration, 93
Israelites, 14. See also Jewish people
  delivery of, 163
  God's demand of, 65
  instructions from God, 60
  lust and pride, 16
  traditions, 16–17

Jehovah, 22
Jerusalem, 63, 86. See also Pentecost
  apostles in, 113
  Jesus in, 165
Jesus Christ, 58. See also blood of Christ; Body of Christ
  baptism, 79–99
  baptism, reason for, 79–84
  baptism's purpose in ministry, 85
  circumcision of, 147
  crucifixion, 140–41
  death of, 59, 128, 131, 163
  Great Commission, 85–94
  image of, 146
  in Jerusalem, 165
  Lord's Supper, 137
  message of repentance, 105
  mission of, 83, 94
  in the name of, 110–12
  new life with, 126
  as Redeemer, 25
  redemption in, 143
  sermon on the mount, 143
  sinlessness of, 80–81
  surrender to, 176, 178
  as threat to traditions, 128
  transcension of execution, 132
  universal vision for the Gospel, 93
Jewish people, 130
  and conversion, 52
  God and, 13–17
  Jesus' message to, 43
  Samaritans, Gentiles and, 120
  traditional way of life, 128
  xclusivism mindset, 93
Jewish proselytes, influence on John the Baptist, 47
Job, 15, 83
John (apostle), 24, 113
John Chrysostom, 212–14
John the Baptist, 93, 120, 142, 152, 173, 188
  on baptism, 57, 78
  baptism, purpose, 48–52
  baptism by, 42–65, 108, 167
  baptism originality of, 43–48
  baptism significance, 64–65
  baptism vs. Jesus' teachings, 63–64
  death, 53
  disciples in Ephesus, 115–16, 119
  disciples of, 57, 80, 153
  execution of, 84
  Jesus baptism by, 79
  Jewish proselytes influence on, 47
  message of repentance, 105
  Qumran community and, 45
  sin in days of, 58–59
Jonah, 76, 77
Jordan River, 10, 42, 44, 80, 137
  Jesus' travel to, 82
Jordan River valley, 44
Joseph (husband of Mary), 83
Joseph of Arimathea, 83
Josephus, 53–54
Josiah, 3–4
Journal of Biblical Literature, 68
Judea, 84

SUBJECT INDEX

justification, 34, 57, 83, 132–33, 159, 175
justified by faith, 178
Justin Martyr, 199–201

kai (Greek; and), 88, 91, 118
katenugeesan (Greek; were pricked), 103n13
kathariasas (Greek), 40
katharidzo (Greek; cleansing), 36
katharisas (Greek; cleansing), 39
Keach, Benjamin, 225–26
Keil, C.F., 22
keirugma (Greek; preaching), 77n26
keirusso (Greek; preach), 77n26, 92
keirux (Greek; preacher), 77n26
Kingdom of God, 57, 65, 98, 101, 157–58
  entrance into, 95–96
  inheritance of, 101
  preaching on, 113
Kingdom of Heaven, 43, 173, 186

labein (received), 114
Lard, Moses E., 231–32
Law of Moses, 43, 48, 60, 143, 149
  influence on John the Baptist, 46–47
  purification rites in, 46
laying on of hands, 125
leprosy, 44, 137
Levi, tribe of, 27
Lewis, Jack, 72
life, blood's importance to physical and spiritual, 130
Lindlom, 88
living (running) waters, 9, 44, 165, 190
  power of, 11
Lloyd-Jones, David Martyn, 247–48
Locke, John, 26n35
logos (Greek; word), 181, 186
Lord's Supper, 137–38
loutrou paliggenesias (Greek; washing of regeneration), 158
love, 148
Lowry, Robert, 132n10
loyalty, 105

Luke, 47, 64, 79
lupeo (Greek; sorrow), 54–55
Luther, Martin, 220–22
Luther Bible, 88

"make disciples" command, 85, 86–87, 90, 92, 94, 111
Malachi, 65
Mantey, Julius, 68–70, 72–73, 76–77, 110, 115–16
Marcus, Ralph, 68–69, 72
martyrdom, 205
  of Ignatius, 198–99
Mary, 79n1
matheiteuo (Greek; make disciples), 92
matheiteusate (Greek; make disciples), 85
McGee, J. Vernon, 130
McIntyre, Luther, 107–9
mei (Greek; is not), 99
mercy, 45, 60, 158
Messiah, 43
  John the Baptist on, 112
meta (Greek), 140
metamelomai (Greek; regret), 54–56
metamorphoo (Greek; transformation), 173
metanoeisan (Greek; converted), 77
metanoeisate (Greek; repent), 107
metanoeo (Greek; repent), 51, 56, 105, 110
metanoia (Greek; conversion), 93, 173
metanoia (Greek; repentance), 51, 54–55, 57, 102
meth (among), 140
meth heimon ho Theos (God with us), 140
Michel, Otto, 55
ministry
  of Jesus, 94, 188
  of John the Baptist, 82
miracles
  by Jesus, 96, 103
  at Pentecost, 102
mission of Jesus, 83, 94
missionary journey of Paul, 115
monon (Greek; only), 124–25, 125

monotheism, 11
moral conversion, 141
moral lifestyle, John's call to, 48
moral standard, and conversion, 85
More Than a Symbol (Fowler), 151
Morris, Wally, 251–52
Moses, 164. See also Law of Moses

Naaman, 137
nacham (Hebrew; repent), 50–51
nahzar (Hebrew; separated), 28
Naiades, 10
Nashville, radio preachers, 106
Nazareth, 82
New Jerusalem, 165
new life, 142
New Testament, 189
　authors of, 142
　on forgiveness, 60
　foundation, 129
　holiness and sanctification in, 33–37
　teachings about baptism, 7
Nicodemus, 16, 94–99, 123n64, 131n7, 158, 186
Nile River, 10
Nineveh, 76
Noah, 83, 160, 161
nun sodzei baptisma (Greek; baptism now saves you), 187

obedience, 168, 250–51
　baptism and, 184
　to God, 82
　of Jesus, 82
Old Covenant, and forgiveness, 62
Old Testament
　and baptism, 198
　on forgiveness, 60, 63
　Hebrew translation into Greek, 29
　holiness/sanctification in, 29–32
　prophets, 64–65
　word meanings in, 29
　Yahweh and, 14
Old Testament Hebrew, 177
omniscience of God, 63
onoma (name), 110
ordinance, 182, 184

Origen of Alexandria, 204–5
oudepo (Greek; not yet), 124, 125
Ovid, 7

pagan religions, 14, 43, 45
　baptismal rituals, 7–12
　conversion from, 47
　reverence for waters, 183
pahlah (Hebrew; set apart), 27–28
pain, 56
paliggenesias (Greek; new genesis), 158
palin (new), 158
paredoken (Greek), 40
participles, 86n29, 87
Partitive Apposition, 109
passive event, baptism as, 172
Paul, 24, 140, 152, 246
　anothen use by, 97
　baptism of, 118, 127
　conversion of, 116–18
　on Damascus road, 117, 127–28
　on distorting gospel, 129
　in Ephesus, 64, 119
　on grace, 133–34
　letters of, 127–28
　message of repentance, 143
　as missionary, 115, 127
　persecution of Christians, 114
　as Pharisee, 128
　in Philippi, 177
　restoration of sight, 116
　on saint's body after death, 132
　on sanctification, 34
　theology of, 127–29
　timing of baptism, 193
Pentecost, 94, 101–5, 110
　Peter's message, 71, 118–19, 153, 188
　timing of baptism, 193
pepisteuka (Greek), 90
persecution of Christians, 102
　by Paul, 114
Peter, 113, 186–87
　on baptism, 71, 111, 166
　on faith and forgiveness, 114
　on holiness, 23–24
　at Pentecost, 118–19, 153, 188

(Peter continued)
    theology of, 107
Pharisees, 52, 84, 94, 123n64
    legalism of doctrines, 143
    Paul as, 128
Phasaelis of Nabatae, 53
Philip, 113–14, 119, 125, 185
Philippi, 177
Philippi jailer, timing of baptism, 193
Philo, 9
physical event
    baptism as, 185–86
    and spiritual reality, 136, 137
    with spiritual significance, 149
physical pain, 51
physical practices, 136
Pilate, 165–66
piscinae, 191–92
pistei (Greek), 178
pisteos (Greek), 178
pisteuo (Greek; believe), 90–91, 176, 178
pisteuonta (Greek; believe), 114
pisteusas (Greek), 92
pistis (Greek; faith), 90, 176, 178
Platt, David, 250–51
pleiroma (Greek; fullness), 148
pleiroo (Greek; fulfill), 83, 148
pneuma hagios (Greek; set apart Spirit), 34
Polhill, John, 108–9
political strife, 65
Polycarp, 202
polytheism, 11, 14
poreuomai (Greek; I go), 86
poreuthentes (Greek; go), 86, 90
post-baptismal growth, 193
Potamoi (Greek river gods), 10
pouring, 192
prayer, Jesus on, 22
preachers, in early church, 101
preaching, 42, 94
    by John the Baptist, 65
    at Pentecost, 102
prepositions, 66–67
priests, 167
    purity of, 30
Procksch, Otto, 236

profanity, 21
propheiteis (Greek), 75
prophesying, 64, 122
prophets, preaching of, 64–65
Protestant traditions, for sacrament, 184
purification, 8, 44, 126
purification rites, in law of Moses, 46
purity, 19–21, 24, 44, 174
    beauty of, 22
    of Christ, 146
    emphasis on, 37
    of God, 18–19, 29
    of priests, 30

qadash (consecrate), 30
qadosh (Hebrew; holiness, sanctification), 26, 28, 57
qadusa (Arabic), 28
qd (Hebrew), 28
qds (Hebrew), 28
Qumran community, 43, 44–46, 47
    disciples, 45
    water purification views, 44

rabbinic traditions, 143
Red Sea, 163
redemption, 102–3, 163
    baptism and, 25
    and Cross, 36
regret, 55
relationship with God, initiation into, 193
relationships, 188–89
religious duties, ceremonial washing before, 30
remorse, 55–56
renewal, 158
repentance, 42, 50, 51, 54–63, 109, 141
    baptism and, 49–52, 104
    as baptism prerequisite, 54, 110
    forgiveness and, 93, 104
    John's call to, 48
    Pentecost and, 102
Restoration Movement, 228
resurrection of Jesus, 103, 140–41, 160, 161, 172

righteousness, 48, 83
   baptism and, 175
   and Cross, 36
   relationships and, 34
ritual bath, 47
rivers, role in religious mythology, 10
Robertson, A.T., 69–70, 73, 108–10, 115–16, 235–36
Roman Empire, new congregations in, 127
Romans, purification by, 8
Rome, 198–99
running (living) waters, 9, 44, 165, 190
   power of, 11

sacrament, baptism as, 182–85
sacramentum (Latin), 182
sacrifice, 46, 217
   of Jesus' death, 62
sacrifices, instructions from God, 60
Sadducees, 52
sainthood, 184
salvation, x, 38, 105, 133, 144, 152, 168, 178–79, 187, 193
   and baptism, 106, 183
   by faith alone, 106
   holiness and, 18
   in New Testament, 51–52
   in Old Testament, 50–51
   themes of, 128
   timing of, 192–93
   by works, 106, 172
Samaria, Philip in, 124
Samaritan woman, 96, 165
Samaritans, 113–14, 153
   baptism of, 116
   conversion of, 119
   Jewish church and, 120
sanctification, 27, 57, 83, 101, 110, 132–33, 135, 142, 158–59, 172, 175
   baptism and, 100, 173–74
   blood of Cross and, 174
   cleansing and, 39
   and Cross, 36
   in New Testament, 33–37
   in Old Testament, 29–33

price for, 105
   vs. holiness, 19
Sanday, William, 232–33
Sanhedrin, 95, 123n64
   attitude towards Jesus, 16
sarx (Greek; flesh), 186
Satan, 155
Saul. See Paul
Schreiner, Thomas R., 248–49
scripture, study of, xi, 2
Semitic languages, 28, 33
Septuagint, 29
Sermon on the Mount, 143
Shepherd of Hermas, 201
shub (Hebrew; repent), 50–51
sick-bed, baptizing on, 206–7
Silas, 177
Simmons, Menno, 223–25
Simon, 113
sin, 54–63, 133, 142, 172, 183. See also forgiveness
   certainty of, 24
   cleansing of, 131, 158
   contamination of, 47
   and death, 56
   and grace of God, 134
   impact of, 155–57
   Jesus and, 81
   pain from, 56
   relationship with God and, 83
   separation from God, 174, 175
   ugliness of, 130
Sindhu River, 10
Smyrnaeans, Epistle of Ignatius to, 199
Socrates, 9–10
sodzei (Greek; it saves), 162
Solomon, 15, 136, 137
sorrow, 54–63
   physical display of, 50
souls in hell, 161
soul-searching, 24
Southern Baptist Theological Seminary, 108
speaking in tongues, 64, 122
spiritual baptism, 135
spiritual birthday, 171
spiritual blessings, 148, 172

spiritual body, human body transformed to, 132
spiritual cleansing, 132
spiritual distress, 51, 65
spiritual event, baptism as, 185–86
spiritual experience, 138
spiritual gifts, 123
spiritual life, 130
spiritual reality, 177
  in New Testament, 137
  and physical activity, 136
spiritual redemption, by Roman crucifixion, 131
spiritual uncleanness, 9
sprinkling, 189, 192
stability, of faith, 148
Stein, Robert H., 248
stipulatio (Latin), 168n98
suffering, behavior in, 160–61
suneideiseos (conscience), 169
suneideiseos agatheis (Greek; good conscience), 168
sunestaurothei (it was crucified with him), 138
sunetapheimen (we have been buried), 138
suskeimatidzo (fashioned according to), 173
Sychar, 165
symbolic burial, 135
symbolic commitment, 136
symbolic event, baptism as, 137

tabernacle, 136, 170
tahor (Hebrew), 29
te (Greek), 88
temple, 136, 154
tenses, 59
Tertullian, 203–4
text
  and interpretation, 122
  prepositions impact on meaning, 66
Theological Dictionary of the New Testament (Otto), 55
Theophilus, 213
Thiessen, Henry C., 239
Tillich, Paul, 2–3

timing of forgiveness, 59
tis (Greek; anyone), 98
to soma humon (the body of you all), 154
tomb, 142
Torrance, Thomas Forsyth, 239–42
tradition, 25, 101
Trallians, Epistle of Ignatius to, 199
transformation, 57, 141, 142
  and baptism, 98, 99, 173
  in relationship with God, 65
transgressions, 61, 147. See also sin
translation. See also English translations of Bible
  challenges of, 25
  rules of, 69
translator, 69
Trinity, 111–12, 118, 120, 182, 190
  defense of, 209
truth, xi
Trypho, 199–201
tsahraph (refined), 2
tsedeq (righteousness, justification), 83n19
Turag River, 10

uncleanness, 22, 27, 146, 174
union
  with Christ, 120
  with God, 178

verbs
  analysis of, 40
  modifier, 113
  tenses, 117
virgin, church as, 35
voice from heaven, 80
Voltaire, Francois-Marie, 26

"wash away," 118
washing, 173
  sanctification and, 158
washing rituals, 8–9
water, 8–9, 183
  as cleansing agent, 186
  purification by, 44
  sin washed away by, 163
  symbolic connection, 164

symbolisms of, 185–86
water ablutions, characteristics, 11
Wesley, John, 226–28
witnessing, 94
words in opposition, 109n24
Wuest, Kenneth S., 237
Wycliffe, John, 71–72

xenos (Greek; strangers, foreigners), 37

yadusu (Arabic), 28
Yahweh, 13–17, 20, 22, 93

Zophar, 15

Scripture Index

Old Testament

Genesis

	50
1	186
1:1	18
1:31	143
2:24	87n34
3:22	198
5:21–24	3n6
6:6–7	50n31
6:9	83n20
6:17–18	164n84
17:10–11	136n20
17:10–14	149
17:11	149n53
18:14	50n26
26:18	50n27
28:15	31n53

Exodus

14:16	163n83
14:26	164n85
15:11	20n5
19:5–6	65n68
20:7	21n10, 22, 22n17

Leviticus

	29, 46
4:20	59, 59n53
4:26	59
4:31	59
4:35	59
5:10	59
5:13	59
5:16	59
5:18	59
6:7	59
10:3	20n6
10:9–10	30n49
11:44	23n25, 65n69
11:44–45	30n46
11:45	23n23
12:3	149n52
13:45–46	36n76
15:31	28n39
19:2	23n24, 30n46
19:12	21n12
19:22	59
20:7	23n25
20:24	27n37
20:26	23n26, 30n46
21	30
21:8	30n50
22:32	21n14
26:11–12	3n7

Numbers

14:19–20	61n56, 62
15:25	59
15:26	59
15:28	59
35:34	14n4

Deuteronomy

4:7	32n56
5:11	22n17
10:8	27n38
10:16	149n54
21:8	59
30:4	31n54
30:6	150n55

1 Samuel

2:2	20n7
8:4–9	16

1 Kings

	50
8:23	15n5
8:27	15n5, 137n22
8:27–29	136n19

2 Kings

	50
5:1–14	137n23
22:1—23:30	3n10

1 Chronicles

16:9–10	21n16
16:25–26	13
23:13	28n40

2 Chronicles

	50
34:1—35:19	3n10

Job

4:12–17	24n28
37:23	15n6

Psalms

	50
1:1	198
4:3	27n36
12:6	2
12:6–7	1
14:1–3	24n29, 24n31
16:8–11	103
18:30	1n1
19	143
31:6	14n1
32:1	61n57, 62
32:2	61n57
32:5	61n57
34:4	32n57
51:3–4	56n44
53:1–3	24n29, 24n31
85:2	62n63
99:9	20n4
100	31n52
100:3	14n2
110:1	103
145:5	21n8

Proverbs

30:5	2
30:5–6	1

Isaiah

	50
6:3	20n3
6:5–7	62, 62n60
7:14	32n58, 139n26
44:1–4	164n87
45:5–7	13
53:9	81n10
55:8–9	122n60
58:11	164n88

Jeremiah

	50
4:4	150n56
29:13–14	32n55

Ezekiel

	30, 50
3:1–19	188n143
3:19	198
14:2–3	50n28
14:6	50n28
36:22–25	31n51
39:7	21n15
44:23	18

Joel

2:28–32	103

Zechariah

3:3	215

Malachi

	65
4:5–6	65n70

Dead Sea Scrolls

Damascus Rule

Vermes

111–12	44n7

Hymns

Vermes

163–64	46n10

Manual of Discipline

Vermes

74–75	44n6

Rule for the Community   45

Ancient Jewish Writers

Josephus   53, 54

Antiquities of the Jews

18.5.2 (18.24)	53n36

Philo   9

On the Cherubim

28.95	9n4

Rabbinic Works

S. Bar.[Syrian Apocalypse of Baruch]

51:3	173n106

New Testament

Matthew

	51, 76, 84, 92, 94, 111, 234
1:19	83n20
1:22–23	139n27
1:23	32n58
3:1, 5	45n8
3:1–2	42n2
3:2	49n25, 74, 85n26
3:4	43n5
3:5	45n8
3:8	252
3:9	48n18
3:11	49n20, 52, 63n64, 68, 72, 72n12, 77, 93, 102n9, 112n30, 152, 239, 251
3:13–15	80n4
3:15	82n17
3:16–17	80n5
4:12	84n24
4:17	42n3, 74, 85n26
5:17	144n36
6:9	22n20
7:28	114
10:5–42	74
10:7	43n4, 74
10:13	75
10:13–14	75
10:14	74
10:25	74
10:32	180n128
10:32–33	74
10:40	75
10:40–42	73, 74, 74n19
10:41	70, 73, 75
10:42	75
11:14	65n71
11:28	25n33
12:41	68, 73, 74, 76–77
16	92
16:1	166n96
17:1–13	65n71
18:5	75
18:20	75n23
21:23–27	48n17
21:24–25	167n97
26:27–28	77
26:28	78
26:29	89, 90
26:39	82n15
27:24	166n94
27:46	140n30
27:51	97n54
28	92
28:16	85
28:17	111
28:18–20	85, 85n27
28:19	75n23, 85, 90n40, 111n28, 118n50, 119, 135, 184, 190, 230, 238
28:20	85

Mark

	51, 53, 84, 94, 234
1:4	49n21, 54n37, 57n47, 58, 70, 70n8, 71, 72n13, 78, 93, 116n41, 152
1:4–5	45n8
1:4–8	42n1
1:4f	69, 235
1:5	80n6
1:8	102n9, 112n30
1:9–11	79n2
1:14	84n25
1:14–15	74
1:15	85n26
9:11–13	65n71
10:2	166n96
11:27–33	48n17
15:34	140n30
15:38	97n54
16:8	88, 89n38
16:9	88

SCRIPTURE INDEX

16:9–20	88, 89
16:15	89
16:15–16	88, 89, 90n40
16:16	89, 91, 92, 98, 164n86, 186, 224

Luke

	51, 53, 76, 84, 92, 94, 234
1:3	97n54
3:2	47n14
3:2–3	45n8
3:3	49n22, 54n37, 71, 72n14, 78, 93, 116n41, 152
3:4	47n14
3:15–16	63n65
3:16	102n9, 112n30
3:21–22	79n2
10:16	75
11:32	68, 76–77
12:3	77n26
20:1–7	48n17
22:17–19	137n21
23:50	83n20
24:46–47	58n48
24:46–48	92, 92n45
24:47	78, 93, 116n42

John

	84, 234
1:12	75n23
1:14	3n8, 186
1:32	80n5
1:32–33	79n3
1:33	48n16, 112n30
2:19–21	154n66
3	98
3:1–10	94–95
3:1–12	16n7
3:1–21	123n64
3:2	16n8, 123n64, 131n7
3:3	57n47, 95, 95n47, 96, 98n59, 99, 158, 186, 193n159
3:4	97n56
3:5	95, 95n47, 97n58, 98n60, 99, 158, 186, 205, 245
3:6	97n57
3:7	96, 193n159
3:18	75n23
3:22	84n21
3:25	84n23
3:28	84n24
3:30	84n24
3:31	96n51
4:1–3	84n22
4:3–26	96
4:10–11	165n89
4:34	82n15
4:48	95n50
5:19	111n29
5:30	82n15
6:38	82n15
7:37–39	165n90
8:33	52n35
10:18	82n15
10:25	76n24
12:44	75
12:49–50	82n15
13:15	82n16
14:30–31	82n15
15:3	67n2
15:10	82n15
16:23	76n24
17:16–17	146n43
19:11	96n52
19:23	96n53
20:31	124n65

Acts

	51, 64, 94, 98, 111, 112, 120, 121, 126, 248
1:4–5	64n66
1:5	112n31
1:6–8	93, 93n46
1:8	94
2	56, 64, 102
2:14	102n10
2:22	103n11
2:22–23	103n12
2:32–33	103n12

(Acts continued)

2:36	103n12
2:37	103n14
2:38	55, 56, 58, 67, 69, 70, 71, 72, 72n11, 73, 74, 77, 78, 101, 101n5, 102, 105, 106, 107, 108, 109, 109n24, 110, 111, 112, 115, 116, 119, 119n51, 125, 153, 184, 224, 226, 235, 239, 245, 251
2:41	104n17, 193
2:47	154n63
3:19	55
4:12	ixn1
4:13	146n41
6:5	113n36
8	120, 124
8:1	102n6
8:4	102n6
8:5	113
8:12	113, 114
8:12–17	113, 113n35, 119, 119n52
8:16	75n23, 116n43, 119, 153
8:16–17	124n67
8:17	119
8:26–38	193
8:36	185n139
8:36–37	179n122
8:37	179n122, 180n122, 224
8:38–39	185n140
9:1–2	128n1
9:17–18	116, 116n48
9:18	118, 134, 193, 246
9:27	76n24
9:28	76n24
10	120
10:1–48	193
10:43	114, 114n38
10:44	119
10:44–48	119, 119n53
10:47	239
10:47–48	185n141
10:48	119, 166n96
12:21	145
13:2	36n72
13:24	49n23
16:18	76n24
16:19	177n117
16:22–34	193
19	120
19:1–6	64n67
19:1–7	119n54, 193
19:4	49n24
19:5	75n23, 116n44, 119, 153
19:5–6	115, 115n40, 119
19:6	119, 122
19:9	128n1
19:23	128n1
22:16	116, 116n48, 117, 118, 134, 157, 158, 193, 240, 245, 246
24:14	128n1
24:22	128n1
26:5	97n54

Romans

1:1	36n73
1:28–32	156, 156n71
2:28–29	150n57
3:10	169n101
3:10–12	24n31
3:22	179n121
3:23	24n29, 155n68, 156, 169n100
4:20	68
5	133
5:1	133n12, 178n120
5:1–2	134n14
5:10–11	141
5:12–21	141
5:21–22	134n13
6	98, 134, 135, 136, 141, 152, 158, 159, 234
6:1 ff	141, 245
6:1–7	134
6:1–11	133, 142, 185, 245
6:1–14	232
6:3	134, 138, 139, 141, 153, 189, 233, 238, 246
6:3 ff	245
6:3–4	71, 116n45, 134, 135, 205, 223, 247
6:3–7	138
6:3–11	186n142
6:4	138, 139, 153, 236, 241

6:4–5	149n50
6:5	139
6:6	134n15, 138, 141, 158n74
6:6–7	157
6:9	139
6:10	58n51, 141
6:11–14	142n32
7:12	183, 183n137
8	120
8:9	112n33, 120n55
8:14	112n33, 120n55
10:9–10	180n123
10:17	224
12:2	173n107
12:18	188n145
13:12	145
16:25	77n26

1 Corinthians

	147
1:10–17	151–55
1:13	75n23, 152n61, 153
1:15	75n23, 153
1:30	36n71, 236
2:4	77n26
5:4	76n24
6	156, 157
6:9–10	34, 156, 159
6:9–11	34n65, 101n4, 155
6:11	34, 76n24, 157, 158, 240, 245
6:19	154n67
8:7	170n102
9:13	183n135
10:2	230
11:1	82n16
11:23	189
12	123, 124, 152
12:7–11	123n63
12:12–14	151–55
12:13	116n47, 134, 152, 152n60, 153, 189, 234, 239, 245, 246, 250
15	132
15:1–8	129n4

2 Corinthians

5:1–4	145
5:21	81n9
7:8–11	54–55, 55n39
9:13	180n125
11:2	35n67

Galatians

	143, 147
1:6–9	129n3, 143n34
1:11–12	128n2
2:19f	241
2:20	146n42
2:26 f	245
3:3	143n35
3:24–27	144n37
3:25–27	142–46
3:26	144, 145
3:26–27	144
3:27	71, 116n46, 144, 145, 153, 230, 238, 245
3:27–29	245
3:27f	135, 239, 246
4:9	97n55
5:19–21	156, 157n72

Ephesians

1:3	137n24, 149n51, 172n104
1:3–14	57n46, 100n1
1:13 f	245
1:22–23	154n64
1:23	149n49
2:12	36n74
4:4–6	136n18
4:11–12	154n65
4:11–16	xii
4:15	193n160
4:30	245
5:1–1	82n16
5:6	166
5:20	76n24
5:25	40
5:25–26	35n66, 39

(Ephesians continued)

5:25f	240
5:26	35, 40, 41, 87, 230–31

Philippians

2:1	76n24
2:8	82n15
3:3	150n58

Colossians

1:3–4	148n46
1:8	148n46
1:8–10	148n48
1:13	245
1:26–27	140n29
2	150, 159
2:1 ff	245
2:5	148n47
2:10–14	147–51
2:11 f	245
2:12	236
2:12–14	186n142
3:11	146n44
3:13	82n16
3:17	76n24, 176n115

1 Thessalonians

4:7	36n70

2 Thessalonians

3:6	76n24

1 Timothy

1:5–11	143
1:15	83n18
4:2	170
6:12	180n124

2 Timothy

1:11	77n26
1:12	90n41, 176n113
2:15	3n9, 4n11
3:15	183n136
3:16–17	1

Titus

1:15	170
3	156, 157
3:3	156, 159
3:3–7	155
3:5	157, 158, 166, 245

Hebrews

	51
4:14	180n126
4:15	81n11
6:1	51n33
9:9–11	47n12
9:9–14	170n103
9:12	58n49, 132n11
9:14	81n14, 132n11
9:24	19n2
10:1	59, 62
10:1–3	59n52
10:3	59
10:3–4	60n55
10:10	174n110
10:10–14	58n50
10:23	180n126
11:1	177, 177n116
11:6	176n114, 178n119
12:1	101n2
13:12	236
13:15	181n129

James

1:17	97n54
2:10	156n69
2:20	36n75

3:15	97n54	**Revelation**	
3:17	97n54		
4:8	36n68		51
4:17	188n144	1:1–2	161
5:10	76n24	4:8	20n3
5:16	182n133	5:8–9	130n6
		7:9	131n8
		7:14	131n8
1 Peter		7:17	165n91
		19:7–9	23n22
1:3—4:11	160	21:6	165n92
1:14–16	173n108	22:1	165n93
1:15–16	24n27	22:21	18
1:16	30n46		
1:18–19	81n13		
1:21	249	**Early Christian Writings**	
2:20	101n3		
2:20–22	82n16	Alexander of Jerusalem	202
2:21–22	81n10		
3:13–18	160		
3:17	160		
3:18	161	Ambrose of Milan	196,
3:18–21	160–70		214–16, 216
3:19	161		
3:20	162		
3:21	25n32, 54n38, 98, 160, 162, 162n81, 169, 170, 186, 225	*Concerning the Mysteries*	
		chap. 3.17, p. 51	214n35
		chap. 7.37, p. 59	214n36
		chap. 7.37, p. 60–61	215n37
2 Peter		*Concerning the Sacraments*	
1:19–21	xin3	chap. 3.10, p. 79	215n38
2:5	161		
		De Sacrtamentis	
1 John		85	215n39
		94	215nn40–41
1:6–7	131n9	96	216n42
1:8	24n30	97	216n43
1:9	181n130		
2:5–6	82n16		
3:5	81n12	*Apostolic Constitutions*	
4:2–3	181n131		
4:15	181n132		196, 211
5:13	75n23	bk. 7, sect. 3, par. 43	211n31
5:16	166n96		

SCRIPTURE INDEX

Aquinas, Thomas   196, 218–19

Summa Theologica
859   219n49
860   219n50

Arius   209

Athanasius of Alexandria   196, 209

Four Discourses
disc. 2, chap. 18   209n28

Athanasius the Great   210

Augustine of Hippo   196, 213, 216

On Christian Doctrine
636–37   217n45

City of God
301   217n46

The Confessions
1   216n44

Enchiridion
42–43   218n47
50   218n48

Basil the Great   196, 209–10, 211

On the Holy Spirit
10.26   210n29
12.28   210n30

Chrysostom, John   196, 212–14

Instructions to Catechumens
par. 2   214n34

Clement of Alexandria   196, 202–3

Instructor [Paedagogus, or Tutor]   203

Cyprian of Carthage   196, 205–7

The Epistles of Cyprian
1.4   206n17
58.2   206n18
69.1   207n20
75.12   207n19

The Treatises of Cyprian
2.23   207n21

Cyril of Jerusalem   196, 207–9

SCRIPTURE INDEX 285

Catechetical Lectures

lect. 3	208nn24–26
lect. 3, par 3	208n23
lect. 17	209n27
Procatechesis, par. 16	208n22

The Didache

"Concerning Baptism"

	197
7:1–4	190n150
7.1–4	197n1

The Teaching of the Lord Through the Twelve Apostles to the Nations   190

"The Thanksgiving (Eucharist)"

	197
9.1, 5	191, 191n153
9.5	197n2

Epistle of Barnabas   195, 198

Epistle of Ignatius   195, 199

"The Epistle of Ignatius to the Smyrnaeans"

8.1	199, 199n5

"The Epistle of Ignatius to the Trallians"

2.8–9	199, 199n4

Erasmus, Desiderius   196, 219–20

The Handbook

30	219n51
36–37	2n4

An Inquiry Concerning Faith

219	220n52

Paraphrase on the Gospel According to Matthew

377–78	220n53

Eusebius   203

Gregory of Nazianzus   196, 209–10, 211–12

Orations

par.4	212n32
par.35	212n33

Gregory of Nyssa   210, 211

Irenaeus   196

Against Heresies

3.12.7	202, 202n10

Jerome 203

Justin Martyr 195

Dialogue with Trypho
    200n6
chapter 1   199–200
First Apology   200–201
chapter 61   200n7

Origen of Alexandria   196, 202, 213

Commentary on Romans   205
Homilies on Numbers   205

Shepherd of Hermas   196

Mandates   201
Visions   201

Tertullian   196, 203–4

On Baptism [De Baptismo]
    204
chapter 1   204n12
chapter 3   204n13
chapter 7   204n14

Theophilus   213

Greek and Roman Literature

Heraclitus of Ephesus   9, 9n5

Herodotus   166

Histories
2.47   8

Ovid

Fasti   7
2.45–46   7n1

Plato

Cratylus
section 402.a   9n6

Plutarch

On Isis and Osiris
5   10n

www.ingramcontent.com/pod-product-compliance
Lightning Source LLC
Chambersburg PA
CBHW071236230426
43668CB00011B/1464